English and Development

CRITICAL LANGUAGE AND LITERACY STUDIES

Series Editors: Professor Alastair Pennycook, *University of Technology, Sydney, Australia* and Professor Brian Morgan, *Glendon College/York University, Toronto, Canada* and Professor Ryuko Kubota, *University of British Columbia, Vancouver, Canada*

Critical Language and Literacy Studies is an international series that encourages monographs directly addressing issues of power (its flows, inequities, distributions, trajectories) in a variety of language- and literacy-related realms. The aim with this series is twofold: (1) to cultivate scholarship that openly engages with social, political, and historical dimensions in language and literacy studies, and (2) to widen disciplinary horizons by encouraging new work on topics that have received little focus (see below for partial list of subject areas) and that use innovative theoretical frameworks.

Full details of all the books in this series and of all our other publications can be found on http://www.multilingual-matters.com, or by writing to Multilingual Matters, St Nicholas House, 31-34 High Street, Bristol BS1 2AW, UK.

Other books in the series

Collaborative Research in Multilingual Classrooms
Corey Denos, Kelleen Toohey, Kathy Neilson and Bonnie Waterstone

English as a Local Language: Post-colonial Identities and Multilingual Practices
Christina Higgins

The Idea of English in Japan: Ideology and the Evolution of a Global Language
Philip Seargeant

Gendered Identities and Immigrant Language Learning
Julia Menard-Warwick

China and English: Globalisation and the Dilemmas of Identity
Joseph Lo Bianco, Jane Orton and Gao Yihong (eds)

Language and HIV/AIDS
Christina Higgins and Bonny Norton (eds)

Hybrid Identities and Adolescent Girls: Being 'Half' in Japan
Laurel D. Kamada

Decolonizing Literacy: Mexican Lives in the Era of Global Capitalism
Gregorio Hernandez-Zamora

Contending with Globalization in World Englishes
Mukul Saxena and Tope Omoniyi (eds)

ELT, Gender and International Development: Myths of Progress in a Neocolonial World
Roslyn Appleby

Examining Education, Media, and Dialogue under Occupation: The Case of Palestine and Israel
Ilham Nasser, Lawrence N. Berlin and Shelley Wong (eds)

The Struggle for Legitimacy: Indigenized Englishes in Settler Schools
Andrea Sterzuk

Style, Identity and Literacy: English in Singapore
Christopher Stroud and Lionel Wee

Language and Mobility: Unexpected Places
Alastair Pennycook

Talk, Text and Technology: Literacy and Social Practice in a Remote Indigenous Community
Inge Kral

Language Learning, Gender and Desire: Japanese Women on the Move
Kimie Takahashi

English and Development

Policy, Pedagogy and Globalization

Edited by

Elizabeth J. Erling and Philip Seargeant

MULTILINGUAL MATTERS
Bristol • Buffalo • Toronto

Library of Congress Cataloging in Publication Data
A catalog record for this book is available from the Library of Congress.
English and Development: Policy, Pedagogy and Globalization/Edited by Elizabeth J. Erling and Philip Seargeant.
Critical Language and Literacy Studies: 17
Includes bibliographical references and index.
1. Language policy—English-speaking countries. 2. English language—Study and teaching. 3. English language—Study and teaching—Foreign countries. 4. English language—Globalization. 5. English language—Variation. 6. Language and languages—Political aspects. I. Erling, Elizabeth J., editor of compilation.
P119.32.E54E54 2013
306.44'9–dc23 2013001851

British Library Cataloguing in Publication Data
A catalogue entry for this book is available from the British Library.

ISBN-13: 978-1-84769-946-6 (hbk)
ISBN-13: 978-1-84769-945-9 (pbk)

Multilingual Matters
UK: St Nicholas House, 31-34 High Street, Bristol BS1 2AW, UK.
USA: UTP, 2250 Military Road, Tonawanda, NY 14150, USA.
Canada: UTP, 5201 Dufferin Street, North York, Ontario M3H 5T8, Canada.

The policy of Multilingual Matters/Channel View Publications is to use papers that are natural, renewable and recyclable products, made from wood grown in sustainable forests. In the manufacturing process of our books, and to further support our policy, preference is given to printers that have FSC and PEFC Chain of Custody certification. The FSC and/or PEFC logos will appear on those books where full certification has been granted to the printer concerned.

Typeset by Integra Software Services Pvt. Ltd., Puducherry, India.
Printed and bound in Great Britain by the MPG Print Group.

For

Marie Annik Erling Gerstenecker

and

Ylva Anaïs Erling Gerstenecker,

both born during the process of bringing this book together

Contents

Figures and Tables

Figures

Tables

Contributors

Daniel Ahimbisibwe is a graduate of Uganda Martyrs University, where he studied local governance and human rights. He is currently a key member of Kitengesa Community Library, where he serves as head librarian and research associate. He is a committee member of the Uganda Community Libraries Association and has presented his work at international conferences in Uganda, Tanzania and Canada.

Jean-Louis Arcand is Professor of International Economics and Professor and Chair of Development Studies at the Graduate Institute of International and Development Studies in Geneva. He is associate editor of the *Journal of African Economies* and the *Revue d'Economie du Développement*, co-editor of the *European Journal of Development Research* and Founding Fellow of the European Union Development Network (EUDN). His research focuses on the microeconomics of development, with a current focus on impact evaluation of social programs in West Africa and the Maghreb. He has been a consultant to the World Bank, the FAO, the UNDP, the Gates Foundation and several national governments. He is currently leading multi-year impact evaluations in Angola, Burkina Faso, Burundi, Cameroon, The Gambia, Mali, Morocco and Senegal, with the topics being investigated ranging from peer mentoring to fight HIV-AIDS, to capacity-building in rural producer organizations to foster food security.

Tom Bartlett is the director of the MA programme in Applied Linguistics at Cardiff University. He has taught English as a Foreign Language in Scotland, Spain and Latin America. From 1999 to 2002 he lived in Guyana, South America, where he was involved in language and development work, which forms the basis of his forthcoming monograph *Hybrid Voices and Collaborative Change: Contextualising Positive Discourse Analysis* (Routledge, 2012). Other recent publications include articles on Positive Discourse Analysis and English as a lingua franca in European universities.

Mary Jane Curry is associate professor at the Margaret Warner Graduate School of Education at the University of Rochester, New York, where she directs the language teacher education program and Writing Support Services. She is co-author of *Academic Writing in a Global Context: The Politics and Practices of Publishing in English* (Routledge, 2010) and *Teaching Academic Writing: A Toolkit for Higher Education* (Routledge, 2003). She has published in journals including *English for Specific Purposes, Written Communication, TESOL Quarterly* and the *International Journal of Applied Linguistics*.

Elizabeth J. Erling is Lecturer of International Teacher Education at the Open University and has produced materials and led evaluations of teaching interventions for 'English in Action', an English-language learning and teacher education development project in Bangladesh (funded by DFID). Her research explores topics in world Englishes, language policy, teacher professional development and English for academic purposes. She has published papers in journals such as *World Englishes, English Today, Language Policy* and *Innovations in Language Learning and Teaching*.

Gibson Ferguson is the director of the MA programme in Applied Linguistics at the University of Sheffield. Early in his career he taught for seven years in rural secondary schools in Malawi and Zambia and since that time has maintained an interest in international development. Among his recent publications is a monograph *Language Planning and Education* (Edinburgh University Press, 2006) and a variety of articles on such topics as English as a lingua franca, English in science and classroom code-switching.

François Grin is Professor of economics at the University of Geneva's School of Translation and Interpretation, as well as visiting professor at the University of Lugano. He has specialized in language economics and language policy evaluation and has published widely in these fields. His latest book, *The Economics of the Multilingual Workplace* (with C. Sfreddo and F. Vaillancourt), was published by Routledge in 2010. He has carried out large-scale projects for scientific research agencies and international organisations such as the Council of Europe, the European Commission, the World Bank Institute and the Organisation internationale de la francophonie.

M. Obaidul Hamid is a lecturer in the School of Education at the University of Queensland, Australia, where he teaches in the area of TESOL. Previously he taught English language and applied linguistics at the University of Dhaka, Bangladesh. He is interested in English as a second/foreign language; English-in-education policy in the context of national development; social perspectives on second language acquisition; and the sociology of English learning. He has published his work in *Current Issues in Language Planning,*

TESOL Quarterly, Language Learning Journal, ELT Journal, English Today and *International Journal of Research and Method in Education*.

Shelley Jones is an Assistant Professor in the Department of Curriculum and Instruction at the State University of New York, College at Potsdam. Her research interests include gender, education and international development; global education; and multimodality.

Zuleikha Kombo Khamis has recently been appointed as the Director of the Zanzibar Institute of Tourism Development (ZITOD). Prior to this she worked for seven years at the State University of Zanzibar. Throughout her career, she has worked as a professional teacher educator in areas of pedagogy and second language learning, gaining wide experience of academic and professional activities in Zanzibar at primary, secondary, teacher education and university level. She has also been involved in developing teaching and learning materials for Zanzibari children. Between 2006 and 2009, she was the Zanzibar Coordinator of the ESRC/DFID research project (RES-167-25-0263), a collaboration with the University of Bristol and the State University of Zanzibar investigating the dynamics of languages in school (under)achievement.

Theresa Lillis is a professor in language and education at The Open University, the United Kingdom. Her research interests are in academic and professional writing, particularly in relation to the politics of access, location and participation. She authored *Student Writing: Access, Regulation and Desire* (Routledge, 2001) and co-authored with Mary Jane Curry, *Academic Writing in a Global Context* (Routledge, 2010). She has published articles in numerous journals including *Language and Education, TESOL Quarterly, Written Communication, Revista Canaria de Estudios Ingleses*, and *International Journal of Applied Linguistics*.

Bonny Norton is Professor and Distinguished University Scholar in the Department of Language and Literacy Education, University of British Columbia, Canada. Her research addresses identity and language learning, critical literacy and international development. In 2010, she was the inaugural recipient of the Senior Researcher Award by the Second Language Research group of AERA (American Educational Research Association) and in 2012 was inducted as an AERA Fellow. Her website can be found at http://educ.ubc.ca/faculty/norton/.

Federica Olivero is the director of MSc in Education, Technology and Society at the University of Bristol. She has done extensive research on the teaching and learning of mathematics and the mediating role played by new technologies through the ESRC Interactive Education Project. Her most recent work has focused on the potentialities of videopapers as an innovative research dissemination tool. She was also part of the ESRC/DFID research project (RES-167-25-0263), investigating the role of language in students' mathematics performance in Zanzibar.

Naz Rassool teaches in the Institute of Education at the University of Reading, the United Kingdom. She has published and supervises PhD students in the fields of language and social development; literacy and social change; language, education and identity formation; the political economy of technology in education; national language-in-education policy frameworks; language, identity and transmigration; and social justice in education. Her books include *Global Issues in Language, Education and Development* (Multilingual Matters, 2007) and *Literacy for Sustainable Development in the Age of Information* (Multilingual Matters, 1999).

Pauline Rea-Dickins is the Gulbanu and Pyarali Jassani Director of the Aga Khan University Institute for Educational Development, East Africa, and a Visiting Professor at the University of Bristol. She has worked extensively in Sub-Saharan Africa as well as the United Kingdom and is widely published in areas of language assessment and language programme evaluation. Her most recent ESRC/DFID research project (RES-167-25-0263) involved a collaboration between the University of Bristol (where she worked for 11 years) and the State University of Zanzibar and investigated the dynamics of languages in school (under)achievement.

Philip Seargeant is Senior Lecturer in Applied Linguistics in the Centre for Language and Communication, The Open University. He is author of *The Idea of English in Japan* (Multilingual Matters, 2009) and *Exploring World Englishes* (Routledge), and editor of *English in Japan in the Era of Globalization* (Palgrave Macmillan, 2011) and *English in the World: History, Diversity, Change* (Routledge, 2012, with Joan Swann).

Martin Wedell has worked on different aspects of international TESOL teacher education for more than 30 years. He is currently Head of International Education at the School of Education, University of Leeds, the United Kingdom. His research interests are summarised in the title of his recent book *Planning for Educational Change: Putting People and their Contexts First* (Continuum, 2009).

Lionel Wee is a professor and Head of the Department of English Language & Literature at the National University of Singapore. His books include *Language Policy and Modernity in Southeast Asia* (Springer, 2006, with

Antonio Rappa), *Language Without Rights* (Oxford University Press, 2011) and *Markets of English* (Routledge, 2012, with Joseph Park). His articles have appeared in *Applied Linguistics*, *Language Policy* and *World Englishes*. He is an associate editor of the *Journal of Sociolinguistics* and sits on the editorial boards of *Applied Linguistics* and *English World-Wide*.

Eddie Williams is Professor of Applied Linguistics in Bangor University. He has worked at the University of Malta and the Centre for Applied Language Studies at the University of Reading, and has carried out research into school-based literacy in English and African languages in many African countries, principally Malawi, Zambia, Rwanda, Ghana and South Africa. He has also researched and published on the links between education and development in many articles and a book, *Bridges and Barriers: Language in African Education and Development* (St Jerome, 2006). He has been a visiting lecturer in many universities, including the University of Rwanda.

Series Editors' Preface

A key question to which we still don't have particularly good answers is the extent to which the widespread learning of English around the world may be beneficial or detrimental. As Tollefson (2000) warned a number of years ago, 'when English is widely seen as a key to the economic success of nations and the economic well-being of individuals, the spread of English also contributes to significant social, political, and economic inequalities' (p. 8). There are a number of different sides to this question, including the role of English in relation to other languages, to economic and other forms of development, and to education more broadly. Widespread education in English may be linked to participation in a global economic order, but it is also a question of favouring one language over others as a second language, using English as a medium of instruction (and thereby potentially harming the educational development of children who struggle to understand the educational content), of pushing other languages and subjects out of the curriculum, and of making some languages increasingly redundant. There is also the question of the kinds of English skillsets that policies promote. Essayist literacies, once the hallmark of elite schooling, and closely tied to the content of English literature, may be of limited utility for job opportunities in particular communities. Conversely, the provision of basic literacies in English may be insufficient – and perhaps intentionally so – to mitigate deeply inscribed social inequalities.

Among applied linguists there seems in fact to be quite widespread agreement on some of the arguments about language in education. In the context of South East Asia for example, Kirkpatrick (2012) warns of the dangers of the emphasis on English in organizations such as ASEAN (Association of South East Asian Nations), which has adopted English as an official language. With the growth of many of these economies, their increased roles in the global economy, and the constant pressure to teach English earlier and younger in a region with wide linguistic diversity, there are real causes for concern that current language education policies favouring only the national language plus English will lead to Asian multilingualism being reduced to bilingualism only in the national language and English. For Kirkpatrick, the best solution would be to adopt 'a language education policy that could be simply summarised as "primary for local, secondary for English".' This, he suggests, would mean that 'at least some local languages would be maintained and strengthened, as they would become languages of education.' Children would also be able to 'learn their respective national languages and become bilingual in Asian languages and, given that many more children would now learn in their mother tongues, primary retention rates would increase.' This would mean that 'more children would become trilingual, with English as their third language' (2012: 342).

There are tensions here, however. Many applied linguists are in agreement that education, especially in the elementary years, is best carried out in the first language. Yet governments are very aware that many people want access to English because it is seen as a language of opportunity. With the growth of private sector English provision, furthermore, many who can afford it may also opt for English education whatever the government decides. As applied linguists, we also need to be cautious here in not getting stuck in arguments only about language policy, or mother tongue education. As Mufwene (2010) reminds us, linguists are all too often insufficiently clear 'about how countries that are rich in ecological, cultural, and linguistic diversity but are economically poor can, with their limited financial means, satisfy both the human rights of their populations to evolve out of poverty and the alleged rights of their languages to each be used in the education system and/or other cultural domains' (p. 914). We need to move away from the reification and exoticization of languages, suggesting that to maintain one's L1 is somehow a guarantor of self-esteem, a consistent worldview, a useful education and economic advancement. As Mufwene (2010) makes very clear, all of this depends on the nature of local ecologies and economic opportunities, the value accorded to different languages, and the movement of people in search of livelihoods. Linguistics, he argues, 'must address issues arising from the real world of socioeconomic inequality more globally and not just from the point of view of languages as maps of world views and illustrations of mental/cognitive variation. The rest of the world happens to see languages as tools at the service of mankind, and this perspective is an equally legitimate one, just as is the view that a language can be an asset or a liability to a person or a population' (p. 927).

When we try to understand the role of English in development, then, we need to take basic economic concerns into consideration. We know, of course, that learning English may bring advantage individually – it is a key gatekeeper to higher education around the world, for example – but at a broader level, we need to ask what the effects of widescale provision of English may be on social and economic development. It has been suggested that the widespread introduction of English into primary sectors around the world could lead to the amelioration of poverty (see Pennycook, 2007, for discussion). The questions raised by a broad and careful examination of the relations between English and development – questions this book addresses in a number of ways – suggest, however, that to focus on individual betterment is to miss the intersecting relations of class, gender, race and the global economy. The questions of English and development, then, need to be considered within the global and local structures of neoliberalism (Block *et al.*, 2012; Chun, 2009; Kubota, 2011): For Piller and Cho 'the global spread of neoliberal free-market doctrines naturalizes the use of English as the language of global competitiveness' (2013: 24). As they go on to argue, with reference specifically to the use of English as a medium of instruction in higher education in South Korea 'neoliberalism with its imperative to compete is a covert form of language policy, which imposes English as a natural and neutral medium of academic excellence' (2013: 24). All of this takes us back to the inescapable concern that inequality between rich and poor has been increasing globally, and that, for example, both the promise of English for white-collar workers in Korea and the belief about benefits of English for less privileged people in the world actually work similarly in reproducing unequal social and economic relations (Park, 2011). The effects of learning English in a schoolroom in rural Indonesia or urban Juba (South Sudan), therefore, have to be seen both in their local particularities and set against the much wider context of global economies and injustices.

The international context in which English operates in relation to development can be seen in two different, though often overlapping, ways. The focus on the international in this book is predominantly though analysis of English language education in relation to social and economic development in a diversity of contexts, such as Bangladesh, Singapore, Uganda and Zanzibar. An alternative focus is on international development projects – with nations and agencies offering aid packages which include a range of educational and economic strictures – through close analysis of the effects of such projects on the ground. Widin (2010) points out that local participants are all too often denied legitimacy within these projects, so that 'insurmountable barriers prevent host-country project team members from participating fully and equally in the decision-making processes of the project' (p. 146). The context of international development projects has also been well covered by an earlier book in this series by Ros Appleby (2010). There we were invited to feel what it was like to teach in the battered classrooms on the campus, with wood smoke and the sounds of roosters drifting through the broken windows; we were given a close portrait of the disparity between the adversity of the locals and the comfort of the expatriate development workers on the development 'gravy train'; we learned of the extraordinary hardships some of these students had faced, and their courage and pain in taking up education again.

Appleby presented us with a powerful critical analysis of the ways in which inequality can be perpetuated through the very processes of international development, and the place of English language within those processes. She also linked the local experiences of language teaching, gender relations, and development with the ambiguous location of women in the language and development industries, offering fresh insight into social, political and historical understandings of English language and gender in a globalised world. As she convincingly argued, 'the dominant emphasis on time in English language teaching, geared towards a liberal vision of progress, has neatly aligned orthodox ELT with mainstream notions of international development, and has tended to overshadow an engagement with a spatial politics that values and affirms a complex, coexisting, transcultural multiplicity' (2010: 210). Here our attention is drawn to the difficult relations between the interests of those that fund development projects and diverse local interests and contingencies. Perhaps most importantly we can see that the educational provisions that may go with what is termed 'development' – education aimed at preparing workers for factory work in local towns, for example – may have a range of outcomes – social, environmental, cultural – that do not necessarily carry the same patina of development for local communities.

Bruthiaux (2002) has argued convincingly that for many of the world's poor, English language education is 'an outlandish irrelevance' and 'talk of a role for English language education in facilitating the process of poverty reduction and a major allocation of public resources to that end is likely to prove misguided and wasteful' (pp. 292-3). Thus we need to distinguish very clearly between individually-oriented access arguments about escape from poverty, and class-oriented arguments about large-scale poverty reduction. The challenge here is to get beyond liberal arguments for access, and look instead at the broad effects of educational provision in all their complexity. As Tupas (2006) points out in the context of the export of labour from the Philippines, for example, the 'hierarchy of skills (including English language skills) that governs the deployment of labour actually perpetuates, rather than reconfigures, both the Philippine social structure (which, in turn, also reproduces such hierarchy), as well as the globalized unequal structure of relations between the Philippines as a labour-producing country and labour-using countries and corporations' (p. 101).

In a recent blog on *Language on the Move*, Ingrid Piller (2013) discusses an earlier study of the relevance of English education in rural Indonesia (Pasassung, 2000). The British Council, it turns out, had been funded by the World Bank to investigate why compulsory English teaching in Indonesian schools was doing so badly. The answer, as is so often the case with such organizations, lay in methodology, and so a stronger dose of communicative language teaching was prescribed for Indonesia's rural poor. Not only do such prescriptions conceal the interests of the textbook writers and central organizations in the provision of English (Phillipson, 2009), but they overlook the social, cultural and economic conditions within which English is being promoted. As Gray puts it, 'ideologies associated with English which take it as self-evident that it is perforce the language of economic prosperity and individual wealth are also those of the ELT industry itself' (2012: 98).

As Pasassung (2000) noted, by contrast, the difficulties with English were part of a much bigger picture including the point that English was quite alien to this rural community in Sulawesi – it had no local use – a problem that included the inappropriacy of the textbooks (a lesson on hotels, of which none of them had any experience, struggled for relevance). Again this is the point that Gray (2012) makes in his critical analysis of the relations between English textbooks, celebrity culture, and neoliberalism, arguing that textbooks all too often promote a cultural imaginary that is precisely part of the neoliberal economic system that is responsible for the continued dispossession of these people. For Piller (2013) all of this conspires 'to turn the compulsory English lessons in the junior high school under investigation into a meaningless waste of time. Not only does compulsory English study under these conditions not produce any results but it attracts a cost: the opportunity cost to spend the time invested into English lessons in a more productive way'.

Within all this too, we need to remember that development should not be reduced to questions only of economic improvement. Measures of development need to address questions of life expectancy, school enrolment (particularly in relation to gender), literacy, child malnutrition, mortality rates and much more. So we are left with the fundamentally hard question of how English education may connect to this, not only as possibly affording individuals more economic opportunity, but also in terms of enabling socioeconomic development more broadly, enabling or lowering literacy rates among girls (English for boys, other languages for girls?), helping or hindering HIV/AIDS information in parts of Africa (Higgins & Norton, 2010), or in the broad arguments of Amartya Sen (2001), what forms of freedom – in terms of a range of social, cultural, political and economic choices – are made possible? Given that we know that improving education for girls is not only a basic issue of human rights – lack of access to education and literacy may be a question of local economies and infrastructure, but the unequal distribution of that access along gender lines is also a fundamental question of rights and discrimination – but also has very clear practical outcomes – improved family health and nutrition, lower mortality rates, increased family income, better educational outcomes in the next generation and so on – we need to consider what the implications of the inclusion or absence of English in such education may be.

This book, then, helps shed light on these difficult issues: who benefits from the global spread of English? As educators, we need answers to these questions, or at least adequate ways of thinking about them. If we could teach English (or other languages) confident that there were clear linguistic, social, cultural and economic benefits to be gained from our instruction, we could continue our programs, safe in the knowledge that they are doing good. If, on the other hand, it was clear that teaching English was an active part of the systematic linguistic, cultural and economic deprivation of our students (they were linguistically, socially, culturally or financially worse off), we would doubtless be better off cancelling our classes. The problem of course is that it is always a much more complex mix, of some gains and some losses. But to say this is too hard or to rest on the assumption that there will always be gains and losses, is not an adequate response to these concerns: we need ways of addressing this, and this book takes us in some very useful steps in the right direction.

Alastair Pennycook
Ryuko Kubota
Brian Morgan

References

Appleby, R. (2010) *ELT, Gender and International Development: Myths of Progress in a Neocolonial World*. Bristol: Multilingual Matters.

Block, D., Gray, J. and Holborow, M. (2012) *Neoliberalism and Applied Linguistics*. London: Routledge.

Bruthiaux, P. (2002) Hold your courses: Language education, language choice, and economic development. *TESOL Quarterly* 36 (3), 275-296.

Chun, C. (2009) Contesting neoliberal discourses in EAP: Critical praxis in an IEP classroom. *Journal of English for Academic Purposes* 8, 112-120.

Gray, J. (2012) Neoliberalism, celebrity and 'aspirational content' in English language teaching textbooks for the global market. In D. Block, J. Gray and M. Holborow *Neoliberalism and Applied Linguistics* (pp. 86-113). London: Routledge.

Higgins, C. and Norton, B. (eds) (2010) *Language and HIV/AIDS*. Bristol: Multilingual Matters.

Kirkpatrick, A. (2012) English in ASEAN: Implications for regional multilingualism. *Journal of Multilingual and Multicultural Development* 33 (4), 331-344.
Kubota, R. (2011) Questioning linguistic instrumentalism: English, neoliberalism, and language tests in Japan. *Linguistics and Education* 22, 248-260.
Mufwene, S. (2010) The role of mother-tongue schooling in eradicating poverty: A response to language and poverty. *Language* 86 (4), 910-932.
Park, J.S-Y. (2011) The promise of English: Linguistic capital and the neoliberal worker in the South Korean job market. *International Journal of Bilingual Education and Bilingualism* 14 (4), 443-455.
Pasassung, N. (2000) Teaching English in an 'Acquisition-Poor Environment': An Ethnographic Example of a Remote Indonesian EFL Classroom. Unpublished PhD Dissertation, University of Sydney
Pennycook, A. (2007) The myth of English as an International Language. In S. Makoni and A. Pennycook (eds) *Disinventing and Reconstituting Languages* (pp. 90-115). Clevedon: Multilingual Matters.
Phillipson, R. (2009) *Linguistic Imperialism Continued*. London: Routledge.
Piller, I. (2013) Is English improving lives in a remote Indonesian village? *Language on the Move* Research Blog: February 1, 2013. http://www.languageonthemove.com/language-globalization/is-english-improving-lives-in-a-remote-indonesian-village
Piller, I. and Cho, J. (2013) Neoliberalism as language policy. *Language in Society* 42, 23–44.
Sen, A. (2001) *Development as Freedom*. Oxford: Oxford University Press.
Tollefson, J. (2000) Policy and ideology in the spread of English. In J.K. Hall and W. Eggington (eds) *The Sociopolitics of English Language Teaching* (pp. 7-21). Clevedon: Multilingual Matters.
Tupas, R. (2006) Anatomies of linguistic commodification: The case of English in the Philippines vis-à-vis other languages in the linguistic marketplace. In P. Tan and R. Rubdy (eds) *Language as Commodity: Global Structures, Local Marketplaces* (pp. 90-105). London: Continuum.
Widin, J. (2010) *Illegitimate Practices: Global English Language Education*. Bristol: Multilingual Matters.

Introduction: English and Development

Philip Seargeant and Elizabeth J. Erling

This book examines the nature and implications of the relationship between English and development. It appraises the role that the language has in the socio-economic development of various countries around the world, and looks at how English-language provision fits within the wider context of development in general. In the last few decades, a number of programmes and initiatives have been promoting English as an important resource for international development. We might begin by asking, however, how the promotion of English within these contexts relates to the achievement of development targets such as those laid out in the Millennium Development Goals (MDGs, 2000). The MDGs include aims such as providing universal education, ending poverty and hunger and ensuring child and maternal health. With the 2015 deadline for achieving these fast approaching, it has become clear that, while much progress has been made, there are still several obstacles to overcome, particularly across large parts of Africa and for many of the least developed countries (Ban Ki Moon in the Millennium Development Goals Report, 2008). In a context where so many of the world's poor still live without basic necessities like fresh water, access to medical care or basic education, one could question why many development programmes include a strong focus on the improvement of language education, and in particular on the English language. What is it that a knowledge of English is thought to contribute to the plight of developing societies?

With this as its starting point, the book looks to investigate the connections between English-language ability and personal as well as national development, as these are both discursively promoted (particularly through language policy) and as they are practically realized in developing societies. The book also addresses the question of what effects the increased teaching and use of English is having on broader educational issues, as well as the impact it has on local language ecologies and cultural identities. It investigates these issues by drawing together a series of original examinations and case studies by a range of scholars working in this burgeoning field. The chapters focus on a range of contexts from regions of the world including Sub-Saharan Africa, South America, South and Southeast Asia, and Eastern Europe. These various contexts represent different points on the continuum of economic and social development, and allow the volume as a whole to identify both generalities and contrasts in the positioning and influence of English as a catalyst for development in the 21st century. In this introduction we look at the key themes and concepts to be explored in the book, along with the research context that is emerging around the role of English in development initiatives.

English as a Global Language

The role of English in development programmes has come about, in part, because of the rise of English as a 'global' language. The current global status of English is the result of an interplay of social, political and historical factors that have had wide-ranging implications for societies around the world (Crystal, 2003). One of the primary consequences of English's global spread is that it now operates as the pre-eminent medium of international communication in the modern world. It is used as a lingua franca by various transnational political and economic associations, while also operating as a medium of global communication in domains such as science, technology, business and academia. Because of this, English-language ability is viewed by many – both at the level of government and the individual – as a fundamental element in the skill set required for full participation in 21st century society. It is often seen as a resource that can contribute to personal, social and economic development in a range of diverse contexts – as something that can provide access to education and to certain sectors of the employment market, and which offers the ability to influence the global economic and political trends, which have resulted in a variety of social inequalities and injustices for individuals and groups around the world. Due to these associations, the learning of English in many contexts is viewed as a means of increasing one's social and cultural capital. This is the case in both Outer Circle countries, where one of the legacies of colonialism is an infrastructure that favours English in key domains such as education, the law and the civil service, and in Expanding Circle societies, where the associations between English and powerful political and economic Anglophone countries boost the esteem in which the language is held (Seargeant, 2012).

Because of its status as a global language and the associations it has in the public consciousness, English-language education policy has long played a role in national development initiatives, the details of which have been well documented (see, for example, de Segovia & Hardison, 2009 for Thailand; Lamb & Coleman, 2008 for Indonesia; Li, 1998 for Korea; Hu, 2005 for China). Around the world, English is thus increasingly promoted as a resource for engagement in globalising economies and societies. As Lillis and Curry (this volume) note, access to English also plays a role in determining who participates in, and benefits from, the global 'knowledge economy'. For these reasons, it is being given increasing prominence in school curriculums. As Wedell (this volume) observes, English is being introduced at ever-earlier levels of formal schooling in, for example, China, Chile, Korea, Japan, Turkey, Oman and parts of India. Further evidence of the increasing role of English in development initiatives is the fact that the role of English as the medium of instruction is currently being extended in certain countries such as Pakistan, South Sudan and the previously Francophone setting of Rwanda (see Williams, this volume).

Given the trends both in the increasing use of English in a range of domains, along with the beliefs people have about the potential the language has to improve their prospects (Erling *et al.*, 2012; Tembe & Norton, 2011; Vavrus, 2002), it is maybe not surprising that in recent years English-language provision has also become an important focus for international development projects. If ever more countries globally are aiming to enhance English-language education as a means of attracting foreign investment and participating in the global economy, developing economies cannot be excluded from this. And it is against this background that, since the early 1990s, there has been a significantly increased focus on English-language education and teacher education projects in development contexts around the globe (see, for example, discussion in Bruthiaux, 2002; Kenny & Savage, 1997; Lo Bianco, 2002; Pincas, 1995; Widin, 2010). Indeed, Bruthiaux (2002: 289) goes so far as to contend that development efforts today have become 'inextricably linked in governmental and academic circles as well as in the media with English language education'.

Language and Development Research: An Emergent Field

Due to the increasing stress on the importance of language-related issues in development, as well as the prominence of English-language teaching in development initiatives, there has, since the late 1990s, been a growing body of research in the field of language and development. Early work in this field (e.g. Pincas, 1995; Kenny & Savage, 1997) mainly reported on and celebrated the outcomes of international development projects, but offered little critical reflection on the part played by language teaching in such projects, or on the political nature of these initiatives and the role of the donor countries (see Appleby, 2010: 31). Since these early studies, however, three main strands of language and development research have emerged:

- Quantitative research, which sets out to measure the relationship between language skills and economic gain.
- Qualitative research, which, drawing on a variety of theoretical approaches from across several disciplines, explores the complex ways in which language, education and development may be linked.
- Critical research, which questions whether English-language teaching programmes in development contexts are successfully fulfilling their objectives, and how they link to political and cultural issues.

These are not, of course, entirely distinct categories, and research often combines aspects from more one than one of them. For the purposes of this overview, however, and for simplicity's sake, let us consider the research field under the following three headings.

Quantitative research exploring links between English and development

With the growing perception that English can play an important role in development – and particularly in economic development – a need has arisen to quantify the 'cost benefit' or 'return on investment' of English-language learning (e.g. Martin & Lomperis, 2002). The nature of this benefit can take different forms. Coleman (2010) provides an overview of research that has attempted to quantify the relationship between English and various indicators of development, such as employability, access to research and information, international mobility, and international collaboration and cooperation. Empirical work mapping this relationship has been undertaken for a variety of different contexts (e.g. Grin, 2001 in Switzerland; Chakraborty & Kapur, 2008 in West Bengal), and has produced results that point to the complexity of the picture. Recent work by Ku and Zussman (2010), for example, found that in a survey of 100 countries in which English is not a first language, the acquisition of English-language skills could be seen as enabling the promotion of foreign trade. They illustrated this by constructing a dataset based on mean national scores in the Test of English as a Foreign Language (TOEFL) spanning 30 years. Controlling for other factors influencing trade, they argue that English proficiency has a strong and statistically significant effect on bilateral trade flows. These results can be compared to the findings in Arcand and Grin's chapter in this volume, which show that widespread proficiency in English throughout populations in countries in postcolonial Sub-Saharan Africa and Asia does not, on its own, appear to be associated with higher levels of economic development for these particular countries, but that widespread use of local languages does. They thus conclude that, in general terms at least, English should not be considered 'special' in terms of economic development or growth. Their novel use of statistical analysis also suggests that previous research on the impact of language on the development process needs to be reviewed, and perhaps has been seriously misinterpreted for many years.

Recent Euromonitor research (2010, 2012) has also attempted to investigate empirically the extent to which promotion of English is an important factor in a country achieving economic growth. In these studies, a scoring system for each country's economy and education system has been created in order to determine the nature of the relationship between the two. The 2010 study concludes that, while economic growth may be slow in the postcolonial contexts that the study reports on, the fact that English is seen as offering a key competitive advantage in a difficult employment environment means that demand for English education in these countries remains high. The 2012 study shows how countries in the Middle East and Africa are seeking to develop their economies and create better living standards and improved social conditions, in part by improving the English-language skills of their populations. Euromonitor reports that each of the governments that the study examined regards English-language skills as an essential part of achieving growth, which will give domestic companies a competitive edge in the global economy as well as attract investment from abroad.

Research such as this indicates that many countries continue to invest in English-language education based on its associations with economic gain. However, other studies probe more deeply and critically into these associations. They show that while there may often be some form of causal relationship between English-language ability and economic development (although, as Arcand and Grin's work shows, even this should not be assumed as self-evident), it needs to be qualified by the fact that the pre-existing social environment inevitably complexifies the relationship. For example, Levinsohn (2007) found that the economic advantages of being able to speak English in South Africa increased as the country opened up to the international economy from 1993 to 2000, but he also found that there was more of an advantage for white than for black South Africans. His work demonstrates that English-speaking ability is not necessarily of equal value for different ethnic groups and thus has a complex relationship with other social variables.

A similarly complex picture was found by Azam and Prakash (2010), who used the India Human Development Survey of 2005 to quantify the effects of English-speaking ability on wages. Their findings show that being fluent in English (compared to not speaking the language at all) increased the hourly wages of men by 34%, and thus had the same economic impact on wages as completing secondary school does, and it had half as much impact as completing a bachelor's degree. And simply being able to speak a little English increased male hourly wages by 13%. They found, however, that returns to English were lower for women, particularly those in rural areas, and were also significantly lower for members of India's Schedule Caste, the historically disadvantaged grouping in Indian society. They thus conclude that 'upward mobility does not come automatically with English skills in India; some obstacles, which likely include long-rooted discrimination against low caste, impede low caste group members even when they have a skill that is valued by the modern labour market' (Azam & Prakash 2010: 18). Any study looking into correlations between language use and development, therefore, has to consider a wide range of contextual factors that influence or affect the causal nature of the relationship.

Taking account of such contextual factors, a number of the chapters in the present volume (especially Chapters 2 and 11) provide further qualifying evidence about the discourse that links English and economic advancement, suggesting that, although this notion continues to be a primary motivating factor behind the ambitions of many language policies, it is far from straight-forward relationship. Studies of this sort suggest, therefore, that care needs to be taken to ensure that policy recommendations and planning interventions take account of a full range of social variables if they are to successfully achieve their aims.

Qualitative research on language, education and development

It is with this need to consider the complexity of each context and relationship that, in addition to quantitative studies, there is also a growing body of qualitative research, which explores the ways in which language, education and development are linked to the changing global labour market, and discusses the social and political consequences of these relationships. Research in this area includes the selections in Harbert *et al.* (2009), which approach the relationship between language and poverty from various disciplinary perspectives to illustrate how the languages that people speak (or, conversely, do not speak) influence their economic status. Rassool (2007) has also examined the relationship between English and development by looking at the way that the spread and use of English in postcolonial contexts has contributed to an ongoing colonial legacy of social and economic inequalities. She argues that language education policies in Africa and the Indian subcontinent during the 19th century have left an enduring challenge for modern educationalists and policy makers, and have contributed to the underdevelopment of these nations and their local languages. Djité (2008) uses a sociolinguistic approach to investigate the relationship between language use and development in Africa. Like Rassool (2007), he outlines the ways in which the reliance on postcolonial languages has affected the development potential of the African continent and, based on this conclusion, calls for a more powerful role for African languages in the development of the region. As both Ferguson and Williams (this volume) point out, these, and other applied linguists (e.g. Mazrui, 2004; Kamwangamalu, 2010), have repeatedly advised against the choice of English as the language of instruction in several African contexts due to the large body of evidence pointing to linguistic issues as a major source of continued educational failure. They also point out, however, that such research has not hindered the popularity of English-language learning or of its use in education because of the strong associations with economic and social capital that adhere to the language. Several of the authors in the current volume are therefore seeking out new solutions that recognise the importance of local languages in literacy development and education without ignoring the strong demand for English.

As Rassool (this volume) demonstrates, much of the research in this area has traditionally drawn on theories from sociolinguistics – such as language shift and minority language rights – when engaging with any language-related issues associated with development. And, as Arcand and Grin (this volume) point out, studies on language economics have often neglected development contexts, while those probing economic development ignore issues of language. Both Rassool, Arcand and Grin and others (e.g. Appleby, 2010; Coleman, 2011) stress the need to look to other disciplinary approaches and perspectives in order to better understand attitudes and assumptions about the role of English in development; and, as indicated above, recent studies have begun to broaden the methodological and theoretical range of the research area. The present book continues in this interdisciplinary vein, drawing on approaches from, for example, economics, the social sciences and development studies in the analysis of the relationship between language and development, thus allowing for a multi-perspective exploration of the topic. Several of the studies (e.g. Erling *et al*., this volume; Lillis & Curry, this volume) also bring together both quantitative and qualitative data in an effort to create more nuanced ways of understanding the relationship between language use and development.

Critical research on English-language teaching programmes in development contexts

Another related body of work to emerge in the field of language and development consists of studies that investigate and critique English-language teaching (ELT) projects and their implementation in development contexts. Nunan (2003), for example, provides a survey of the English-language education programmes in several countries in the Asia-Pacific region, which indicates that the significant resources invested in these programmes are not achieving the designated goals due to inadequate teacher training and a general lack of support for teachers. He further cautions that many countries invest considerable resources in providing English education at the expense of other aspects of the syllabus, and that these resources rarely produce the desired instructional goals.

Brock-Utne (2000) also critiques ELT in development programmes for privileging Western languages and practices. She argues that 'donor agencies have been so concerned with supporting international languages that they have hampered educational development, destroyed local textbook production in indigenous languages and weakened local cultures' (in Crossley & Watson, 2003: 87). In this vein, ELT projects have been accused of a form of linguistic imperialism (Phillipson, 1992) for failing to recognise the value of local languages and cultures (see Phillipson, 2012). Moreover, scholars like Appleby (2010) have claimed that these projects are, in effect, supporting Western hegemony through the promotion of Western cultural ideals such as a bias towards monolingualism and the use of the major European languages (especially English) as mediums of instruction. Examining the context of East Timor, Appleby analyses the ways in which social and economic inequalities can in fact be perpetuated rather than alleviated through international development processes and the role they allocate to English.

Another study with a similar critical approach is Widin's (2010) examination of the role and practices of a particular development programme – an Australian-funded project intended to enhance the quality of English-language teaching in Laos – in which she questions its stated rationale of 'building up' English teaching provision in order to improve social and economic growth in the region. As is discussed in many of the chapters in the current volume, Widin's work thus problematises common-sense assumptions that suggest that improvements in English-language ability will necessarily lead to increased opportunities for individuals or nations, and explores why and how ideologies of English as a language for international development persist and are perpetuated.

Concepts and Themes

Having described the current research context, and before moving to an overview of the structure of the book, it is worth outlining a number of the key concepts and themes around which the studies are centred, and considering the factors that shape practices and debate in the field. These include the notion of development itself, and how it relates to education, literacy development and language learning.

The meaning of development

The concept of 'development' is much contested, and its definition has shifted over time (Hettne, 2009: 1; see also chapters by Bartlett, Ferguson and Rassool, this volume). In basic terms, development can be understood as a planned process of change, which leads to improvements in the economic and social conditions of people who live in poverty. When modern development initiatives were taken after World War II, as part of the process of decolonisation which began in the late 1940s, they focused almost exclusively on economic growth, and aimed at an increase in productive capacity and labour productivity (Thomas, 2000: 33). Viewed within this rather narrow context, development was measured in terms of a nation's gross domestic product (GDP). In response to charges of ineffectuality, however, as well as criticism that these programmes were imposing a normative, externally established, capitalist model on the societies they were attempting to aid (Hettne, 2009: 12), the goals of development were broadened. While economic growth was still seen as a fundamental element in the process, it was no longer considered sufficient in and of itself. As such, a new generation of initiatives took the improvement of people's lives more generally as their goal. The concept of development thus expanded to include social factors such as improving the health of populations, mitigating environmental degradation, reducing inequality and promoting democratisation. (For a thorough history of the evolution of international development, and a discussion of the contentiousness of the term, see Appleby, 2010; Crossley & Watson, 2003; Escobar, 1995; Hettne, 2009; Rassool, 2007; Thomas, 2000.)

An important influence in the shift of focus in development studies has been Amartya Sen's (2001) work, which frames development as 'freedom' – a process of expanding people's choices which, in turn, can strengthen other freedoms, thus perpetuating change and growth. Partially as a result of Sen's influence, more recent trends in development have attempted to promote inclusiveness and to incorporate the voices and opinions of those at whom the initiatives are aimed. These approaches aim to include more participatory, 'grassroots' projects that are structured so as to involve indigenous traditions of knowledge and community perspectives, and to promote empowerment and self-reliance in the communities being targeted (see Bartlett, this volume, for further discussion). In the present era, development initiatives have also sought to alleviate poverty by promoting involvement in global dialogues and facilitating developing countries to participate in and shape the global economic system. And this shift in focus in development discourse to choice, awareness and participation makes the role of language – and the need for a global lingua franca – more salient.

Achieving or sustaining economic development is a primary goal for all nations and is often explicitly stated as such in national economic and education policies. Assisting other countries to achieve economic and social development is an additional goal of the foreign policy of several countries, particularly the former colonial powers and the relatively wealthy 'Western' nations, which are often collectively referred to as 'First World' countries. In addition, fostering development has also become the focus of several international organisations, such as the World Bank and UNESCO. Such internationally planned, funded and/or executed projects are often referred to as 'international development'. In the modern globalised era, however, there is often also an international dimension to national development initiatives, and as such, the division between 'national' and 'international' development is not always clear or entirely distinct. Indeed, Hettne (2009: 7) suggests that the use of the modified term 'international' or 'global' development within the field today has come to indicate new trends of the sort outlined above, which seek to address issues of participation, dialogue and partnership building, and to negotiate the relationship between local concerns and a globalising world. Issues of this sort are a key concern for all the chapters in the present volume, as they explore their manifestation in the contexts of regions ranging from Sub-Saharan Africa to Singapore.

Education and development

The means by which all initiatives in the sector attempt to achieve their idea of development consist of a number of key components, the most important of which, for the purposes of this present collection, is education. Since 1945 and the creation of UNESCO, educational provision has been seen as a central element in development programmes (Crossley & Watson, 2003: 85). In the course of decolonisation processes, the former colonial powers often assisted with the 'building up' of the education systems of countries they had previously colonised (Rassool, 2007). During this period, several bilateral aid agencies were founded in Europe and North America, each of which formulated their own educational priorities and agendas. In 1971, the World Bank published its first Education Sector Working Paper, which highlighted the role of education in development and established the World Bank as a leading institution in this field (Crossley & Watson, 2003: 86).

The role of education in development was traditionally perceived primarily as a means of securing economic growth. The relationship between education and development was largely based around the assumptions of human capital theory, formulated by the economist Theodore Schultz. In this, education is regarded as an investment in the developing country's human resources. As Schultz (1963: 10) writes, 'the economic value of education rests on the proposition that people enhance their capabilities as producers and as consumers by investing in themselves and that school is the largest investment in human capital'. From this theoretical perspective, the promotion of education has as its goal the enhancement of skills and knowledge amongst the labour force, 'thus stimulating possibilities for increased production, raised incomes as well as economic and social mobility' (Rassool, 2007: 91).

More recent conceptions of development still give education a central enabling role in economic advancement, but also extend its significance to other areas. For example, Williams and Cooke (2002) list a number of development advantages associated with education, including improvements in health awareness, the reduction of birth rates and environmental benefits. And Sen (2001) sees the most important role for education being that of increasing human capability and therefore access to choice. Furthermore, information and knowledge – and not industrialised production – are now seen as a key resource for economic growth (see Lillis & Curry, this volume).

These more complex and plural notions of the relationship between development and education extend beyond the effect on a nation's GDP and are thus difficult to measure. Educational economists have therefore been devising more nuanced means of understanding and calculating the returns on investment in education. Working within this framework, research conducted by Little and Green (2009: 166) has produced results showing that the role of education has been significant in leading several developing countries to 'successful engagements with the global economy', while work by Hanushek and Woessmann (2008) has found that the cognitive skills of a population can have a strong and robust influence on the economic growth of a country. They thus conclude that there is a significant correlation not simply between education and development, but between *quality* education and development.

There is, however, a lack of universal agreement within the discipline that investment in education necessarily guarantees economic development. This is often the case when there is unequal access to educational opportunity across a society due to socio-economic factors such as a rural–urban divide or the availability of quality teachers. In addition, some scholars suggest that certain forms of education work to reproduce rather than alleviate social inequalities, particularly when educational models from donor countries are uncritically introduced in developing nations (see, for example, Appleby, 2010: 26; Djité, 2008; Rassool, 2007). And crucially, in certain circumstances, linguistic impediments to education can be obstacles to economic advancement (Mohanty, 2009: 12). This can be the case particularly when the language promoted as the medium of instruction is not the first language of the majority of the community. Pinnock and Vijayakumar (2009) argue that this issue has not been sufficiently recognised in development initiatives and that access to the medium of instruction is actually a prerequisite for quality education and hence for development more generally. They therefore suggest that medium of instruction is one of the most important factors that needs to be addressed when attempting to foster learning. And in certain contexts this issue is now being addressed. In Namibia, for example, where English has been the official language of instruction since 1993, recent research identified teachers' low levels of English as an important factor in persistently low student performance and thus in the country's development. As such there has been a call for a return to instruction through the mother tongue, at least at the primary level (Harris, 2011). Further issues around the importance of policies concerning the medium of instruction and the impact they can have on other aspects of the education system are discussed in several chapters in this volume, including those by Ferguson, Rea-Dickins *et al.* and Williams.

Literacy and development

Closely tied to the promotion of education for development is the promotion of literacy, which is also inherently linked to issues of language learning and use. In 1957, a UNESCO report demonstrated that a world map indicating areas of poverty overlapped greatly with the world map of illiteracy. The authors of the report thus put forward the contention that the higher the levels of literacy in a country, the greater the likely level of economic development (Crossley & Watson, 2003: 86). There followed from this several campaigns to promote access to basic education, functional literacy and universal primary education – ideas which still figure prominently in campaigns such as Education For All (EFA) and the Millennium Development Goals.

While the promotion of literacy is still high on the agenda in programmes targeting poverty reduction, the concept of literacy that is now being promoted has been modified in light of theoretical work within the discipline. Whereas the earlier incarnation of the concept was in terms of a purely functional approach – which was often criticized for not taking into account social factors that shape the ways people actually engage with the act of reading and writing (Street, 2001) – more recent approaches have framed literacy as a range of socially situated practices. Within this paradigm, literacy is seen as 'a necessary condition to equip people to participate in the local, national, and global economy, culture and polity' (Kellner, 2000: 249). The shift in focus raises the question as to which language(s) best allow for participation in local, national and global activities, and the relative advantages of a 'global' language such as English and of local languages. Recent work has also highlighted the extent to which literacy practices are shaped by the contexts in which they are developed and used. It has also shown how unequal access to linguistic and educational resources can result in the 'grassroots literacies' that develop in Third World contexts effectively marginalising people from full participation in the social mainstream (Blommaert, 2008; see also Rassool, this volume).

Literacy campaigns and the promotion of basic education have escalated in number and received greater international attention since the World Conference on Education For All in Jomtien, Thailand in 1990. One of the outcomes of this conference was to set a goal of providing universal access to primary education as an important means of eradicating poverty (UNESCO, 2005). The campaigns for Universal Primary Education (UPE) and Education for All were prompted by evidence that even relatively small amounts of education can make a significant improvement to the lives of the poor (Buchmann, 1999) and that individuals who have completed primary school tend to have

> higher earnings, more modern attitudes, better spacing of births in the family, better health and more nutritious diets than illiterate peers. They save more of their incomes, adopt new technologies more easily and are more likely to get involved in community affairs and hold politicians to account. (Moon & O'Malley, 2008: 4; see Palmer *et al.*, 2007, and Ferguson, this volume, for a critique of this position however)

Furthermore, in response to the rapid changes occurring in communications technology, the concept of literacy today is not restricted solely to language-related concerns, but also to competence in the use of digital communication technologies. Indeed, Castells (1999: 3) argues that in the current age the availability of and ability to use Information and Communication

Technologies (ICTs) are a prerequisite for economic and social development and that '[e]xclusion from these networks is one of the most damaging forms of exclusion in our economy and in our society'.

English is also framed within the discourse of development as a means of allowing access to technology, and English and ICT provision are often closely linked in development programmes today as a means of helping to reach the United Nations' Millennium Development Goals. As Graddol (2006: 72; 2010) notes, information technology and English have become part of a 'basic education' or 'functional literacy', as they are both needed today to engage with the global economy, as well as to gain access to the products of knowledge generation (see Norton *et al.*, this volume).

The Content of the Book

The 11 chapters in the current volume extend and expand upon many of these debates and areas of investigation. They set out to show that, while English is consistently promoted as a key resource for development in the era of globalisation, the relationship between the language and development is a complex one, with local variables influencing the effect and meaning it can have in different contexts. As such, empirical research (of the sort showcased here) on the impact of English and English-language education initiatives on the linguistic ecologies and language ideologies that exist in the communities at which these initiatives are targeted can play an important role in informing policy and, in this way, contribute to the success and sustainability of such programmes. In engaging with these issues, the chapters in the book all show a commitment to initiatives informed by an understanding of local contexts and an intent on providing support that allows communities to engage on a global scale while remaining sensitive to local needs and practicalities.

Approaching these issues from a variety of disciplinary perspectives, the chapters offer critical examinations of the current and historical relationship between English and development. Of particular interest for all the contexts covered are attitudes and beliefs about English as a global language and the question of how this concept influences language education policies and practices. Several chapters also examine issues around the use of English as a medium of instruction and the impact this may have on development when English is not the main language of the community. Another common theme is an exploration of how communities, in the face of a global language being used in so many new domains, are able to find ways to negotiate a careful balance between local and global languages in order to participate in their own development. A summary of the main themes addressed in the chapters follows.

Ferguson, in Chapter 1, provides a thorough introduction to current thinking and practices concerning the relationship between education and development, and explores the notion of educational quality and the issues and controversies surrounding the choice of language for medium of instruction in schools. He aims to uncover why, despite ample evidence that English-medium instruction can impact negatively on the quality of education, the demand for the language remains such a powerful force, and what impact it has on development initiatives.

In Chapter 2, *Rassool* examines the hegemony of English as a 'world language' within the broader discourse of language and development in postcolonial societies. In doing so, she questions some of the common frameworks used to analyse the ways in which language is involved in contemporary processes of societal development, and, arguing for the need for a wide-ranging methodological approach, employs a Bourdieusian framework to look at how the position and status of English in particular developmental contexts relates to changes taking place within the global economy.

In the next chapter, *Williams* continues the examination of the social and educational impact of language policy decisions about the choice of medium of instruction. Presenting data from Malawian, Zambian and Rwandan schools, he shows how English as the medium of instruction has had a negative effect on the education of the majority in these countries, and that there is thus little evidence that education policies structured around this principle enhance national unification or development. Drawing on these findings, he then explores potential alternative policy approaches aimed at securing a country's sociocultural base (especially in terms of its linguistic culture) while enabling it to participate more equitably in the global economy.

Erling, Hamid and *Seargeant*, in Chapter 4, consider the extent to which assumptions about English that are articulated in official language policies (i.e. those produced by governmental organisations, funding bodies and academic institutions) relate to the grassroots discourse on English that is constructed by the people at whom such development initiatives are aimed. Drawing on data collected in part from a large-scale international development project in Bangladesh, the chapter explores local language ideologies about the use of English and ELT, and surveys both the local aspirations about the English language, and also the perceived role the language plays in the lives of those who have invested in its learning.

Chapter 5 turns to an examination of the role played by assessment in personal and national development, and how English is used as gatekeeping mechanism in many postcolonial countries. In the context of Sub-Saharan Africa, where a significant number of children have to demonstrate their school achievement through formal examinations administered through a second or even a third language, *Rea-Dickins, Khamis* and *Olivero* explore the ways in which working through an unfamiliar language impacts on students' abilities to be taught and examined. As the chapter points out, these issues are not restricted solely to educational successes and failures, as there is also a broader impact on the social and economic lives of individuals and their overall well-being.

In Chapter 6, *Wedell* examines how, despite the lack of any clear evidence of links between national English-language levels and development, educational policy statements in many countries suggest that developing citizens' English-language proficiency is a prerequisite for national development and national ability to meet the demands and effects of globalisation. But with the increasing focus on English, he points out that policy makers rarely seem to recognise widespread failure in the implementation of educational change, and that, if they wish reform to be effective, the education system needs to be viewed as a whole. Thus, any plans for implementing (English) curriculum reform need to consider the needs of *all* those likely to be more or less directly affected by the changes.

Bartlett, in his chapter, shifts the focus to a new context and area of exploration. Whereas the previous chapters interrogate the often uneasy relationship between policy intentions and practical realities, Bartlett examines how the locally specific use of English can foster a discourse that will benefit both local communities and international development organisations. Using the sociolinguistic concept of 'voice', and drawing on examples from fieldwork in the North Rupununi Savannahs of Guyana analysed within the framework of Systemic Functional Linguistics, the chapter looks at hybrid discourse patterns utilising English in which the different forms of symbolic capital possessed by local participants and professional development workers can be combined to construct a collaborative approach to development. The chapter points particularly at ways that English can be appropriated by different communities, and the important role that this process can have in development.

The next chapter, by *Norton, Jones* and *Ahimbisibwe*, examines ways in which access to health awareness can be increased through the development of IT competence and English-language use. It reports on an action research study undertaken in a rural Ugandan village, which explores how a group of young women gain access to information about HIV/AIDS through global health websites, which are available in English. The study illustrates how literacy skills in both English and technology give access to global knowledge deposits – in this case health and medicine information – and how these skills can be facilitated and fostered by development programmes.

Chapter 9 again shifts focus slightly, examining a case in which development over the past several decades has been very successful but where controversies about the positioning of English still occupy debates over policy. In this chapter, *Wee* looks at the way English has been promoted in Singapore's language policy as a key means of achieving socio-economic mobility and for ensuring the nation's continued access to scientific-technological developments. Because of this, however, the government has become concerned that Singlish, an informal local variety of English, is having a detrimental effect on society and could therefore have a negative effect on the country's further development. Wee argues that the government's anti-Singlish stance, however, construes the global value of English too narrowly, and that use of this nativised variety actually contributes to a sense of what is authentic about Singaporean identity and is thus an advantage in the government's drive for further 'global' development.

The following chapter, by *Lillis* and *Curry*, again focuses on the often-contentious role that English can play in access to knowledge resources and the effects this has on development. The authors examine how English is bound up with global academic publishing and embedded in research evaluation systems, which are increasingly being driven transnationally by Anglophone-based frameworks of evaluation. Drawing on both quantitative and qualitative research into the politics of academic production and evaluation, the chapter discusses the relevance of debates over the topic to international development. It shows how the dominance of English as the medium of scholarly exchange may be leading to the stratification of opportunities for securing publication and, as a result, in the kinds of knowledges produced and published in different parts of the world.

In the final chapter in the volume, *Arcand* and *Grin* use econometric procedures in an attempt to establish empirically verifiable links between the English language and development. As intimated above, they find that in postcolonial contexts, widespread competence in English is *not* necessarily associated with a higher level of economic development (measured by GDP). Instead, their analysis points to the fact that societal multilingualism, or use of local languages, actually increases income per capita in these contexts. As a complement to the qualitative studies, which begin the book, the statistical measurements presented in this chapter add further insightful detail to the overall picture of the complex and multifaceted relationship that can exist between English – and English-language education – and development. They also suggest that there are solid grounds for considering linguistic diversity as conducive to economic development – and that causes for slow growth should, in future research, be sought elsewhere.

The range of themes and contexts covered in these chapters, then, is an indication not only of the complexities in the relationship between English and development, but also the challenges for language professionals working within such contexts. Given the history of English, the political and practical issues resulting from its spread are now having an effect on people and societies in diverse contexts across the world, and the increasing use of the language in development contexts, promoted in part by a discourse of 'English as a language for international development' (Seargeant & Erling, 2011), means that this particular aspect of the study of English in the world is becoming a critical topic within the wider disciplines of both development studies and English-language studies. It is hoped that the collected chapters in this book, with their focus on the politics, pedagogies, economics and social impact of English-language provision in development contexts, can contribute to the expansion of this important area of study, and in doing so can also provide solid academic foundations on which the practical work of development can build in the contemporary world.

References

Appleby, R. (2010) *ELT, Gender and International Development*. Bristol: Multilingual Matters.

Azam, M.C.A. and Prakash, N. (2010) The returns to English-language skills in India. Bonn: Institute for the Study of Labor. Discussion Paper No. 4802. http://ideas.repec.org/p/iza/izadps/dp4802.html

Blommaert, J. (2008) *Grassroot Literacy: Writing, Identity and Voice in Central Africa*. Abingdon: Routledge.

Brock-Utne, B. (2000) *Whose Education for All? The Recolonization of the African Mind*. New York: Falmer Press.

Bruthiaux, P. (2002) Hold your courses: Language education, language choice, and economic development. *TESOL Quarterly* 36 (3), 275-296.

Buchmann, C. (1999) Poverty and educational inequality in Sub-Saharan Africa. *Prospects* 24 (4), 503-515.

Castells, M. (1999) Information technology, globalization and social development. United Nations Research Institute for Social Development (UNRISD). Discussion Paper no. 14. www.unrisd.org/unrisd/website/document.nsf/(httpPublications)/F270E0C066F3DE7780256B67005B728C

Chakraborty, T. and Kapur, S. (2008) English language premium: Evidence from a policy experiment in India. Washington University St. Louis. www.isid.ac.in/~pu/conference/dec_08_conf/Papers/ShilpiKapur.pdf

Coleman, H. (2010) *The English language in development*. British Council: Teaching English. http://www.teachingenglish.org.uk/transform/books/english-language-development

Coleman, H. (ed.) (2011) *Dreams and Realities: Developing Countries and the English Language*. London: British Council.

Crossley, M. and Watson, K. (2003) *Comparative and International Research in Education: Globalisation, Context and Difference*. London: Routledge.

Crystal, D. (2003) *English as a Global Language*. Cambridge: Cambridge University Press.

Djité, P. (2008) *The Sociolinguistics of Development in Africa*. Clevedon: Multilingual Matters.

Erling, E.J., Seargeant, P., Solly, M., Chowdhury, Q.H. and Rahman, S. (2012) *Attitudes to English as a language for international development in rural Bangladesh*. London: British

Council. http://www.teachingenglish.org.uk/publications/attitudes-english-a-language-international-development-rural-bangladesh
Escobar, A. (1995) *Encountering Development: The Making and Unmaking of the Third World.* Princeton, NJ: Princeton University Press.
Euromonitor (2010) *The Benefits of the English Language for Individuals and Societies; Quantitative Indicators from Cameroon, Nigeria, Rwanda, Bangladesh and Pakistan*. London: Euromonitor International.
Euromonitor (2012) *The Benefits of the English Language for Individuals and Societies; Quantitative Indicators from Algeria, Egypt, Iraq, Jordan, Lebanon, Morocco, Tunisia and Yemen*. London: Euromonitor International.
Graddol, D. (2006) *English Next*. London: British Council.
Graddol, D. (2010) *English Next India*. London: British Council.
Grin, F. (2001) English as economic value: Facts and fallacies. *World Englishes* 20 (1), 65-78.
Hanushek, E.A. and Woessmann, L. (2008) The role of cognitive skills in economic development. *Journal of Economic Literature* 46 (3), 607-668.
Harbert, W., McConnell-Ginet, S., Miller A. and Whitman, J. (eds) (2009) *Language and Poverty*. Bristol: Multilingual Matters.
Harris, P.G. (2011) *Language in schools in Namibia: The missing link in educational achievement?* Windhoek: The Urban Trust of Namibia. http://www.osisa.org/sites/default/files/language_in_ schools_in_namibia_-_the_missing_link_in_educational_achievement.pdf
Hettne, B. (2009) *Thinking about Development*. London: Zed Books.
Kamwangamalu, N.M. (2010) Vernacularization, globalization, and language economics in non-English-speaking countries in Africa. *Language Problems and Language Planning* 34 (1), 1-23.
Kellner, D. (2000) New technologies/new literacies: Restructuring education for a new millennium. *Teaching Education* 11 (3), 245-265.
Kenny, B. and Savage, W. (eds) (1997) *Language and Development: Teachers in a Changing World*. London: Longman.
Ku, H. and Zussman, A. (2010) Lingua franca: The role of English in international trade. *Journal of Economic Behavior and Organization* 75, 250-260.
Lamb, M. and Coleman, H. (2008) Literacy in English and the transformation of self and society in post-Soeharto Indonesia. *The International Journal of Bilingual Education and Bilingualism* 11 (2), 189-205.
Levinsohn, J. (2007) Globalization and the returns to speaking English in South Africa. In A. Harrison (ed.) *Globalization and Poverty* (pp. 629-646). Chicago, IL: University of Chicago Press.
Little, A. and Green, A. (2009) Successful globalisation, education and sustainable development. *International Journal of Educational Development* 29, 166-174.
Lo Bianco, J. (2002) *Voices from Phnom Penh, Development and Language: Global Influences and Local Effects*. Melbourne: Language Australia.
Martin, W.M. and Lomperis, A.E. (2002) Determining the cost benefit, the return on investment, and the intangible impacts of language programs for development. *TESOL Quarterly* 36 (3), 399-429.
Mazrui, A. (2004) *English in Africa: After the Cold War*. Clevedon: Multilingual Matters.
Mohanty, A. (2009) Perpetuating inequality: Language disadvantage and capability deprivation of tribal mother tongue speakers in India. In W. Harbert, S. McConnell-Ginet, A. Miller and J. Whitman (eds) *Language and Poverty* (pp. 104-124). Bristol: Multilingual Matters.

Moon, B. and O'Malley, B. (2008) *Every Child Needs a Teacher: The Primary Teacher Supply and Training Crisis in Sub-Saharan Africa*. London: Commission for UNESCO.

Nunan, D. (2003) The impact of English as a global language on educational policies and practices in the Asia-Pacific region. *TESOL Quarterly* 37 (4), 589-613.

Palmer, R., Wedgwood, R., Hayman, R., King, K. and Thin, N. (2007) *Educating Out of Poverty? A Synthesis Report on Ghana, India, Kenya, Rwanda, Tanzania and South Africa*. London: Department for International Development (DFID).

Pincas, A. (ed.) (1995) *Spreading English: ELT Projects in International Development*. Hertfordshire: Prentice Hall.

Pinnock, H. and Vijayakumar, G. (2009) *Language and Education: The Missing Link*. London: Save the Children and CfBT Education Trust. http://www.unesco.org/education/EFAWG2009/LanguageEducation.pdf

Rassool, N. (2007) *Global Issues in Language, Education and Development: Perspectives from Postcolonial Societies*. Clevedon: Multilingual Matters.

Schultz, T.W. (1963) *The Economic Value of Education*. New York: Columbia University Press.

Seargeant, P. (2012) *Exploring World Englishes: Language in a Global Context*. Abington: Routledge.

Seargeant, P. and Erling, E.J. (2011) The discourse of 'English as a language for international development': Policy assumptions and practical challenges. In H. Coleman (ed.) *Dreams and Realities: Developing Countries and the English Language* (pp. 248-267). London: British Council.

Sen, A. (2001) *Development as Freedom*. Oxford: Oxford University Press.

Street, B. (ed.) (2001) *Literacy and Development: Ethnographic Perspectives*. London: Routledge.

Tembe, J. and Norton, B. (2011) English education, local languages and community perspectives in Uganda. In H. Coleman (ed.) *Dreams and Realities: Developing Countries and the English Language* (pp. 114-136). London: British Council.

Thomas, A. (2000) Meanings and views of development. In T. Allen and A. Thomas (eds) *Poverty and Development into the 21st Century* (pp. 23-48). Oxford: Oxford University Press.

United Nations (UN) (2008) *Millennium Development Goals Report*. New York: United Nations. http://www.un.org/millenniumgoals/2008highlevel/pdf/newsroom/mdg%20reports/MDG_Report_2008_ENGLISH.pdf

United Nations (UN) (2000) United Nations Millennium Development Goals (UNMD). www.un.org/millenniumgoals/

Vavrus, F. (2002) Postcoloniality and English: Exploring language policy and the politics of development in Tanzania. *TESOL Quarterly* 36 (3), 373-397.

Widin, J. (2010) *Illegitimate Practices: Global English Language Education*. Bristol: Multilingual Matters.

Williams, E. and Cooke, J. (2002) Pathways and labyrinths: Language and education in development. *TESOL Quarterly* 36 (3), 297-322.

1 English, Development and Education: Charting the Tensions

Gibson Ferguson

Introduction

As one might expect, given divergent perspectives on the global diffusion of English (see e.g. Phillipson, 1992; Pennycook, 2000), the relationships of English to development are contested and controversial. On the one hand, an almost unanimous community of applied linguists see the continued use of English as a medium of education in primary schools in Sub-Saharan Africa, and elsewhere, as impairing the quality of education, and hence as holding back development. On the other hand, there are abundant official discourses that portray English-language skills as essential for economic competitiveness, for entry into the knowledge economy and for access to foreign investment and technology. Not uncommonly such views are buttressed by development experts who argue the benefits of widespread English-language skills. An example would be Green *et al.* (2007: 218), whose report for the UK Department for International Development (DFID) concludes:

> Are there any straightforward lessons to be learnt regarding the benefits of promoting particular kinds of skills through education? Two points seem to emerge clearly from our analysis.
>
> First widespread fluency in English language has proved to be a considerable asset in many developing countries, especially for the growth of service industries, as India is now finding. Some successful developers, like Singapore and Hong Kong, had this advantage built into their education systems through colonial inheritance and public policy decisions from the start since English was a major language of instruction ....

At the popular level, meanwhile, there is a seemingly insatiable demand for English-medium education and/or the early introduction of English as a curricular subject (see e.g. Trudell, 2007; Muthwii, 2004; Probyn, 2001, 2005; Annamalai, 2004; Nunan, 2003 with respect to Cameroon, Kenya, South Africa, India and East Asia). And this pressure has been reflected in policy: for example, in the drift to English-medium education in South African schools despite official multilingualism (Kamwangamalu, 2004), in the ever earlier introduction of English as a curriculum subject in East Asian countries and in the rapid growth in private English-medium schools in India, Tanzania and elsewhere (see e.g. Graddol, 2010; Lassibille *et al.*, 1999).

If the relationships of English to development are controversial, they are also complex and difficult to ascertain reliably. One reason lies in the very variable relationship of education, hence of English, to development across different societies with different economies and labour markets, different education systems and different sociolinguistic ecologies. The failed neo-liberal 'Washington consensus' approach to development,[1] positing (almost) universal recipes for economic growth, has long since given way to more nuanced understandings of development, and of the role of local factors – governance, social cohesion and social capital, culture, equality, etc. – as conditioning the potential for, and the pathways toward, development (see e.g. Robertson *et al.*, 2007). Thus, there are likely to be few policy prescriptions that are universally applicable, and the relationship of English to development is not a constant across societies.

Another source of complexity lies in the very definition of development. Narrow economic conceptions seem to have given way to broader conceptions that embrace improved governance, security, better health, social cohesion, environmental sustainability and so on.[2] Similarly, poverty can be defined from various perspectives – narrowly as a lack of income, or more broadly as a complex of multiple, interlocking deprivations – as precarious livelihoods, isolated places, hungry and sick bodies, low physical security, disrespect by the powerful, discriminatory social relations and disempowering institutions (see Narayan *et al.*, 2000: 2). Our purpose here, however, is not to interrogate these definitions – there is insufficient space for that – but rather simply to note them, and observe that if development is indeed multifaceted, it is possible that English relates to the facets in varying ways – perhaps advancing development in some directions while thwarting it in others.

It is apparent already, then, that in discussing English and development one enters a terrain bestrewn with tensions, even contradictions – for example, between access and quality, equity and efficiency, educational research and public pressure, aspiration and economic reality. This chapter explores some of these tensions. Our focus is mainly on Sub-Saharan Africa, but because English-language skills are typically acquired through the formal educational system, it is useful to first briefly review what is known about the relationship between education and development generally.

Education and Development: The Wider Context

For many years, influenced substantially by human capital theory,[3] education has been seen as having positive benefits for development. A historically influential methodology for probing the economic benefits of education has been rate of return analysis, a form of analysis that matches life-time earnings against the cost of education. Broadly speaking, these analyses indicate positive social and private returns to investment in education at all levels (Psacharopoulos & Patrinos, 2002), especially at the primary level.[4] This finding, in combination with the rise of the poverty reduction agenda (see Robertson *et al.*, 2007) and the international adoption of the Millennium Development Goals (MDGs), has led to a particular investment focus on the basic education sector, a key driver, so it is thought, of poverty reduction. Meanwhile, alongside the putative economic benefits, there are claims of indirect benefits: for example, education has been linked to enhanced agricultural productivity, better maternal health and reduced child mortality (see e.g. World Bank, 2005a; King & Palmer, 2006b).

However, while there is a broad consensus that education is positively associated with development, there remain uncertainties around the precise nature of this association, three aspects of which can be singled out for comment. The first is methodological, and concerns the reliability of the data on which rates of return analysis are based, particularly in Sub-Saharan Africa (see e.g. Bennell, 1996). Samples may not be truly representative of the populations under study (Psacharopoulos & Patrinos, 2002), and the methodology is limited in not taking account of the non-economic benefits and costs of education. Thus, while rate of return of analysis may be one useful tool for guiding investment decisions, it generally needs to be supplemented by other methodologies.

A second area of uncertainty concerns the precise components of education that contribute most to poverty reduction and development:[5] literacy, general analytical abilities, or specific technical skills (inclusive of language skills). Answers are elusive, however, not just because of the methodological challenges but because such contributions are likely to vary across locations, and, most pertinently, across time. Palmer *et al.* (2007), for example, suggest that information technology skills and scientific literacy may become more economically relevant due to globalisation, the rise of knowledge-based economies and the onset of rapid technological change. One might also speculate – no more than that – that the same economic changes may be increasing the economic utility of English-language skills, a point of view that Green *et al.* (2007) in the quote at the beginning of the chapter seem to endorse. That said, the dearth of tracer studies and of rates of return analyses for English-language education means that we lack detailed empirical evidence of how English functions for individuals in terms of life-outcomes, and of its benefits and costs for society as a whole.

A related question has to do with the developmental contribution of the different levels of education. As noted previously, governments and donor agencies have historically tended to prioritise primary/basic education, and indeed this is enshrined in the MDGs. But such prioritisation, and the attendant dangers of an unbalanced expansion of one sector of education to the detriment of others, has recently received critical attention from a number of commentators (e.g. King & Palmer, 2006a; Palmer *et al.*, 2007), and indeed the World Bank itself (World Bank, 2005b), who, noting the interlocking nature of different education levels, point out the essential contributions of secondary and tertiary education. There are, first of all, benefits for primary education in that the prospects of continuing to a higher level of education incentivise primary school completion (World Bank, 2005b). The secondary/tertiary levels also provide trained teachers for primary schools, not to mention trained health professionals, IT professionals, business leaders, scientists and the like. Studies also show a range of indirect benefits (externalities): for example, women with secondary education tend to delay marriage, have fewer children and experience lower child mortality (Benefo & Schulz, 1996); secondary school study is also associated with greater use of agricultural technologies and the creation of more profitable enterprises (Palmer *et al.*, 2007).

Conversely, the limitations of an education restricted to primary level are becoming more apparent. A number of country-specific studies (Fryer & Vencatachellum, 2002; World Bank, 2004b[6]) suggest that rates of return to primary education may be falling and those for secondary and tertiary on the rise, reasons for which include the very low quality of much primary education and the sheer numbers of primary graduates. At the same time, economic and technological change is altering the demand for particular kinds of skills, and in many places primary education alone confers little advantage in finding a waged job.

This growing appreciation of the contributions of secondary education (see e.g. King & Palmer, 2006a; Palmer *et al.*, 2007) and the increased emphasis on the role of primary education as an essential preparation for further study is not without implications for English-language education. Secondary education, after all, is, in Africa, very much the domain of English-medium education, and thus the quality of instruction and the outcomes of schooling will be partly dependent on how well pupils and teachers are prepared for the use of this medium.

The third, and probably most crucial, aspect of the education–development association we focus on is the importance of context. It is now relatively well-understood that education can facilitate development (see e.g. King & Palmer, 2006b; Palmer *et al.*, 2007) – but only in an enabling environment. Put simply, quality education can promote the acquisition of skills and knowledge but does not guarantee their purposeful utilisation. There is no direct causal pathway from education to development, as is perhaps illustrated by the case of Kenya, where despite considerable investment in schooling over the past 20 or 30 years, there has, arguably, been little impact on incomes or social cohesion (see e.g. Oketch, 2007: 137).

Disabling factors, ones that block the developmental potential of education, are various and include poor governance, weak institutional capacity, a stagnant macro-economic environment that does not generate employment opportunities, a deteriorating ecology and a non-progressive, non-egalitarian political environment (e.g. arbitrary decision making, policy fluctuation, weak civil society). More specific factors may impede the realization of particular potential gains: for example, the benefits of literacy, whether in local languages or English, may be reduced if there is no literacy environment (e.g. few or no newspapers, books or printed materials, no electric light) to sustain literacy skills. The benefits to agricultural productivity similarly may not be realised if there is lack of access to credit, fertilisers, extension services, agricultural markets, etc.

If the above factors are part of the disabling/enabling external context, then the quality of education is surely one of the critical internal factors governing the relationship of education to development, and it is here that the applied linguistics literature on the effects of English-medium education in Sub-Saharan Africa and elsewhere is especially relevant. Accordingly, it is to this that we now turn.

The Quality of Education and the Language of Instruction

It is now widely accepted, and has been for some time (UNESCO, 1953), that a local (or familiar) language is the most educationally effective language of instruction in early education and, indeed, possibly throughout primary education. The key arguments, briefly, are that cognitive development is best fostered in a language the child knows well. Instruction through a familiar language improves the quality of interaction between pupil and teacher, narrows the gulf between home and school, integrates the school better into the local community and gives recognition to the pupil's home language and culture (see e.g. Benson, 2000). It is also sometimes suggested, in line with Cummins's linguistic interdependence hypothesis (Cummins, 1979), that consolidation of academic literacy skills in the first language can facilitate subsequent acquisition of the same skills in the further languages learned.

These arguments are increasingly bolstered by empirical evidence. For example, Williams (1996) shows that Year 5 primary pupils in Malawi, where Chichewa is the medium up to Year 4, have no worse reading abilities in English and better Chichewa/Nyanja abilities than Year 5 pupils in Zambia, where the official medium from Year 1 is English. Experimentation with local language or bilingual media of instruction in Nigeria, Mozambique and Burkina Faso has had broadly favourable results (see Fafunwa *et al.*, 1989; Benson, 2000, 2002; Alidou & Brock-Utne, 2006). In a Botswana study, Prophet and Dow (1994) taught a set of science concepts in Setswana and in English. On testing they found that the class taught in Setswana outperformed a matched Year 1 secondary class taught in English, who also had difficulties in expressing their ideas in class.

Conversely, a body of evidence points to the weak performance of pupils in English-medium education in many African countries, especially where skills in the language are poorly developed through primary school and where there is little exposure to the language beyond the school. An illustrative, and much cited, early study here is that of Criper and Dodd (1984: 1) from Tanzania, who report that:

> Most pupils leave primary school unable to speak or understand simple English. A selected few enter secondary school but they are so weak in English that they are unable to understand lessons or read textbooks in English. Teachers more often than not teach in Kiswahili and give notes in English.[7]

If Tanzania, where Kiswahili is the medium throughout primary education, is a particularly severe case, similar problems have been reported elsewhere in Africa. Williams and Cooke (2002: 307), for example, report on adverse findings from Zambia, Zimbabwe, Zanzibar, Mauritius and Namibia.

Further studies implicate poor L2 English-language skills in patterns of classroom interaction that are not conducive to learning. A recent example would be Hardman *et al.*'s (2008) study of primary classrooms in Nigeria, which documents styles of classroom interaction – not unfamiliar from previous studies (see e.g. Brock-Utne & Alidou, 2006) – characterised by a teacher-centred, lecturing pedagogy with passive pupils offering very short choral (or individual) responses to teachers' questions. Meanwhile, Rea-Dickins *et al.* (2009) documents how pupils in Zanzibar are disadvantaged in maths and science examinations by having to process, and respond to, questions in English only, thus casting doubt on the validity and reliability of the examinations themselves.

There is, then, a body of evidence that English-medium instruction, in Africa, if not elsewhere,[8] impairs the quality of education, and that education in a familiar language may be, as common sense would suggest, more effective. On this basis many commentators (e.g. Rubagumya, 1990; Arthur, 1994; Trappes-Lomax, 1990; Heugh, 2006) have argued, so far with little success, for a shift from 'early-exit' policies, under which pupils transition to English medium after perhaps three to four years of primary schooling, to 'late-exit' policies, allowing a considerably prolonged period of local language media of instruction up to and including secondary education.

However, while plausible – even compelling – in educational terms, these arguments, and the applied linguistics literature from which they derive, have limitations stemming from their partial engagement with the political, economic and social contextual factors that constrain major shifts in language education policy, central among which is the persistent, apparently unquenchable, public desire for English-language education. It is to an exploration of these that we now turn.

Constraints on Policy Change: The Wider Political and Economic Context

Many, but not all, commentators arguing for the extension of the use of local languages of instruction acknowledge that the poor quality of education in many developing countries has multiple causes. These may be worth commenting on in a little more detail than is customary in the applied linguistic literature, if only to reinforce the point that a single intervention such as changing the medium of instruction may have little effect unless embedded in a wider reform programme.

Among these multiple causes, ironically,[9] has been the drive for universal primary education (UPE) and the consequent rapid, and poorly planned, rise in pupil enrolments (e.g. a 143% rise in Uganda between 1996 and 2003 (ODI, 2006)[10]), the overall effect of which has been to exacerbate already severe problems of teacher supply and material shortages. The result, in many cases, is classes with over 50 pupils, few desks for pupils to sit at, a shortage of classrooms useable in rainy weather (in a relatively prosperous Ghana only 66% of classrooms are useable during rain (World Bank, 2004a)), and a low textbook–pupil ratio, this being a key input impacting on pupil achievement (Fuller, 1987; Fuller & Heyneman, 1989). Teacher quality has also been impaired. In many countries a high proportion of primary teachers are untrained.[11] Many are not educated beyond junior secondary school, and as a consequence often have low levels of English proficiency even though they teach in nominally English-medium systems. High mortality from HIV in some countries has further exacerbated difficulties in supplying sufficient qualified teachers (e.g. Malawi and Zambia, see Bennell *et al.*, 2002; Williams, 2006), while high levels of teacher turnover in remoter rural schools compound the difficulties (Bennell *et al.*, 2002).

The problems extend beyond shortages of teachers and materials to encompass issues of school culture and teacher methodology, endemic even where a local language of instruction is utilised – as in Tanzania. These include teacher absenteeism[12] (which in Ghana has been on the rise despite improvements in material conditions (World Bank, 2004a)), weak teacher morale and commitment, and low-level corruption in school management. Meanwhile, though there is evidence that the use of local languages can enhance the quality and quantity of pupil talk (EdQual, 2010), it is unsurprising, given the numbers of underqualified teachers, that many – even when teaching in a local language – have a limited pedagogical repertoire and fall back on the inefficient pedagogical discourses to which they themselves were exposed as pupils.

That systems utilising a local language of instruction are not immune from such problems is partly evidenced by the case of Tanzania, where there are reports of pupils leaving primary schools with poor maths and English skills. Lassibille *et al.* (1999: 26) remark, for example, that 'a major handicap faced by all schools, public and private alike, is that most students enter secondary school with a poor basis for good performance'. And Rubagumya (2003) appears to attribute the growth of private English-medium primary schools not so much to the attraction of English but to parental perceptions of a deterioration in the quality of state primary education, which in this case is delivered in Kiswahili.

This somewhat depressing litany of problems has not been compiled for its own sake, however, but to make two straightforward points. The first is that, because educational underachievement has multiple and complex, interlinked causes, a change in the policy on the language of instruction for upper primary or secondary level is unlikely of itself to resolve the issue of low quality. It needs to be accompanied by simultaneous change in educational practices and resourcing, the two being interdependent. And, as I have argued previously (Ferguson, 2006), placing too great a burden of expectation on a single, if necessary, policy intervention is likely to lead only to disappointment. The second point is that, given the range of challenges to be addressed, the scale of spending needed to remedy basic material shortages, and the high proportion of budgetary expenditure allocated to recurrent costs (e.g. salaries, books), it seems likely that a relatively complex intervention like replacing English with a local language of instruction will require external donor support. It is also likely to tax to the maximum the analytical and implementational capabilities of stressed ministries of education. That said, if cost alone were a barrier to change, it could, and would, in all probability have been overcome by now. The trouble is there are other constraints to which we now turn.

The Persistence of English and Public Attitudes

It is commonly, and rightly, observed (e.g. see Tollefson & Tsui, 2004) that policy on medium of instruction is as much, or more, driven by socio-political factors as educational evidence, and it is to these that applied linguistics commentators usually turn for an explanation of what, for them, is a perplexing, even perverse, retention of English as a language of instruction. Most frequently invoked here, are vested interests (so-called 'elite closure' (Clayton, 1998; Myers-Scotton, 1990)) and misguided/ill-informed public attitudes toward English in education.

The vested interest argument, to take this first, proposes that the retention of English-medium education helps elites maintain their privileged status by excluding the mass of the population, who have less easy access to the language and hence to the opportunities it confers. They are thus better able to reproduce their privilege in the succeeding generation.

The argument has a certain plausibility, and may partly explain the lack of 'political will' that some commentators (e.g. Brock-Utne, 2010) adduce as a reason for inertia on language education policy. But there are difficulties. First, direct evidence of a covert motivation is, by its very nature, not easy to secure, and second, and more importantly, the expansion of secondary schooling in Africa is beginning, if slowly and partially, to widen access to English, which, in turn, is reducing the potency of English as an instrument of 'elite closure'. It is necessary, therefore, to consider other probably more powerful constraints, among them the public hunger for English.

There is no shortage of evidence of the attractiveness of English-language education in Africa, and across the world. In Tanzania, for example, private English-medium schools – catering principally to the children of political and business elites – are on the increase (Vavrus, 2002). The same is true of India, where Graddol (2010: 84) notes that the proportion of pupils attending private schools, most of them English medium, has risen from roughly

16% in 2005 to 26% in 2008. From South Africa, Broom (2004) reports sustained pressure for schools to transition to English medium as early as possible. From China, Hu and Alsagoff (2010) report initiatives to introduce school-level English-medium programmes in response to popular demand, and in other states in Asia English is introduced as a curricular subject at ever earlier ages (Nunan, 2003). In Europe, meanwhile, English is already almost universally taught as a curricular subject, but in addition CLIL programmes,[13] using English as one teaching medium, are multiplying rapidly, while the number of English-medium programmes in European higher education has tripled over five years to 2400 in 2007 (Wächter & Maiworm, 2008).

Increasing demand, however, does necessarily mean that it is rational, and a number of commentators (e.g. Wolff, 2006; Brock-Utne, 2010) argue that parents' preference for English-medium education is ill-informed and misguided. There is much to commend in this argument – at least as regards the educational evidence, which is often complex and counter-intuitive, especially for parents with little formal education. And certainly much more could be done to inform parents following the strategies outlined by Linehan (2004) for the Zambian primary reading programme, which successfully persuaded parents of the merits of initial literacy in Zambian languages.

That said, there are many who – though conscious of the educational difficulties posed by instruction through English – nevertheless insist on the need for English-medium education because of the longer-term socio-economic benefits it appears to promise – for example, the individual cited by Brock-Utne (2005: 174). Two issues demand examination here: (1) to what extent do socio-economic benefits accrue to individuals through the acquisition of English-language skills; (2) does the considerable expense of teaching English, and in English, yield commensurate benefits for society as a whole.

Socio-economic benefits accruing to the individual

It has been estimated that the informal economy accounts for roughly 93% of all new jobs in Sub-Saharan Africa (see Palmer *et al.*, 2007: 5). This is educationally relevant, for most informal sector employment does not call for, nor particularly reward, high level of English-language skills. Thus, it seems quite possible that in the end the majority derive little direct economic benefit from the acquisition of English. To substantiate this claim empirical evidence based on studies of the private (and social) rates of return to English-language kills would be useful, but to my knowledge there are as yet few such African-based studies focusing on English as opposed to education in general[14] and similarly few relevant tracer studies.

But, in any case, to understand the attractions of English one has to move beyond the benefits actually accruing to consider aspirations and the opportunities foregone if one has no English. The fact is that in many economies English functions as a gatekeeper to employment in the formal public sector (e.g. the civil service), to work in service industries (e.g. tourism, call centres, banking) and, most importantly, to upper secondary and higher education, which typically offers the greatest private returns. To a rural parent the idea of a son/daughter (or other relative) obtaining a civil service post with a regular salary is a most enticing prospect, bearing in mind here Oketch's (2007: 152) point that the incomes of many rural households need supplementation from non-farm sources, which often takes the form of remittances from those in salaried employment.

The widespread parental preference for English-medium instruction cannot, then, be seen as irrational, for, while parents may well realize that English-language skills do not guarantee a good job, they also know that without English one is definitively excluded from a host of opportunities. Moreover, the behaviour of elites in sending their children to private English-medium schools – sometimes outside the country – constitutes a further signal to the population of the potential of English.[15] The trouble is, of course, that though rational at the individual level, these preferences, when aggregated, may help sustain a system of education that doubly disadvantages the majority, first because it may impair the quality of mass education, and second because instruction in English tends to favour the elite, who have easier all-round access to the language than the rural poor.

English, one could also argue, has attractions that go beyond the strictly economic. For many young people, speaking English – of whatever variety – carries a social cachet, connoting social prestige, urban sophistication, 'international cool', upward mobility, and the middle class identities they see enacted by their teachers. Conversely, the standardised varieties of local languages taught in school are not only often different from the mixed urban vernaculars actually spoken in daily life such as Street Swahili, Sheng, Town Bemba, Tsotsitaal, Is'camtho, and Street Setswana (see e.g. Makoni *et al.*, 2007; Cook, 2009) but are perceived as lacking symbolic capital, as indexing undesired rural, static, narrowly ethnic and local identities. More seriously still, many parents – no doubt influenced by their historical inferiorisation – persist in seeing local languages as an educational and economic dead-end, affording little in the way of well-paid employment.

Changing these attitudes, and hence perceptions of local languages in education, requires no less than a long-overdue revalorisation of African languages but this, in turn, is most unlikely to be accomplished by top-down language planning alone or by imposing local language instructional media on an unenthusiastic public. Rather it will require first an economic reconfiguration to change the economic status/market value of these languages so as to incentivise their learning, but also their use in prestigious public domains to raise their prestige, and an increase in the quantity of entertainment/reading material available to enhance their attractiveness. But all this, as Alexander (2008, 2009[16]) suggests, depends on significant politico-economic change, whose implementation is, to say the least, uncertain. Revalorisation of local languages seems likely, then, to be a long-term, uncertain and politically contingent project, though this does not mean, of course, that proactive measures of the kind advocated by Alexander (2008) (e.g. linguistic infrastructure projects – translation, terminology elaboration, etc) should cease. Rather that the pull of English is likely to remain strong irrespective of the benefits it actually confers on individuals.

Benefits accruing to society

Moving to the societal level, one comes across an abundance of official state discourses extolling the social benefits of widely distributed English-language skills. The Tanzanian government national website, for example, proclaims that 'English is essential, as it is the language which links Tanzania and the rest of the world through technology, commerce and also administration'.[17]

And the 2000 Secondary Education Master Plan 2001-2005 avers that

> Tanzania cannot afford being illiterate in English while surrounded by countries which speak English fluently and hope to remain an active and effective member of key and strategic economic blocks that use English, including SADC (*Southern Africa Development Community*) and the Commonwealth.[18]

Leaving aside interesting questions regarding the discoursal properties of these statements and the rhetorical work they perform, we need to consider to what extent such claims have substance. Evaluation is exceedingly difficult, however, for a variety of reasons – for example, the lack of relevant data on the specific contribution of English to economic performance, controversy regarding the appropriacy of economic criteria in estimating the impact of English, and variation between the economies of different societies and their level of development, all of which influences the developmental contribution of English.

Nonetheless, it is possible – at a general level – to build a plausible argument not only that English-language skills can enhance economic performance but that with globalisation their importance is, if anything, increasing. Briefly put, the argument is that globalisation changes the relationship between national economies and the global market (see Green *et al.*, 2007), and in so doing increases the relative importance of foreign trade, foreign direct investment and export earnings, all of which have some dependence on international language skills. Also, in increasingly knowledge-based economies, technological skills and knowledge transfer, which both require communication skills in international languages, become more significant drivers of development (see e.g. World Bank, 2002; Palmer *et al.*, 2007). Meanwhile, higher and upper secondary education, where English is likely to remain a significant medium for the foreseeable future, is increasingly recognised (see e.g. World Bank, 2002) as making a vital contribution to development: for example, by supplying trained professionals (e.g. teachers, doctors, technicians, business managers) for other sectors, and by developing analytical capacities that are valuable for accessing global knowledge and reinterpreting it for local use. It follows, then, that English-language skills have a facilitative, if indirect, role in development in these particular areas.

If such general arguments are unpersuasive, then one could invoke specific examples. A case in point might be India, where the last two decades have witnessed a remarkable growth in service industries based around outsourcing (e.g. call centres, back-office work), and in the software industry centred in Bangalore, a consequence of which has been the expansion of a relatively prosperous, urban middle class. Of course, such success owes much to previous investment in technical and higher education but a relatively wide base of English-language skills has probably also been facilitative as Som Mittal, President of NASSCOM,[19] appears to suggest:

> As India aspires to grow 8-9% and integrates with the global economy, the service industry will grow, and the moment you talk about service industry, it is about people interacting with people, and in communication, language becomes important. And that's ... true for people who are in tourism, for people driving taxis, for people who are guides, for people in hotels. ... it could become a hindrance if we didn't have more people able to communicate in English and understand English. (cited in Graddol, 2010: 115)

The above arguments should not suggest, however, that local languages cannot also function as valuable resources for development and empowerment. In fact, as Stroud (2002) and Bruthiaux (2002) persuasively argue, they play an important role in the informal economy, and they allow poor, marginalised communities to engage more fully in development processes leading to more sustainable and locally relevant development. From a development perspective, then, there is no necessary opposition between local and international languages. Both can have useful functions in different contexts.

That said, claims for a facilitative role for English need not, and should not, obscure the fact that English-language education is always costly and often wasteful. Indeed, anyone observing the low quality of much primary education, the weak English-language skills of primary teachers and the poor language outcomes could find reason to conclude that teaching English as a subject at primary school, let alone using it as a medium, constitutes a waste of scarce resources and should therefore be suspended. Just such a recommendation has in fact been contemplated by external consultants invited to advise on language education policy – for example, Davies (2009) in Nepal, and Criper and Dodd (1984) in Tanzania. However, in both cases no such proposals were actually brought forward – in the Tanzanian case because '... it was universally rejected by all the Tanzanians we spoke to, both professionals and others' (Criper & Dodd, 1984: 22).

Meanwhile, English, or English-medium education, imposes well-understood social costs. Specifically, while English has the not negligible advantage of being ethnically neutral, it is far from neutral socio-economically. Urban elites find it easier to accumulate the capital that English represents either because their way of life affords greater environmental exposure to the language or, more importantly, because, in societies where secondary education is neither free nor universal, they are better placed to gain entry to high-quality secondary education, where the acquisition of English literacy skills is a central priority.

These factors – the poor quality of English teaching in primary schools, the varied and inequitable access to English through secondary education, the limited number of jobs in which high-level English-language skills are demonstrably necessary – would appear to suggest some drastic curtailment of the presence of English in the curriculum along the lines proposed by Bruthiaux (2002: 293), who argues that the priority for poverty alleviation is basic literacy in local languages and that English-language education should be targeted at specific populations who '... have a realistic chance of participating in international exchanges soon'.

However, efficient though it sounds, this kind of proposal has a number of weaknesses. First, it fails to take account of equity considerations and the aspirations of poorer communities, who identify English-language skills as an instrument, however flawed and uncertain, for accessing a better life. And if English is to be targeted at specific populations, how are those excluded going to be reconciled to the frustration of their aspirations? Second, in systems where secondary education encompasses both private and state-funded schools – as is now common in Africa owing to constrained state provision – any restriction of English in secondary school is likely to precipitate further moves to private English-medium education, at least on the part of those who can afford it. This, in turn, is quite likely to produce a version of what Ramanathan (2007), speaking of India, refers to as the 'English-Vernacular Divide': English-medium schooling for the middle class, vernacular medium for the masses. Finally, the root cause of inequality, one might argue, is not so much differential access to English – though this is indeed an effect – but rather the restricted access the rural poor in Africa have to secondary and higher education,[20] the most appropriate remedy for which is to widen participation and in so doing democratise access to English.

To sum up, we have argued that there is clear evidence of a massive popular demand not just for English but for English-medium education, the root cause of which is the perception, largely justified given current market ecologies (see Mufwene, 2008), that without English-language skills one's labour mobility and employment prospects are restricted. Meanwhile, on a different 'scale-level' (see Blommaert, 2010) – that of society as a whole – there are, as we have suggested, development benefits that flow from having a certain proportion of the population equipped with English literacy skills, though that proportion may in fact be considerably smaller than the secondary school population.

On the other hand, English-language education, particularly the use of English as a primary schooling medium, has considerable costs: it reduces further the quality of what is already a weak primary education sector, it tends to advantage urban elites over the rural poor, it may constrain the development/intellectualisation of local African languages and it diverts resources from under-resourced areas. Educational evidence, and efficiency considerations, point, then, to some circumscription of the educational role of English. But equity considerations, popular demand shaped by a dominant market ecology and the need to prepare students for higher studies in English point in the opposite direction – toward wider, democratised access to English. How, and to what extent, these tensions can be reconciled in language education policy is the subject we now turn to in conclusion.

Conclusion and Implications for Language Education Policy

At various points in the preceding discussion, we have suggested that English and local languages are both valuable for different purposes: English because it promotes socio-economic mobility and because it may facilitate a necessary shift to a more knowledge-intensive economy; local languages because they contribute to more effective early learning and to greater local engagement in sustainable development. This being so, policies that assume a necessary opposition between English and local languages are likely to be flawed. More productive would be to embrace complementarity as a policy principle and to focus the debate not on which medium is best but on how best to foster bilingual skills across the school years. In the field of education, this implies bilingual education, which, research suggests, is more effective when conducted in a framework of additive bilingualism where literacy in a familiar language is consolidated prior to the introduction of English. This would require that local languages remain the principal language of instruction during the first six years of primary school with English perhaps introduced by the Year 4 as a subject of instruction (see e.g. Clegg, 2007; Heugh, 2006). From Year 6 onward English could be gradually phased in as a medium of instruction in a limited number of subjects initially, with a slow shift to more subjects in English in secondary school.

There would, of course, be many practical difficulties in implementing such proposals – not all of which we can discuss here. One of the more serious would likely be parental resistance, the best response to which, as argued previously, is to make more strenuous efforts to inform and persuade parents of the educational advantages of a delayed and phased introduction of English as a language of instruction. Whether such efforts would convince is uncertain but at least an attempt should be made. Meanwhile, though there are definite costs to extending the use of local languages, as many commentators have remarked, there are even heavier costs attached to retaining the status quo, to persisting with a medium that young primary pupils find difficult to understand.

It is useful to recall here that bilingual education already has a de facto unofficial existence in many African classrooms, taking the form of classroom code-switching (CS) by teachers who instinctively realise that this helps pupils learn content subjects through an imperfectly understood official L2 medium. And, notwithstanding negative official attitudes, the evidence suggests that teachers are right (see Ferguson, 2003) – that, used sensitively, CS is a useful resource for mitigating the difficulties of studying content subjects through a foreign language. There are sound reasons, then, for officials to moderate their hostility to CS, to acknowledge the reality and prevalence of CS, and, indeed, to incorporate awareness of CS as a resource into teacher education curricula. After all, such language mixing is common in communities beyond the school, and it makes sense to mobilise the full range of teachers' and pupils' linguistic resources in the service of learning.

Many applied linguistics commentators would broadly concur with the drift of policy outlined above, but, undoubtedly, differences remain on a number of issues, only one of which finds mention here. This is the argument, advanced by some, that effective teaching of English as a secondary school subject, as opposed to its use as a medium, is sufficient to equip students with the necessary proficiency to study through the language at university.[21] Experience suggests, however, that this is unduly optimistic. There is already concern that students graduating from nominally English-medium secondary schools have insufficient proficiency to cope with university study and this has prompted the establishment of communication skills units in African universities (e.g. in Kenya and South Africa) catering to the needs of first year students and focusing on both English and academic literacy skills. In Europe, meanwhile, the rising popularity of CLIL stems in part from the not-unfounded perception that subject-teaching alone is an insecure foundation for the cultivation of bilingual skills.

In any event, whatever the views of the academic community, English is likely to persist as a language of instruction in many African secondary schools for reasons already alluded to, and, this being so, measures to mitigate some the difficulties of studying through a L2 medium become a priority for applied linguistics investigation. Among these, one might include greater acknowledgement of CS as a pedagogic resource, greater flexibility around the use of multiple languages in assessment (see e.g. Rea-Dickins *et al.*, 2009), a phased and gradual introduction of English-medium instruction, the use of textbooks linguistically adapted for L2 medium use (see e.g. Chimombo, 1989), teacher education that gives more attention to learner than teacher activity, greater emphasis on preparing pupils for the vocabulary challenges of L2 medium study – not to mention greater efforts to educate parents and officials of the advantages of bilingual education.

Returning finally to development, we have suggested throughout the preceding discussion that the relationship of English to development is complex, imperfectly understood and heterogeneous – neither uniformly positive nor negative, and strongly context dependent. The relationship can profitably be explored at three levels at least – those of the individual, the local community and the state.

With reference to individuals first, it is highly likely that English functions differently for different individuals depending on their social position, empowering some and excluding others, the principal mechanism of which is the gatekeeping role English plays in many societies regulating access to higher education and the formal economy. Removing, or restricting, English is not, however, the optimal solution to the resulting inequality, the reason being that inequality is not ultimately rooted in language. More effective would be to widen participation in secondary/higher education and in this way assist the democratisation of English skills. At local community level, meanwhile, there are plausible reasons to believe that local languages may make a stronger contribution to development than English (see e.g. Bruthiaux, 2002). But, that said, it is unproductive to portray local languages and English as necessarily in opposition, with English cast as the villain. To reiterate, both have value in different ways, and can play complementary roles – hence the desirability of bilingual approaches. Neither is it helpful to construct English as the 'other', as a colonial or as a European language. It has long since cast off its historical moorings in Europe and been creatively incorporated into the heterogeneous linguistic resources deployed by many Africans (Blommaert, 2010). At the state level, finally, there are grounds for believing that many national economies, particularly the more outward-facing ones, benefit from English-language skills in the population, though it remains a matter of conjecture just what proportion of the population need these skills for the wider economic benefits to accrue – probably rather less than official discourses imply.

That some of the observations above have the status of conjecture is itself indicative of the gaps in our knowledge, gaps which – given the important role English plays in African societies and education systems – surely deserve filling. Useful, in particular, would be more detailed empirical evidence on how English performs for different individuals and how it contributes to national economies, questions that call for ambitious multidisciplinary research extending beyond the normal ambit of applied linguistics. Meanwhile, heavily influenced by socio-economic forces that currently assign greater labour market mobility and prestige to the language over local languages, English seems likely to persist as a medium in secondary education at least. Language policy alone without accompanying socio-economic change is unlikely to alter this situation, and, as this is unlikely in the short term, applied linguists might be well advised to work to ameliorate current language education practice while continuing their advocacy of change in language education policy.

Notes

(1) Key features of the neo-liberal 'Washington consensus' approach to development include a trust in market disciplines, a distrust of state intervention in the economy and, conversely, support for economic deregulation, trade liberalisation and tight fiscal control of public expenditure.

(2) A relatively recent and influential conception of development is Sen's capabilities approach, where poverty is seen as capability deprivation (see Sen, 1999).

(3) Human capital theory embodies the notion – very simply put – that education enhances skills and capabilities, leading to greater productivity, and, in turn, rising incomes.

(4) Historically speaking that is. As argued later, there is some evidence that rates of return to primary education are falling and returns to secondary/tertiary increasing.
(5) Rates of return analysis most commonly analyses the returns to education generally and rarely the returns deriving from the school-based acquisition of specific skill sets (e.g. English-language skills).
(6) These studies are in Ghana and South Africa, respectively.
(7) Worthy of note here is that though the official medium in secondary school is English, the actual de facto medium is a mixture of Kiswahili for oral communication and English for reading/writing, a kind of 'translanguaging', which is far from restricted to Tanzania. Brock-Utne (2010) takes Criper and Dodd (1984) to task for recommending a programme of English-language support rather than a switch to Kiswahili medium at secondary school but in so doing she overlooks the prevailing policy of the time (1982-1984), which had recently reaffirmed the continuation of English as medium in secondary education.
(8) Education through a second language medium is, of course, undertaken in many places (e.g. in Singapore, in Canadian immersion programs, in European CLIL-style programs, in private schools in Africa) with a considerable degree of success, which suggests that it is not instruction in a second language per se that negatively impacts on educational quality but rather the conditions under which it is conducted.
(9) This is ironic in view of the desirability of expanding access to basic education. Hence the tension between access and quality.
(10) Meanwhile, the introduction of free primary education in Malawi and Lesotho led to a leap in enrolments in the first year of operation of 68% and 75%, respectively (Avenstrup *et al.*, 2004).
(11) For example, in Uganda in 2003, 37% of primary school teachers remained without formal training (ODI, 2006).
(12) Teacher absenteeism is attributable to a range of factors apart from low commitment – such as ill-health, late payment of salaries, supplementation of low teacher salaries by taking on additional paid work.
(13) CLIL stands for Content and Language Integrated Learning and is a form of bilingual education in which up to 50% (sometimes more) of the curriculum is delivered in the second language. It is claimed that this is a more effective way of learning a second language than through conventional teaching of the language as a subject.
(14) There are studies in other contexts: for example, Grin (2001) shows that in the Swiss labour market English-language skills are associated with significantly higher earnings, independently of the effects of education.
(15) Academic commentators calling for the extension of local language instruction and the restriction of English, typically in perfect written standard English, may find themselves in an uncomfortable position here, for they could be viewed by some as living exemplars of the advantages, and privileges, conferred by an extended education in English.
(16) Alexander (2009: 52) writes: 'Unless African languages are given market value … .no amount of policy change at school level can guarantee their use in high–status functions, and thus, escape from the dominance and the hegemony of English …'.
(17) Accessed at www.tanzania.go.tz/educationf.html on 31 November 2010.
(18) Accessed at http://moe.go.tz/pdf/SEMP%202001%202005%20verII.pdf on 31 November 2010.
(19) NASSCOM stands for National Association of Software and Services Companies, and is a consortium representing the Indian IT-BPO industry.

(20) For example, Palmer *et al.* (2007: 61-62) report that in Ghana the poorest 45% of the population have no access to tertiary education, and 60% of the entrants into the five public universities come from just 18 elite boarding secondary schools.

(21) An obvious rejoinder would be that university education should be delivered through an indigenous national language. In the medium term, however, as we have previously suggested, this is quite unrealistic.

References

Alexander, N. (2008) Creating the conditions for a counter-hegemonic strategy: African languages in the twenty-first century. In C. Vigouroux and S. Mufwene (eds) *Globalisation and Language Vitality: Perspectives from Africa* (pp. 255-272). London: Continuum.

Alexander, N. (2009) The impact of the hegemony of English on access to and quality of education with special reference to South Africa. In W. Harbert, S. McConnell-Ginet, A. Miller and J. Whitman (eds) *Language and Poverty* (pp. 53-66). Bristol: Multilingual Matters.

Alidou, H. and Brock-Utne, B. (2006) Experience I – teaching practices – teaching in a familiar language. In H. Alidou, A. Boly, B. Brock-Utne, Y. Dialo, K. Heugh and H. Wolff (eds) *Optimising Learning and Education in Africa – the Language Factor* (pp. 85-100). Paris: Association for the Development of Education in Africa (ADEA).

Annamalai, E. (2004) Medium of power: The question of English in education in India. In J. Tollefson and A. Tsui (eds) *Medium of Instruction Policies* (pp. 177-194). Mahwah, NJ: Lawrence Erlbaum.

Arthur, J. (1994) English in Botswana primary classrooms: Functions and constraints. In C. Rubagumya (ed.) *Teaching and Researching Language in African Classrooms* (pp. 63-78). Clevedon: Multilingual Matters.

Avenstrup, R., Liang, X. and Nellemann, S. (2004) *Free Primary Education and Poverty Reduction: The Case of Kenya, Lesotho, Malawi and Uganda*. Washington, DC: World Bank.

Benefo, K. and Schultz, T. (1996) Fertility and child mortality in Cote d'Ivoire and Ghana. *World Bank Economic Review* 10 (1), 123-158.

Bennell, P. (1996) Rates of return to education: Does the conventional pattern prevail in Sub-Saharan Africa? *World Development* 24 (1), 183-199.

Bennell, P., Hyde, K. and Swainson, N. (2002) The impact of the HIV/AIDS epidemic on the education sector in Sub-Saharan Africa: A synthesis of the findings and recommendations of three country studies. Centre for International Education, University of Sussex Institute of Education. http://www.harare.unesco.org/hivaids/webfiles

Benson, C. (2000) The primary bilingual education experiment in Mozambique, 1993-1997. *International Journal of Bilingual Education and Bilingualism* 3 (3), 149-166.

Benson, C. (2002) Real and potential benefits of bilingual programmes in developing countries. *International Journal of Bilingual Education and Bilingualism* 5 (6), 303-317.

Blommaert, J. (2010) *The Sociolinguistics of Globalization.* Cambridge: Cambridge University Press.

Brock-Utne, B. (2005) Language-in-education policies and practices with a special focus on Tanzania and South Africa – Insights from research in progress. In A. Lin and P. Martin (eds) *Decolonisation, Globalisation: Language-in-Education Policy and Practice* (pp. 173-193). Clevedon: Multilingual Matters.

Brock-Utne, B. (2010) Research and policy on the language of instruction issue in Africa. *International Journal of Educational Development* 30 (6), 636-645.

Brock-Utne, B. and Alidou, H. (2006) Experience II – active students – learning through a language they master. In H. Alidou, A. Boly, B. Brock-Utne, Y. Dialo, K. Heugh, and H Wolff (eds) *Optimising Learning and Education in Africa – the Language Factor* (pp. 101-117). Paris: Association for the Development of Education in Africa (ADEA).

Broom, Y. (2004) Reading English in multilingual South African primary schools. *International Journal of Bilingual Education and Bilingualism* 7 (6), 506-528.

Bruthiaux, P. (2002) Hold your courses: Language education, language choice, and economic development. *TESOL Quarterly* 36 (3), 275-296.

Chimombo, M. (1989) Readability of subject texts: Implications for ESL teaching in Africa. *English for Specific Purposes* 8 (3), 255-264.

Clayton, T. (1998) Explanations for the use of languages of wider communication in education in developing countries. *International Journal of Educational Development* 18 (2), 145-157.

Clegg, J. (2007) Moving toward bilingual education in Africa. In H. Coleman (ed.) *Language and Development: Africa and Beyond. Edited Proceedings of 7th International Language and Development Conference* (pp. 1-11). Addis Ababa: British Council.

Cook, S. (2009) Street Setswana vs. School Setswana: Language policies and the forging of identities in South African classrooms. In J. Kleifgen and G. Bond (eds) *The Languages of Africa and the Diaspora: Educating for Language Awareness* (pp. 96-116). Bristol: Multilingual Matters.

Criper, C. and Dodd, W. (1984) *Report on the Teaching of the English Language and its Use as a Medium in Education in Tanzania.* London: ODA/British Council.

Cummins, J. (1979) Linguistic interdependence and the educational development of bilingual children. *Review of Educational Research* 49 (2), 222-251. Reprinted in Baker, C. and Hornberger, N. (eds) *An Introductory Reader to the Writings of Jim Cummins* (pp. 63-95). Clevedon: Multilingual Matters.

Davies, A. (2009) Professional advice vs Political imperatives. In J. Alderson (ed.) *The Politics of Language Education: Individuals and Institutions* (pp. 45-63). Bristol: Multilingual Matters.

EdQual (2010) *The Impact of Language of Instruction, Teacher Training, and Textbooks on Quality of Learning in Africa*. EdQual Policy Brief 2, University of Bristol, School of Education. http://www.edqual.org/publications/policy-briefs/pb2.pdf

Fafunwa, B., Iyabode Macauley, J. and Sokoya, J. (eds) (1989) *Education in the Mother Tongue: The Primary Education Research Project (1970-78)*. Ibadan, Nigeria: University Press Ltd.

Ferguson, G. (2003) Classroom codeswitching in post-colonial contexts: Functions, attitudes and policies. In S. Makoni and U. Meinhof (eds) *Africa and Applied Linguistics, AILA Review* 16 (1), 38-51. Amsterdam: John Benjamins.

Ferguson, G. (2006) *Language Planning and Education.* Edinburgh: Edinburgh University Press.

Fryer, D. and Vencatachellum, D. (2002) Returns to education in South Africa: Evidence from the Machibisa Township. http://www.commerce.uct.ac.za/Research_Units/dpru/WorkingPapers/PDF_Files/wp76.pdf

Fuller, B. (1987) What school factors raise achievement in the Third World? *Review of Educational Research* 57 (3), 255-292.

Fuller, B. and Heyneman, S. (1989) Third World school quality: Current collapse, future potential. *Educational Researcher* 18 (2), 12-19.

Graddol, D. (2010) *English Next – India.* London: British Council.

Green, A., Little, A., Kamat, S., Oketch, M. and Vickers, E. (eds) (2007) *Education and Development in a Global Era: Strategies for 'Successful Globalisation'.* London: Department for International Development (DfID).

Grin, F. (2001) English as economic value: Facts and fallacies. *World Englishes* 20 (1), 65-78.

Hardman, F., Abd-Kadir, J. and Smith, F. (2008) Pedagogical renewal: Improving the quality of classroom interaction in Nigerian primary Schools. *International Journal of Educational Development* 28 (1), 55-69.

Heugh, K. (2006) Theory and practice – language education models in Africa: Research, design, decision-making, and outcomes. In H. Alidou, A. Boly, B. Brock-Utne, Y. Dialo, K. Heugh and H. Wolff (eds) *Optimising Learning and Education in Africa – the Language Factor* (pp. 56-84). Paris: Association for the Development of Education in Africa (ADEA).

Hu, G.W. and Alsagoff, L. (2010) A public policy perspective on English medium instruction in China. *Journal of Multilingual and Multicultural Development* 31, 365-382.

Kamwangamalu, N. (2004) The language policy/language economics interface and mother tongue education in post-apartheid South Africa. *Language Problems and Language Planning* 28 (2), 131-146.

King, K. and Palmer, R. (2006a) *Education, Training and their Enabling Environments: A Review of Research and Policy.* Post-Basic Education and Training Working Paper Series – No 8 Centre of African Studies, University of Edinburgh. www.dfid.gov.uk/r4d/PDF/Outputs/PolicyStrategy/King_Palmer.pdf

King, K. and Palmer, R. (2006b) *Skills Development and Poverty Reduction: The State of the Art. Post*-Basic Education and Training Working Paper Series – No9. Centre of African Studies, University of Edinburgh. www.cas.ed.ac.uk/__data/assets/pdf_file

Lassibille, G., Tan, J. and Sumra, S. (1999) Expansion of private secondary education: Experience and prospects in Tanzania. http://siteresources.worldbank.org/EDUCATION/Resources1135281552767

Linehan, S. (2004) *Language of Instruction and the Quality of Basic Education in Zambia*. Paris: UNESCO.

Makoni, S., Brutt-Griffler, J. and Mashiri, P. (2007) The use of 'indigenous' and urban vernaculars in Zimbabwe. *Language in Society* 36 (1), 25-49.

Mufwene, S. (2008) *Language Evolution: Contact Competition and Change.* London: Continuum.

Muthwii, M. (2004) Language planning and literacy in Kenya: Living with unresolved paradoxes. *Current Issues in Language Planning* 5 (1), 34-50.

Myers-Scotton, C. (1990) Elite closure as boundary maintenance: The case of Africa. In B. Weinstein (ed.) *Language Policy and Political Development* (pp. 25-32). Norwood, NJ: Ablex.

Narayan, D., Chambers, R., Shah, M. and Petesch, P. (2000) *Voices of the Poor: Crying Out for Change.* New York: Oxford University Press for the World Bank.

Nunan, D. (2003) The impact of English as a global language on educational policies and practices in the Asia-Pacific region. *TESOL Quarterly* 37 (4), 589-613.

Oketch, M. (2007) Promise unfulfilled: Educational improvement and economic decline in Kenya. In A. Green, A.W. Little, S.G. Kamat, M. Oketch and E. Vickers (eds) *Education and Development in the Global Era: Strategies for 'Successful Globalisation'* (pp. 131-162). London: Department for International Development (DFID).

Overseas Development Institute (ODI) (2006) *Policy Brief 10 – Universal Primary Education: Uganda.* London: Overseas Development Institute.

Palmer, R., Wedgwood, R., Hayman, R., King, K. and Thin, N. (2007) *Educating Out of Poverty? A Synthesis Report on Ghana, India, Kenya, Rwanda, Tanzania and South Africa.* London: Department for International Development (DFID).

Pennycook, A. (2000) English, politics, ideology: From colonial celebration to postcolonial peformativity. In T. Ricento (ed.) *Ideology, Politics and Language Policies: Focus on English* (pp. 107-119). Amsterdam: John Benjamins.

Phillipson, R. (1992) *Linguistic Imperialism*. Oxford: Oxford University Press.

Probyn, M. (2001) Teachers' voices: Teachers' reflections on learning and teaching through the medium of English as a second language. *International Journal of Bilingual Education and Bilingualism* 4 (4), 249-266.

Probyn, M. (2005) Language and the struggle to learn: The intersection of classroom realities, language policy, and neo-colonial and globalisation discourses in South African schools. In A. Lin and P. Martin (eds) *Decolonisation, Globalisation: Language-in-Education Policy and Practice* (pp. 153-172). Clevedon: Multilingual Matters.

Prophet, R. and Dow, J. (1994) Mother tongue language and concept development in science: A Botswana case study. *Language, Culture and Curriculum* 7 (3), 205-217.

Psacharopoulos, G. and Patrinos, H. (2002) Returns to investment in education: A further update. *World Bank Policy Research Working Paper* 2881. Washington, DC: World Bank.

Ramanathan, V. (2007) A critical discussion of the English-vernacular divide in India. In J. Cummins and C. Davison (eds) *International Handbook of English Language Teaching* (pp. 51-61). New York: Springer.

Rea-Dickins, P., Yu, G. and Afitska, O. (2009) The consequences of examining through an unfamiliar language of instruction and its impact for school-age learners in Sub-Saharan African school systems. In L. Taylor and C. Weir (eds) *Language Testing Matters: The Social and Educational Impact of Language Assessment* (pp. 190-214). Cambridge: Cambridge University Press.

Robertson, S., Novell, M., Dale, R., Tikly, L., Dachi, H. and Alphonce, N. (2007) *Globalisation, Education and Development: Ideas, Actors and Dynamics*. London: Department for International Development (DFID).

Rubagumya, C. (ed.) (1990) *Language in Education in Africa: A Tanzanian Perspective*. Clevedon: Multilingual Matters.

Rubagumya, C. (2003) English medium primary schools in Tanzania: A new 'linguistic market' in education? In B. Brock-Utne, Z. Desai and M. Qorro (eds) *Language of Instruction in Tanzania and South Africa* (LOITASA). Dar es Salaam: E&D.

Sen, A. (1999) *Development as Freedom*. Oxford: Oxford University Press.

Stroud, C. (2002) *Toward a Policy for Bilingual Education in Developing Countries*. New Education Division Documents Number 10. Stockholm: Swedish International Development Agency.

Tollefson, J. and Tsui, A. (eds) (2004) *Medium of Instruction Policies: Which Agenda, Whose Agenda?* Mahwah, NJ: Lawrence Erlbaum.

Trappes-Lomax, H. (1990) Can a foreign language be a national medium? In C. Rubagumya (ed.) *Language in Education in Africa: A Tanzanian Perspective* (pp. 94-104). Clevedon: Multilingual Matters.

Trudell, B. (2007) Local community perspectives and language of education in Sub-Saharan African communities. *International Journal of Educational Development* 27 (5), 552-563.

United Nations Educational, Scientific and Cultural Organization (UNESCO) (1953) *The Use of Vernacular Languages in Education*. Paris: UNESCO.

Vavrus, F. (2002) Postcoloniality and English: Exploring language policy and the politics of development in Tanzania. *TESOL Quarterly* 26 (3), 373-397.

Wächter, B. and Maiworm, F. (2008) *English Taught Programmes in European Higher Education: The Picture in 2007*. Bonn: Lemmens.

Williams, E. (1996) Reading in two languages at year five in African primary schools. *Applied Linguistics* 17 (2), 182-209.

Williams, E. (2006) *Bridges and Barriers: Language in African Education and Development.* Manchester: St Jerome Press.

Williams, E. and Cooke, J. (2002) Pathways and labyrinths: Language and education in development. *TESOL Quarterly* 36 (3), 297-322.

Wolff, H. (2006) Background and history – Language politics and planning in Africa. In H. Alidou, A. Boly, B. Brock-Utne, Y. Dialo, K. Heugh and H. Wolff (eds) *Optimising Learning and Education in Africa – the Language Factor* (pp. 26-55). Paris: Association for the Development of Education in Africa (ADEA).

World Bank (2002) *Constructing Knowledge Societies: New Challenges for Tertiary Education.* Washington, DC: World Bank.

World Bank (2004a) *Books, Buildings, and Learning Outcomes: An Impact Evaluation of World Bank Support to Basic Education in Ghana*. Washington, DC: World Bank.

World Bank (2004b) *Skills Development in Sub-Saharan Africa*. Washington, DC: World Bank.

World Bank (2005a) *Education Sector Strategy Update: Achieving Education for All: Broadening Our Perspective*. Washington, DC: World Bank.

World Bank (2005b) Expanding Opportunities and Building Competencies for Young People: A New Agenda for Secondary Education. Washington, DC: World Bank.

2 The Political Economy of English Language and Development: English vs. National and Local Languages in Developing Countries

Naz Rassool

Introduction

During, at least, the last two decades English as a lingua franca has been in ascendance in international forums, business and trade. This association of English language fluency with maximizing economic returns has raised the language's investment potential for both individuals and governments throughout the world. For individuals, the benefits of English language proficiency are seen to lie in the scope that it provides them to improve their employability within local, national and international labour markets and, related to this, the potential that it offers for increasing levels of individual salary income. Governments, especially in non-English-speaking developing countries such as Pakistan, Southern Sudan and Rwanda, or modernizing countries such as China, Taiwan, South Korea, the Gulf States and economies in transition throughout Eastern Europe, are increasingly regarding English language proficiency as a means of maximizing both *economic* and *social capital* and are adopting it as medium of education in schools and tertiary education.

For nation states *economic capital* benefits are associated with the ability that English language proficiency offers countries to broaden their international business and trade opportunities. Economic capital benefits are also associated with the access that English provides to the development of high technological, scientific and management skills, and therefore the ability to participate more effectively in the highly competitive global labour market. As such, English language proficiency is increasingly regarded as representing a factor in improving the quality of human capital (Chiswick, 2008). Further, English as a lingua franca is seen also as contributing to the ability of countries to develop their *social capital* through international networks that are of benefit to local business and trade and through this to attract foreign direct investment (FDI). FDI is widely regarded as playing a central role in economic development through technology and knowledge transfer – improving technological capability and aiding countries' capacity building – thus enhancing productivity (Coe, 2007; Singh, 2005; Sun, 2002; UNCTAD, 2008). English language proficiency has therefore become viewed as central to countries' development within the global knowledge-based economy. In countries such as South Korea, Taiwan and China, the perceived importance of fluency in English as a prerequisite to economic success and social mobility within a competitive global market has resulted in families choosing to send their children to be educated in English-speaking countries such as the UK, USA, Australia, Canada and New Zealand, as well as India and South Africa (Moon, 2010). In South Korea this 'English fever' has been accompanied by the establishment of *yeongeo maeul* ('English villages') by city councils and provincial governments enabling the acquisition of English in an immersion approach (Moon, 2010; Shim & Park, 2008).

How valid are the assumptions about the significance of English language proficiency to development in countries that have a non-English language base and/or are multilingual? What are the implications of adopting English as a medium of education, and/or in the curriculum throughout the different sectors in education, and incorporating it into everyday life for (a) educational achievement, (b) sociocultural relations and (c) social and economic development in these countries in the long term?

Seeking to address these questions, this chapter examines the hegemony of English as a 'world language' within the broader discourse on language and development in postcolonial societies, and how this relates to changes taking place within the global economy. In order to define the chapter's terms of reference, the next section briefly examines some of the main analytical frameworks within academic discourse in relation to the scope they provide for analyzing the multidimensional ways in which language is involved in processes of societal development within a changing global economy. The overall intention is to extend the analytical framework in which language and societal development is discussed by drawing on concepts and theories within the broader Social Sciences.

English and Academic Discourse Frameworks

Bordered knowledges

In academic discourse, the rise in the international status of English traditionally has been analyzed within discrete theoretical frameworks providing perspectives limited to subject disciplines within the humanities and Social Sciences including *sociolinguistics* (Canagarajah, 1999; Rajagopalan, 2004) *language and culture* (Edwards, 2009; Graddol, 1997; Pennycook, 1994), bi- and multilingualism (García, 2008; García & Baker, 2007), as well as *language shift and maintenance across generations in immigrant populations* (Fishman, 1972, 1991, 1999; Li Wei, 1994; Rassool, 2000, 2004) and *minority language rights and education* (May, 2008; Skutnabb-Kangas, 2000, 2010; Skutnabb-Kangas *et al.*, 2009). Analyses in the *sociology of language* have centred mostly on macro-level language planning and policy (Kaplan & Baldauf, 1999; Tollefson, 1991).

A growing area here is what is referred to as the *'economics of language'* or *'language economics'* (see Arcand & Grin, this volume). Studies in the economics of language, largely, have been conceptual analyses (Coulmas, 1992; Grin, 2006; Ozolins, 2003) or survey-based inquiries on the links between language use amongst minority groups and the labour market as well as language fluency and earnings amongst immigrant groups (Casey & Dustmann, 2007; Chiswick, 2008; Chiswick & Miller, 2003). Studies such as those by Vaillancourt (1980) and Grin and Vaillancourt (1997) examine language as an intrinsic element of human capital, whilst other studies in the field centre on the economic costs and benefits of teaching and learning another language (Church & King, 1993; Selten & Pool, 1991). The constraints of this approach lie in the econometric model that underpins analyses focused on labour market effects and outcomes. Although the 'economics of language' framework is undoubtedly useful in highlighting key issues related to the labour market, its quantitative approach does not and cannot deal with *explanations* for these occurrences. The framework excludes micro-factors within people's lives in relation to society and culture that influence individual and group choices and outcomes. In practice, it has translated into arguments advocating the need for immigrants in Anglophone countries to become fluent in English as soon as possible (Grin, 2006). Research in the economics of language seemingly then underscores assimilation into the dominant host culture without consideration of the benefits of bilingualism for supporting learning, cultural enrichment and the potential impact of bilingual workers on labour supply within an interactive and interdependent global economy.

Although collectively the frameworks discussed above have been significant in helping to expand the focus on language in society and culture, and have provided different ways of looking at the role of language in society, the economy and culture, the problem is that each of these perspectives is framed by a particular subject-discipline replete with its own knowledge categories, registers, distinct methodologies and epistemology. Subject-disciplines represent bounded discourses replete with their own terms and frames of reference as well as their own worldviews. Foucault (1970: 59) argues that each subject-discipline frames 'a domain of objects, a set of methods, a corpus of propositions considered to be true, a play of rules and definitions, of techniques and instruments'. Each subject-discipline therefore projects a particular view of what constitutes research, and different sets of variables operate within each frame of reference to arrive at conclusions that generally are not integrated in a way that does justice to the multidimensional reach of language involvement in contemporary society and culture (Rassool, 1999). How, for example, is language, and particularly English in the world today, linked with societal 'development'? Answering this question requires a broader, integrated analytical framework that takes account of multidimensional factors involved in social and economic development.

Multidisciplinary Frameworks

Bourdieu's (1991) seminal work on the sociology and the economics of linguistic exchanges addressed these issues by inserting social scientific concepts into discourse about language in society and culture. Bourdieu (1986) argued that the notion of capital accumulation in all its forms – not only the economic – represents the key organizing principle of society and culture. He focused on both the materiality of language (i.e. its currency or exchange value) *and* its symbolic (hegemonic) power. Language is seen as representing an aspect of cultural capital, which in turn includes the accumulated skills, knowledge, understanding and qualifications to be exchanged within the labour market. Cultural capital, and by that fact, linguistic capital, is accumulated over a period of time, costs money, and is invested in by individuals as well as the state through the educational process, and thus it has an economic value. He positioned the accumulation of linguistic capital in relation to the demands of linguistic markets, and argued that linguistic exchanges obtain their value in relation to the pricing of linguistic capital in particular linguistic markets and the symbolic profit associated with this. As will be seen later, this concept is central to analyses of the value of English in the contemporary world.

Different linguistic markets prevail in everyday life, each, in turn, associated with specific social roles linked with both private and public spheres of interaction (Bourdieu, 1986, 1991). These two spheres are hierarchically organized in everyday social life with the public sphere traditionally associated with languages and discourses of power. For example, national and official languages are imbued with the power of the state (Billig, 1995; Bourdieu, 1991), whereas local language varieties obtain value only within their communities. Those who are fluent in the country's official language possess the requisite *linguistic capital* within the nation's *formal* language markets. Used in formal state institutions such as the government and judiciary as well as in the media, education, business and industry, politically validated languages represent *preferred* linguistic capital as opposed to informal ways of speaking or minority languages within the private sphere. All other languages and varieties of different speech communities within society are measured against the norms established by the standardized official language. Linguistic exchanges therefore reflect and embody the power of wealth and authority of the speakers in relation to their social position within society. In other words, language *reflects power relations* within society; not all endogenous languages are equal; some have greater currency than others within particular contexts of social exchange. While this argument continues to hold in nation states, language relations have gained in complexity within the global terrain in which English is in ascendance at the moment.

The valorization of English as an international lingua franca means that, as an exogenous language, English, in many societies, now represents a potent form of *language capital* within the global language market – and proficiency in Standard English constitutes high-value *linguistic capital*. As will be discussed later, this applies not only to societies with colonial ties to Britain where English has remained the official language, and countries that have adopted English as a de facto official language, but also non-English-speaking countries that aspire to become strong competitors within the global economic market.

Within this changing context, interdisciplinary frameworks integrating the sociology of language, politics, economics and history with societal development have been emerging since the 1990s (Djité, 1993; Heugh, 1999, 2003; Rassool, 1999, 2007; Romaine, 2008). Building on this, the rest of the chapter discusses the *political economy* of English in development as this relates to developing countries within the context of broader changes taking place within the global context. Political economy here refers to the ways in which political and economic forces influence the choice of language policies and the impact that these have on development within society and culture. The focus then is on the interrelationship between language, the individual, communities and society as well as between local, regional, national and international social, economic and language markets. The next section discusses the concept of social 'development' and its relationship with language within the context of the nation state. This will be followed by a discussion of how the concept has evolved within the framework of globalization.

What is 'Development' and How is it Related to Language Per Se, and to English in Particular, in the World Today?

Development is a contested concept within the Social Sciences and depends on the ideological framework as well as the context within which it is articulated. Historically, the concept of development has its locus within the modern nation state that evolved during the 19th century and is underpinned by the principles of having an 'ethnie [ethno-national group] – or peoples claiming a sense of their own history, culture and loyalties' (Billig, 1995: 26; Smith, 1994) who are living within a defined territory having fixed internationally recognized geographical and political boundaries. The nation state also has sovereignty and political legitimacy. Development within this framework, at least since the 19th century, has been defined in relation *to a strengthening of the material or economic base of the nation state mainly through industrialization and through this to benefit society as a whole*.

A more critical perspective on development is provided by Todaro (1999: 87) who stressed the need to reduce levels of 'poverty, inequality and unemployment within the context of a growing economy'. Todaro identified three core values of development including 'life sustenance' (the ability to provide for basic needs), 'self-esteem' (to be a person) and 'freedom from servitude' (to be able to choose) aimed at lessening absolute poverty and inequality in income distribution.

Central to the idea of development within the nation state is the need for a common language through which different language groups can be integrated into a common culture, with a common legal, political and economic system to serve the interests of the overall sovereign nation (Anderson, 1983; Billig, 1995). The need for the nation state to maintain social cohesion is important to secure social equilibrium, and through this to create the social and political stability necessary for development to take place. Having a common language is seen as central to this process, especially for its role in shaping 'nationhood'. The particular language choice made by the nation state to serve as the common language, that is, the official and/or national language, defines the language medium in education. Language in the education process serves to socialize citizens into a common value and belief system and thus plays a major role in integrating different ethnolinguistic and religious groups into society as a whole – and through this to build social cohesion and thereby create the necessary conditions for development.

Within the context of the nation state, language as a medium of communication also *embodies power*; it provides the means through which political power is exercised, for example, through the promulgation of laws and regulations. This means that the extent to which people are able to engage with, and within, the formal structures of society relies on their literacy levels and their ability to communicate effectively in the *official language* adopted by the state. This is the fundamental prerequisite for citizens to be able to participate effectively in the democratic process, and to become productive workers, enabling them to have access to power and resources within society. In other words, the distribution of linguistic and, ipso facto, cultural capital in society is central, on the one hand, to building a *strong civil society* and, on the other hand, to the *accumulation of knowledge and skills to be exchanged within the labour market*. A key factor in social and individual development therefore relates to the *choice of official language*, and the extent to which it is made available to all groups within society, as well as the levels of literacy achieved. The unequal distribution of linguistic capital (language proficiency, communicative competence and literacy levels) amongst the majority of the population contributes to disparities between different social groups in relation to levels of access to the *formal* labour market. As will be seen below, this is evident in many developing countries where English has been adopted as the official language, but has not been distributed equally in educational provision to all groups within society. This, in turn, contributes to the underdevelopment of labour power and, consequently, the underutilization of human capital. These factors raise major issues for social and economic development in developing countries having a non–English language base but where English features as the official language.

Many of the developing countries throughout Sub-Saharan Africa and South Asia previously were British colonies in which English became the official language. This meant that English was used in all the formal state institutions such as the law courts, government and civil service, and that it was also the main language of trade and commerce. Acting as a symbol of higher aspirations and upward social mobility, English constituted potent linguistic and symbolic capital and became the language-medium of choice in education amongst colonized peoples (see Rassool, 2007). However, other than elite groups, access to education was limited to elementary levels. Together, these factors, combined with a limited educational, cultural and social infrastructure, contributed to large-scale underdeveloped human resources within colonized societies. This inheritance became the starting point for social and economic development in postcolonial countries.

English and Development in Postcolonial Societies

Because of their colonial history, postcolonial societies, at least in part, had internalized a colonial hegemonic consciousness; they had assimilated aspects of the dominant colonial culture, including the expectations and aspirations of a subject people. This is best described as the shaping of the 'colonial habitus'. In most cases this is expressed in the continuing high value attached to English, and the general apathy in relation to the harmonization and development of local languages in countries throughout Sub-Saharan Africa. Despite the rhetoric constructed around language and nationhood in the immediate aftermath of decolonization, most (ex-British) postcolonial societies throughout Sub-Saharan Africa and South Asia opted to retain the colonial language (English) as at least one of the official languages and, in many instances, it constituted the only official language.

For some, the choice of English as the official language following decolonization had its rationale in divisions that had been created during colonial rule. In Sub-Saharan Africa the arbitrary state boundaries that emerged from the Congress in Berlin in 1885 resulted in countries comprising various ethnic, linguistic and tribal minority factions contributing to conflicts and divisions which, potentially, could destabilize the emerging postcolonial state (Rassool, 2007). In this situation, many postcolonial governments considered that adopting an ex-colonial language as a common language, a 'neutral' means of communication (de Varennes, 1996), could help to overcome ethnic cleavages and secure national unity, as well as maintain links with the international community. Many postcolonial leaders were influenced also by the widely held belief 'that the best way to [...] quick progress was to adopt or maintain the so-called "already developed" colonial languages, as the exclusive media of education' (Mateene, 1999: 176).

Modernization theory (Schultz, 1963), which prevailed at that time, centred on investment in education and technology as the main means for developing countries to 'catch up' with advanced economies. The concept of modernization revolved around the need for geo-political reorganization (rural-urban), technological restructuring, building an effective infrastructure and the reconstitution of cultural relations to suit the diverse needs of a more complex scientific society (Todaro, 1999). A key principle of modernization theory therefore was the need to develop rationality as a basis for logically informed economic planning to replace traditional forms of thinking and organization (Todaro, 1999). Language and literacy were seen as playing a central part in achieving social modernization.

Indeed, the drive for rapid economic growth and societal modernization provided the main rationale for retaining English in education, over and above the development and mainstreaming of local African languages. Having to acquire knowledge in a language that few speak in their families and communities has meant that learners have been negotiating the learning process in what, in practice, is a foreign language. It therefore is not surprising that many of these countries have continued to sustain high levels of illiteracy.

Since literacy is a major factor in skills acquisition, 'illiteracy puts formal training out of reach for many people in the informal economy' (International Labour Organization [ILO], 2008: 35). In Pakistan, for example, the country's focus on English as the medium of education has contributed to high levels of illiteracy amongst the population as a whole – 53% in 2005; 57% in 2009 (Pakistan Economic Survey, 2009-2010) – and the highest levels of employment are recorded in the informal sector, 73.3% against 26.7% in the formal sector (Pakistan Labour Force Survey, 2008). This reflects the urban–rural divide with regard to language use, with English and Urdu representing the languages of choice for the urban elite – and English more particularly since it is associated with progressivism and modernity (Mansoor, 2005; Rahman, 2000). In Pakistan, English medium schools are dominated by children from the upper-middle classes, the military and government elite. Moreover, elites of the provincial state institutions including the railways, customs, telecommunications and police departments run their own English medium schools (Rahman, 2002). The urban poor and rural communities tend to become literate mainly in the regional languages, which, in part, is due to the prevalence in these areas of large numbers of unqualified or underqualified teachers who themselves lack fluency in English, and also the lack of adequate teaching and learning resources (Mansoor, 2005). The problem for these communities is compounded by the fact that English represents the medium of education at tertiary level. As a result, the educational opportunities of some learners are curtailed, which, in turn, has major implications for employment opportunities within the labour market. This provides some explanation for the high levels of employment in that country's informal sector.

This is the case also in postcolonial Zambia where, based on a research study carried out by Australian academics and funded by UNESCO (UNESCO, 1964), English was adopted as the national language, and became the medium of education. Ever since then, there have been concerns about the low levels of literacy in that country. Many of the educational concerns historically have revolved around the possible linkage between high levels of illiteracy and the fact that children were learning to become literate first through English which, in practice, they were not familiar with. However, the Zambian government in 1977, whilst aware of these concerns, produced a report, *Educational Reform: Proposals and Recommendations,* stating that 'while acknowledging that it is generally accepted by educationalists that learning is best done in the mother tongue ... this situation is found to be impracticable in multilingual societies such as the Zambian society' (MOE, cited in Linehan, 2004: 2).

Following continued high levels of illiteracy and skills development in the country over the next decade, research funded by the World Bank found that 'the use of English as a medium of instruction negatively affected the pupils' reading and arithmetic skills, and was 'unlikely to support good learning, especially in the critical early primary grades ... it orientates the entire school process in a direction that only a small percentage of pupils will follow. Culturally, it undercuts the local languages and the values they embody' (Kelly, 1991, cited in Djité, 2008: 61). Since that time there have been several NGO-funded programmes, notably the influential Molteno Project, focused on using local languages as a means to literacy at least in Grade 1. In response to this, the policy initiative *Educating Our Future* (1996) underscored the need for initial literacy and numeracy to be developed through a language that was familiar to learners. This was subsequently implemented in the *New Breakthrough to Literacy (NBTL)* programme (1999) centred on fast-tracking one-year initial literacy (Grade 1) courses in seven official languages. This has had a major impact on improving literacy development as well as helping to break down the barriers amongst parents demanding a 'Straight-for-English' approach (Linehan, 2004). Whilst people are now more receptive to the use of local languages in education, the hegemony of English as the vehicle to higher learning and economic success nevertheless continues to permeate the consciousness of most peoples in Zambian society 'with slogans such as "If you want to get ahead, get an English head"' (Williams, 1986, cited in Djité, 2008: 62). Although school completion rates improved from 63.6% in 2000 to 72% in 2004, largely through the introduction of the universal primary education programme (UPE), which is Goal 2 of the Millennium Development Goals, the country still has a major skills deficit with only 53.3% of the adult population being literate (IMF, 2007). This is reflected in the skills uptake within the formal labour market. As is the case in Pakistan, in Zambia '[s]eventy to eighty per cent of the labour market is informal workers, with this group consisting mostly of self-employed subsistence farmers and their unpaid family workers' (Burger *et al.*, 2005: 5). Clearly then, Zambia's reliance on English as the medium of education could be questioned in relation to its low yield in the provision of highly skilled workers able to participate in the redefined global labour market. This will be discussed in further detail later.

Elsewhere, in Nigeria proposals by the Lagos State House of Assembly to use Yoruba as a language of debate in the House, in accordance with Section 97 of 1999 Constitution of the Federal Government level in Nigeria, were rejected on the grounds that the 'Yoruba language is not appropriate for the conduct of business of the House of Assembly, since Lagos is a cosmopolitan city. *Besides, its use is capable of demeaning and reducing the intellectual capacity of legislators'* (reported in *The Guardian*, 10 December 1999, cited in Djité, 2008: 63, my emphasis). Implicit in this is the belief that English has intrinsic value not only to social and economic development but also individual cognitive abilities. This reflects the extent to which the social construction of the inherent superiority of English has become part of the hegemonic consciousness amongst governing elites within Nigerian society – and the de facto marginalization of local languages.

The situation is not much better in developing countries that, ostensibly, have adopted multilingual policies in education. In South Africa, in spite of the adoption of 11 official languages and a nominal multilingual educational policy, the main language of the public sphere remains English. As a result of the marginalization of local languages within society during the Apartheid period, the high value attached to English as the language of resistance against Apartheid hegemony and its current high status as a 'global language', the majority of parents still prefer their children to be educated in English (Busch, 2010). As in the case of Pakistan discussed above, lack of English proficiency of teachers in state schools presents a major problem. Heugh's (2003: 197) study found that 'only 5% of rural teacher trainees have the requisite English language literacy skills and that 51% of the Grade 12 school leavers who applied for admission to technikons in 1990 had adequate ESL literacy levels (Grade 8 or above)'. With the exception of a few Afrikaans-medium universities, education at tertiary level takes place in English. This, combined with the 'catastrophic literacy and proficiency levels in English (now the only language of access to tertiary education, the formal economy and the civil service), means that educational transformation is an illusion' (Heugh, 2003: 213). In these situations, English is often taught via the medium of the local language (Harbert *et al.*, 2009), or through rote learning 'with mindless repetition replacing problem solving and inventiveness' (Linehan, 2004; see also Williams, this volume).

What does this mean for societal development?

This disparity in provision for English language teaching serves to deepen existing class differences and, indirectly, to regulate access to the labour market. A recent study (Casale & Posel, 2010) found that demand for English proficiency operates as a de facto screening out of workers in the labour market in South Africa. The study suggests that in South Africa with its Apartheid history 'English language proficiency acts as a signal to employers of the quality of education that the worker has received ... [since it would] reflect whether the individual was educated in a formerly advantaged school or university previously reserved for Whites, a private institution, or one of the better formerly disadvantaged schools or universities' (Casale & Posel, 2010: 18). English language proficiency, in this instance, serves not only as a powerful signifier of educational 'quality' but also signifies the imputed ability of workers to enter skilled sectors in the labour market. Most of those excluded from access to the labour market in this way would be groups who had been socially, politically and economically disadvantaged historically. In this instance, English has become a powerful symbolic social marker, and serves as a mechanism of exclusion, or inclusion, which is socially divisive and, in practice, unequal in relation to labour market access to the majority black population.

On a surface level then, it would seem that many ex-British postcolonial countries are defined by a linguistic market dominated by English as the official language, which means that it 'becomes the theoretical norm against which all linguistic practices are objectively measured' (Bourdieu, 1991: 45). Moreover, as is evident in the discussion above, there is a taken-for-granted correlation between the language of education, that is, Standard English, and that of labour markets as well as formal political institutions. This factor is 'critical in reinforcing the status of specific languages [e.g. English] as legitimate, official, or standard, while also leading to the devaluation of other linguistic practices' (Park & Wee, 2008: 246). Clearly then, English constitutes a potent form of symbolic capital; it represents the unquestioned linguistic 'norm' within all formal sectors in society. In practice though it serves to prevent the development of skilled labour supply within these countries, thus inhibiting the possibility of labour market diversification. I return to this point later.

Furthermore, the truth claims about the 'neutrality' of English playing a major role in integrating different ethnic groups within society is not borne out in practice. Ethnic cleavages in many of these countries have remained, despite the adoption of English as a supranational 'neutral' language. The past two decades have shown the extent to which ethnic conflicts in various postcolonial countries – for example, Kenya and Uganda – have created political instability, thus undermining possibilities for social and economic development. This factor, combined with high levels of illiteracy and the impact of this on skills levels available in the formal labour market, raises questions regarding the validity of English as the exclusive official or dominant language within postcolonial societies that have an indigenous multilingual base.

Whilst these tensions in language policy and educational provision have remained unresolved within postcolonial nation states, changes have been taking place globally, altering processes of capital accumulation as well as the concept of 'development' fundamentally. Within this context of change, the value of English has been enhanced, making it the preferred language capital within global language markets. As will be seen below, there are multiple implications related to this dominant position of English in the world today with regard to the social and economic development of countries generally – and particularly those having a different linguistic and sociocultural base.

Globalization and the Role of English in Development

Whilst the concept of the nation state still prevails, the current phase of globalization has extended social relations beyond national boundaries creating interdependence and cooperation amongst nation states. Castells (1999: 5) argues that

> Globalization is a new historical reality – not simply the one invented by neo-liberal ideology to convince citizens to surrender to markets, but also the one inscribed in processes of capitalist restructuring, innovation and competition, and enacted through the powerful medium of information and communication technologies.

Nevertheless, there is a synergy between information technology and neoliberalism. The diffusion, through international agencies such as the World Bank and IMF, of neoliberal monetary policies grounded in the principles of free enterprise, free trade and the deregulation of money markets to national economic management approaches now provides the ideological basis for the information technology–driven modernization of economies. Underpinning this is the neoliberal belief in the primacy of the market as key regulating mechanism thus freeing capital and in the process stimulating the development of new flexible accumulation strategies facilitated by information technology (Morley & Rassool, 1999). Since the emergence of information technology during the 1980s, the concept of development has extended to new capital accumulation regimes involving rapid information, knowledge and finance flows within a dynamic interactive global environment. As will be discussed below, language as a means of communication features as a central variable within different sectors of the globalized economy including business, trade, manufacturing, the culture industries and the service sector.

Information technology has fundamentally altered the nature of work and the organization of work regimes. In manufacturing, for example, expertise is dispersed horizontally within work teams, which integrate different skills and knowledge expertise. This means, for example, that designers have to communicate amongst different experts as well as with those involved at various levels of production, management and marketing. Some of this expertise is geographically dispersed across regions, countries and continents, as experts work together on international or transnational projects. The centrality of communication to this production process suggests that individual and group language exchanges taking place within these contexts, together with expert knowledge, skills and awarenesses, represent valuable forms of cultural capital that are exchanged within the labour market. Language barriers within this framework therefore represent barriers to economic development.

The capability of microelectronics technology to produce a diverse range of quality products has generated discerning consumers and competitive commodity markets as a result of cheaper products continually entering the global marketplace. Subsequently, advertising, product presentation, management and marketing have become new core areas within the redefined labour market. These changes in the nature of work and the work process have generated labour market demands for new sets of technological and business knowledge, problem solving skills, 'multiliteracies' (Gee, 1996), transferable skills and communication competence, as well as worker awarenesses of the labour market and work process (Rassool, 1999). That is to say, the emphasis is on the self-development of human capital, that is, that workers are responsible for updating their own skills profile in order to sustain their employability within an evolving labour market. This requires workers' ability to be reflective and reflexive in relation to changes in the labour market. Operating within the technological workplace requires language and communication skills such as sophisticated literacy skills, information processing skills, knowledge of different subject registers, specialist knowledges, intercultural communication skills, labour market awarenesses, data handling, decision making skills, problem solving skills, research skills, analytical competence, interpreting meanings and oracy skills (speaking and listening) (Rassool, 1999). Possessing higher order thinking skills, linguistic flexibility, incorporating language fluency and communicative competence, in this context, can be seen as being integral to the notion of individual worker capability.

If this is the case, then the extent to which a society can participate in the competitive globalized economy depends significantly on its levels of *linguistic capability,* in addition to its productive capacity, collectively and individually. A society's linguistic capability includes the accumulated stock of language and communicative competence – the cultural capital – to exchange within different sectors of the global labour market. This includes, for example, negotiations taking place within the financial and business sector, or the interpersonal and intercultural communication skills and knowledges required within the service sector. Building a country's linguistic capability as part of its collective cultural capital therefore contributes to its productive capacity. As such, operating within an interactive global workplace has implications for the choice of language of communication and literacy.

Within this redefined interactive global terrain, English as a preferred lingua franca or language of wider communication, in business, trade and industry, as well as in international political forums, has assumed major exchange value. Consequently, English has been adopted formally by an increasing number of countries as their first foreign or additional language. Regarded thus as a 'global language' (Crystal, 1997; Graddol, 1997), English has high status and represents preferred language capital within interconnected and, at the same time, highly competitive economic markets. Within this context fluency in English can be seen as representing potent linguistic capital.

What does this mean for postcolonial developing countries in terms of their ability to participate effectively within the competitive and highly dynamic economic markets within the global context? How capable are they with regard to maximizing human capital in order to support their economic growth and social development? As can be seen below, there are new opportunities to be exploited as well as constraints to be overcome.

English Language Market Opportunities in Economic Development in Postcolonial Countries

Development and innovations within the field of information and communication technologies, and their diffusion within and across countries, coupled with trade liberalization, have contributed to businesses in industrialized countries outsourcing a major part of their information technology service needs to comparatively cheaper labour importing countries such as India, China, Malaysia and the Philippines (Chadee & Raman, 2007). The impetus for businesses choosing to outsource is the pressure to maintain their place within a highly competitive market, thus creating the need to raise productivity and profitability while lowering operational costs. This is called 'business process outsourcing' (BPO). India in particular, with its large population, can provide a large pool of highly skilled, English-speaking workers; has a well-developed IT sector; and has a reputation for high-quality, low-cost labour, which makes it competitive within the BPO IT offshore service providers (supply) market (Chadee & Raman, 2007). The fact that India can provide a large supply of workers who are proficient in English gives it a competitive edge over a country such as China (also in the BPO market) where English language proficiency is not currently as widely spread amongst workers. According to Coe (2007: 16) 'the fact that the English language itself is unique as the *lingua franca* of international business suggests that other developing countries without large English-speaking populations may find it difficult to replicate the success of India in onshoring service jobs from developed English-speaking countries'. As such, India provides an example of how a postcolonial country with English as one of its official languages has used this, together with investment in education, to redefine its economic strategy and the structure of its economy – and through this, develop the country's capacity to participate more equally within the global economic market by creating new market niches. Here the state also provided strategic support for the development of private enterprise, facilitated by the dot-com boom and cheaper internet-telecom tariffs during the 1990s (Farrell *et al*., 2005), thus decreasing the country's reliance on income from the informal sector. This contrasts sharply with the underdeveloped human resource base in Zambia, South Africa and Pakistan discussed above, where the informal sector of the economy continues to predominate.

India provides an example of how English, the ex-colonial language, was appropriated, redefined and integrated into a new development paradigm. This illustrates that within the interactive and competitive global arena, language markets, as is the case with other markets, are dynamic and therefore subject to change according to shifts in material conditions within the world. It also raises the question as to whether English has become a commodity, like any other commodity in the world today, gaining capital in relation to its instrumental value, and therefore is stripped of its colonial hegemony.

What does this mean for national language policy? In India, most state schools follow the 'Three Language Formula' (the home/regional language; English; and Hindi in non-Hindi-speaking states and any other modern

Indian language in Hindi-speaking states) advocated by the federal government – which leads to the transition to English as medium of education in the upper secondary school (Azam *et al.*, 2010). This approach supports additive bi- or multilingualism and languages are regarded as an integral part of human resource development. As can be seen, the need for highly skilled labour in BPO underscores the significance of quality education and creating niche areas such as IT, science, business and management studies. Indeed '[h]uman resources have been identified as the most critical source of competitiveness for software and services industries ... The quality of the labour force also matters particularly in a knowledge based industry' (Chadee & Raman, 2007).

The benefits have been major to the country as a whole as is described by NASSCOM's 2011 report, which states that

> The IT-BPO sector has become one of the most significant growth catalysts for the Indian economy. In addition to fuelling India's economy, this industry is also positively influencing the lives of its people through an active direct and indirect contribution to the various socio-economic parameters such as employment, standard of living and diversity among others. The industry has played a significant role in transforming India's image from a slow moving bureaucratic economy to a land of innovative entrepreneurs and a global player in providing world class technology solutions and business services. The industry has helped India transform from a rural and agriculture-based economy to a knowledge based economy.

Yet, at the same time, there is a need for caution regarding the link between English language proficiency and higher wage incomes. The report on a recent study on the returns to English language skills in India, for example, states that

> We do find that English proficiency raises wages in India, but the returns are considerably lower for more recent entrants into the labor market. For the marginal worker deciding whether to invest in English skill, the relevant return would be the one estimated for the recent entrants. Thus the implication is that providing English classes to adults may not necessarily raise their wages. For recent entrants, English skills help increase wages only when coupled with high education; those who have not completed their secondary schooling would not see wage increases due to acquisition of English-language skills. Policymakers should be aware of these language-skill complementarities when designing policies. (Azam *et al.*, 2010: 21)

The report further states that there are 'lower returns for scheduled castes compared to other social groups, and lower returns for women in rural areas compared to urban areas' (Azam *et al.*, 2010: 22). Evidently then there are wider issues, related to equity in society, that need to be considered in relation to the truth claims made about the benefits of English language proficiency.

Singapore and Malaysia are two other postcolonial countries who have maximized their economic development potential through BPO industries utilizing a highly skilled labour force that is proficient in English, a strong business infrastructure and government support (see Wee, this volume). Alongside this are the business and trade networks established within the region relying on local and regional languages as media of communication. Local knowledge is an important factor to being able to penetrate local markets in different countries, as can be seen in the advice given to the international banking sector by Stephen Roach, Asia chairman and former chief executive at Morgan Stanley, the global financial services firm: 'There is no substitute for local knowledge, local talent and local presence … local language skills, and familiarity with customs and regulations' (cited in Wilson, 2010). In other words, although English is the dominant language in the contemporary world, knowledge of different languages plays an important role in the economy. As stated earlier, other languages are particularly useful in building regional networks for trade and business and are thus important for countries to build social capital. This indicates that postcolonial developing countries need to revise their stance on the intrinsic value and 'superiority' of English and instead focus on developing their multilingualism (including English) and a high-skills base in line with emerging markets within the global economy – and, equally important, have good governance with leaders having an informed vision for societal development, and strategic educational planning focused on human resource development. In this regard, the development of educational, social, economic and political infrastructure in postcolonial countries throughout the Sub-Saharan Africa region is urgent if they are not to continue to exist outside global economic and labour markets. The significance of this lies in the fact that the information technology–driven development paradigm that dominates the world today 'allows the overall system to link up everything that is valuable according to dominant values and interests, while disconnecting everything that is [deemed to be] not valuable, or becomes devalued'; this includes countries and regions (Castells, 1999: 5). Globalization has redefined the role of the nation state fundamentally and affects the way that it operates; it has redefined the concept of development.

Conclusion

Examining the political economy of language and development within the changing global economy has illustrated the usefulness of an interdisciplinary analytical framework that draws on concepts and theories within the broader Social Sciences. In this regard, the discussion has integrated concepts, theories and perspectives from sociolinguistics, language and culture, the sociology of language, development studies, economics (including labour market theory), politics, history and education. This is a developing area within the Social Sciences and it is hoped that the analysis has contributed to the debate by extending the discourse framework. The discussion throughout the chapter has linked the construction of 'English as a global language' to older colonial hegemonies and also provided evidence of the ways in which English has been redefined within the economic planning framework of some postcolonial countries, allowing them to maximize their labour power, make use of opportunities in emerging markets and, in the process, restructure their economies to the benefit of societal development. The study shows that whilst the value of English has been enhanced in the changing and highly competitive global economy, there are important functions that local languages play in building regional business and trade networks. It has shown that societal development depends to a significant extent on the society's linguistic capability as well as its skills profile in line with emerging labour market trends. For postcolonial governments in countries throughout Sub-Saharan Africa and in Pakistan, education, language and development policy choices clearly are significant with regard to the extent to which they can allow these countries to profit from emerging opportunities within the labour market, in, for example, India, Singapore and Malaysia, and create new niche markets within the information technology–driven development paradigm. Old hegemonies, grounded in the nation state and modernity, are clearly being challenged in a very fundamental way within the interactive and interdependent global economy. It follows then that developments within this changing terrain are analysed and interpreted within interdisciplinary frameworks that take into account the complex tapestry of emerging realities.

References

Anderson, B. (1983) *Imagined Communities: Reflections on the Origin and Spread of Nationalism*. London: Verso.

Azam, M., Chin, A. and Prakash, N. (2010) *The Returns to English-Language Skills in India*. Discussion Paper Series CDP No 02/10. London: Centre for Research and Analysis of Migration, Department of Economics, University of London.

Billig, M. (1995) *Banal Nationalism*. London: Sage Publications.
Bourdieu, P. (1986) The economics of linguistic exchanges. *Social Sciences Information* 16 (6), 645-668.
Bourdieu, P. (1991) *Language and Symbolic Power* (G. Raymond and M. Adamson, trans.). Oxford, Cambridge: Polity Press.
Burger, R., Burger, R. and Van den Berg, S. (2005) *A Note on Trends in the Zambian Labour Market between 1991 and 1998* (DFID-WB Collaboration on Knowledge and Skills in the New Economy). Stellenbosch: University of Stellenbosch, Department of Economics.
Busch, B. (2010) School language profiles: Valorizing linguistic resources in heteroglossic situations in South Africa. *Language and Education* 24 (4), 284-294.
Canagarajah, S. (1999) *Resisting Linguistic Imperialism in English Teaching*. Oxford: Oxford University Press.
Casale, D. and Posel, D. (2010) *English Language Proficiency and Earnings in a Developing Country: The Case of South Africa*. Paper presented at the 5th IZA/World Bank Conference: Employment and Development, Bonn.
Casey, T. and Dustmann, C. (2007) *Intergenerational Transmission of Language Capital and Economic Outcomes*. Discussion paper IZA DP No. 3074. Bonn: Institute for the Study of Labour.
Castells, M. (1999) *Information Technology, Globalization and Social Development*. UNRISD Discussion Paper No. 114. Geneva: United Nations Research Institute.
Chadee, D. and Raman, R. (2007) *Can IT Service Providers in India and China Co-operate to Compete?* Paper presented at the ANZAM Annual Conference, Sydney, Australia, December 2007.
Chiswick, B.R. (2008) *The Economics of Language*. Discussion Paper IZA DP No. 3568. Bonn: Institute for the Study of Labour: An Introduction and Overview.
Chiswick, B. and Miller, P. (2003) The complementarity of language and other human capital: Immigrant earnings in Canada. *Economics of Education Review* 22, 469-480.
Church, J. and King, I. (1993) Bilingualism and network externalities. *Canadian Journal of Economics of Education Review* 2 (6), 337-345.
Coe, D. (2007) *Globalisation and Labour Markets: Policy Issues Arising from the Emergence of China and India*. OECD Social, Employment and Migration Working Papers No. 63. Paris: OECD 12-Nov-2007.
Coulmas, F. (1992) *Language and Economy*. Oxford: Blackwell Publishers.
Crystal, D. (1997) *English as a Global Language*. Cambridge: Cambridge University Press.
Djité, P. (1993) Language and development in Africa. *International Journal of the Sociology of Language* 100 (101), 16-32.
Djité, P. (2008) *The Sociolinguistics of Development in Africa*. Clevedon: Multilingual Matters.
Edwards, V. (2009) *Learning to be Literate*. Bristol: Multilingual Matters.
Farrell, D., Kaka, N. and Stürze, S. (2005) *Extending India's Leadership of the Global IT and BPO Industries*. The McKinsey Quarterly. Mumbai: McKinsey Global Institute.
Fishman, J. (1972) *The Sociology of Language: An Interdisciplinary Social Approach to Language in Society*. Rowley, MA: Newbury House.
Fishman, J. (1991) *Reversing Language Shift*. Clevedon: Multilingual Matters.
Fishman, J. (1999) The new linguistic world order. *Foreign Policy* 1, 26-40.
Foucault, M. (1970) *The Order of Things. An Archaeology of the Human Sciences*. London: Tavistock Publications.
García, O. (2008) Multilingual language awareness and teacher education. In J. Cenoz and N. Hornberger (eds) *Encyclopedia of Language and Education* (2nd edn, Vol. 6, pp. 385-400), Knowledge about Language. Berlin: Springer.

García, O. and Baker, C. (eds) (2007) *Policy and Practice in Bilingual Education: Extending the Foundations*. Clevedon: Multilingual Matters.

Gee, J.P. (1996) *Social Linguistics and Literacies: Ideology in Discourses* (2nd edn). London: Taylor & Francis.

Government of Pakistan (GOP) (2008) *Pakistan Labour Force Survey (2005-2007)*. Islamabad: Federal Bureau of Statistics.

Government of Pakistan (GOP) (2010) *Economic Survey 2009-2010*. Islamabad: Federal Bureau of Statistics.

Graddol, D. (1997) *The Future of English? A Guide to Forecasting the Popularity of the English Language in the 21st Century*. London: British Council.

Grin, F. (2006) Economic considerations in language policy. In T. Ricento (ed.) *An Introduction to Language Policy* (pp. 77-94). Oxford: Blackwell.

Grin, F. and Vaillancourt, F. (1997) The economics of multilingualism: Overview and analytical framework. *Annual Review of Applied Linguistics Annual Review of Applied Linguistics* 17, 43-65.

Harbert, W., McConnell-Ginet, S., Miller, A. and Whitman, J. (eds) (2009) *Language and Poverty*. Bristol: Multilingual Matters.

Heugh, K. (1999) Languages, development and reconstructing education in South Africa. *International Journal of Educational Development* 19, 301-313.

Heugh, K. (2003) *Language Policy and Democracy in South Africa: The Prospects of Equality within Rights-based Policy and Planning*. Stockholm: Centre for Research on Bilingualism, Stockholm University.

International Labour Organization (ILO) (2008) *Skills for Improved Productivity, Employment Growth and Development*. Report V presented at the International Labour Conference 97th Session, 2008, Geneva.

International Monetary Fund (IMF) (2007) *Zambia: Poverty Reduction Strategy Paper*. IMF Country Report No. 07/276. Washington, DC: The International Monetary Fund.

Kaplan, R. and Baldauf, R. (eds) (1999) *Language Planning in Malawi, Mozambique and the Philippines*. Clevedon: Multilingual Matters.

Kelly, M. (1991) *Education in Declining Economy: The Case of Zambia 1975-1985*. Washington, DC: The International Bank for Reconstruction and Development and the World Bank.

Li Wei (1994) *Three Generations Two Language One Family: Language Choice and Language Shift in a Chinese Community in Britain*. Clevedon: Multilingual Matters.

Linehan, S. (2004) *Language of Instruction and the Quality of Education in Zambia*. Paper commissioned for the *EFA Global Monitoring Report 2005, The Quality Imperative* 2005/ED/EFA/MRT/PI/29. Paris.

Mansoor, S. (2005) *Language Planning in Higher Education: A Case Study of Pakistan*. Oxford: Oxford University Press.

Mateene, K. (1999) OAU's strategy for linguistic unity and multilingual education. *Social Dynamics* 25 (1), 164-178.

May, S. (2008) *Language and Minority Rights*. New York: Routledge.

Moon, S. (2010) Education, language, identity and culture: An ethnographic case study of Korean Sojourner families in the UK. Unpublished PhD thesis, University of Reading.

Morley, L. and Rassool, N. (1999) *School Effectiveness: Fracturing the Discourse*. New York: Routledge.

The National Association of Software and Services Companies (NASSCOMM) (2011) *The IT-BPO Sector in India – Strategic Review*. New Delhi: NASSCOMM.

Ozolins, U. (2003) Language and economics: Mutual incompatibilities, or a necessary partnership? *Current Issues in Language Planning* 4 (1), 67-83.

Park, J.S. and Wee, L. (2008) Appropriating the language of the other: Performativity in autonomous and unified markets. *Language & Communication* 28, 248-257.

Pennycook, A. (1994) *The Cultural Politics of English as an International Language*. Harlow: Longman Group Limited.

Rahman, T. (2000) *Language and Politics in Pakistan*. Oxford: Oxford University Press.

Rahman, T. (2002) *Language Teaching and Power in Pakistan*. Paper presented at the World Congress on Language Policies, Barcelona, Spain.

Rajagopalan, K. (2004) The concept of World English and its implications for ELT. *ELT Journal* 58 (2), 111-117.

Rassool, N. (1999) *Literacy for Sustainable Development in the Age of Information*. Clevedon: Multilingual Matters.

Rassool, N. (2000) Contested and contesting identities: Minority languages vs. the teaching of 'world' languages within the global cultural economy. *Journal of Multilingualism and Multicultural Education* 21 (6), 386-398.

Rassool, N. (2004) Sustaining linguistic diversity within the global cultural economy: Issues of language rights and linguistic possibilities. *Comparative Education, Special Issue: Postcolonialism and Comparative Education* 40 (2), 199-214.

Rassool, N. (2007) *Global Issues in Language, Education and Development: Perspectives from Postcolonial Societies.* Clevedon: Multilingual Matters.

Romaine, S. (2008) Biodiversity, linguistic diversity and poverty: Some global patterns and missing links. In W. Harbert, S. McConnell-Ginet, A. Miller and J. Whitman (eds) *Language and Poverty* (pp. 127-146). Bristol: Multilingual Matters.

Schultz, T. (1963) *The Economic Value of Education*. New York: Columbia University Press.

Selten, R. and Pool, J. (1991) The distribution of foreign language skills as a game equilibrium. In R. Selten (ed.) *Game Equilibrium Models* (Vol. 4, pp. 64-84). Berlin: Springer.

Shim, D. and Park, J.S. (2008) The language politics of 'English fever' in South Korea. *Korea Journal* Summer, 136-159.

Singh, A. (2005) *FDI, Globalisation and Economic Development and International Rules of the Game*. March 2005, Working Paper No. 304. Cambridge: University of Cambridge.

Skutnabb-Kangas, T. (2000) *Linguistic Genocide in Education – Or Worldwide Diversity and Human Rights?* Mahwah, NJ: Lawrence Erlbaum.

Skutnabb-Kangas, T. (2010) Education of indigenous and minority children. In J.A.G. Fishman and O. García (eds) *Handbook of Language and Ethnic Identity. Disciplinary and Regional Perspectives* (2nd edn, Vol. 1, pp. 186-204). Oxford: Oxford University Press.

Skutnabb-Kangas, T., Phillipson, R., Panda, M. and Mohanty, A. (eds) (2009) *Social Justice through Multilingual Education*. Bristol: Multilingual Matters.

Smith, A.D. (1994) *Nations and Nationalism in a Global Era*. Oxford: Polity Press.

Sun, X. (2002) Foreign direct investment and economic development: What do the states need to do? *Capacity Development Workshops and Global Forum on Reinventing Government on Globalization, Role of the State and Enabling Environment Sponsored by the United Nations.* December 10-13, 2002. Marrakech, Morocco: Foreign Investment Advisory Service, United Nations.

Todaro, M.P. (1999) *Economic Development in the Third World*. Harlow: Longman.

Tollefson, J.W. (1991) *Planning Language, Planning Inequality: Language Policy in the Community*. London: Longman.

United Nations Conference on Trade and Development (UNCTAD) (2008) *Development and Globalisation: Facts and Figures*. UNCTAD/GDS/CSIR/2007/1. New York and Geneva: United Nations.

United Nations Educational, Scientific and Cultural Organization (UNESCO) (1964) *Report of the UNESCO Planning Mission: Education in Northern Rhodesia*. Lusaka: Government Printer.

Vaillancourt, F. (1980) *Difference in Earnings by Language Groups in Quebec, 1970. An Economic Analysis.* Quebec: Centre international de recherche sur le bilinguisme.

Varennes, F. de (1996) *Language, Minorities and Human Rights*. The Hague: Kluwer Law International.

Williams, G. (1986) Language planning or language appropriation? *Journal of Multilingual and Multicultural Development* 7 (6), 509-518.

Wilson, E. (2010) *Global Banks: Risky business emerging markets: News, analysis and opinion online*. http:///www.emergingmarkets.org

3 Political Perspectives on Language Policies and Development in Africa

Eddie Williams

Introduction

One of the many current debates concerning Africa is whether the 19th-century colonization by Europeans had profound and far-reaching effects, or whether it was a superficial and relatively brief episode in the life of a continent that has harboured humans since their earliest days. Two phenomena attributable to colonization are, however, obvious to the observer of the here-and-now in Africa: first that the borders of modern African states are by and large those arising from the agreements between European powers following the General Act of the Berlin Conference in 1885, where no Africans were present, and second that the languages of the colonialists, primarily English, French and Portuguese (the Germans having lost their African colonies following the First World War), have, since that time, enjoyed high status and widespread use in the formal institutions of the ex-colonies. Although the 1960s saw the end of most European colonies in Africa, European languages retained their dominance; indeed, in the case of the British ex-colonies, English dominance has since been buttressed by its having become the language of globalization, and having spread beyond the 'Anglophone' countries.

This chapter will examine educational practices involving English in three countries: Malawi, Zambia and Rwanda. They are presented as examples of central and eastern African countries with differing language-in-education policies, but where English plays a dominant role, with, as will be argued, concomitant adverse effects on the development of their people. After outlining relevant background issues, evidence based on classroom observation and testing is adduced to illustrate how the use of English as a medium of instruction is a barrier, rather than a bridge, to education and development.

We then address the question of why African governments persist in using English (or other ex-colonial languages) as media of instruction despite such negative evidence, and despite numerous declarations from African educationists decrying the practice. While conceding that generalizations need to be treated with caution in the African context, the answers generally are to do with politicians' concerns with national unification and their notions of language in development. However, the question of why Africa's development has been so problematic cannot be reduced to simple issues of educational language practice and political goals: the reality is more complex. The chapter accordingly closes by focusing on one element in this complex, which development specialists consider crucial, namely social capital, and the role it plays in the well-being of states.

The Role of Education in Development

In recent decades the term 'development' has come to be viewed from two perspectives. In the first, development is conceived of as increased prosperity, measured in terms of national economic growth (Arndt, 1987), whether this be purely neo-conservative market-driven development, or development moderated by state intervention in the interests of fairness, with the hope that wealth will 'trickle down' to the poorest. The second view, championed by, among others, Thomas and Potter (1992), sees development as related to the meeting of human needs, and involves not only a reduction in material poverty and inequitable distribution, but also factors such as increases in democratic participation, levels of education and health, mortality rates, the status of women, and environmental sustainability. The human needs conception also encompasses the view that vulnerability, powerlessness, and isolation are important aspects of deprivation. The two perspectives are not incompatible, and development agencies currently work from an integrated model: the UN, for example, includes both human and economic criteria in its country descriptions (see UNICEF, 2010; UNDP, 2010), while the persuasive statistics of Rosling (2009) suggest that the two perspectives are related.[1]

Despite a few dissenting voices, the general consensus is that education has a role to play in development, although the precise pathways of its effects are contested. Thus Anderson's (1966: 347) claim that 'about 40% of adult literacy ... is a threshold for economic development' is ironically characterized as the 'magical figure of 40%' by Rogers (1990: 3), although Anderson elaborates that 'that level of education would not be a sufficient condition in societies lacking other support systems'. Indeed, subsequent research (e.g. Knight & Sabot, 1990; Lockheed *et al.*, 1980; Moock & Addou,

1994) supports Anderson's view, and demonstrates that adequate education is a necessary, but not sufficient, condition for both human and national economic development. Research has also made the crucial demonstration that education can be a cause of economic development, as opposed to simply correlating with it (Hicks, 1980; Wheeler, 1980). In a particularly wide-ranging review, Azariadis and Drazen (1990), having examined the development history of 32 countries from 1940 to 1980, concluded that a threshold level for a number of factors including the educational quality of the labour force was a necessary, but not sufficient, condition for rapid economic growth. What they see as particularly significant is that none of the countries which failed to meet the threshold level of educational quality managed to achieve rapid growth. Crucially, however, it should be noted that for education to make a positive contribution to development, it must be effective education: the argument in this chapter is that much education in Africa in not effective, and that language education policies are one reason for this.

Background

The language in education policies in Malawi, Zambia and Rwanda

In order to facilitate understanding of the research findings, some background on the language situation and language policies in the three countries where this research was carried out is appropriate. In common with almost all African countries, Malawi and Zambia have a number of indigenous languages. Ethnologue (Lewis, 2009) lists 16 indigenous languages for Malawi, and 43 for Zambia, although different authorities claim higher numbers, depending on their definition of 'language'. A major language used in education in both countries is Chichewa (Chewa), also known as Nyanja (Chinyanja).[2] Despite the different labels, the languages are the same (the entry for Chewa in Crystal, 1987: 452 says 'See Nyanja'), although there are very minor differences in spelling. The Chichewa/Nyanja language is found on both sides of the Malawi–Zambia border (a case of an ethnolinguistic group being divided by colonial boundaries).

The language policy in Malawi for the eight years of primary schooling is that from Years 1 to 4 Chichewa is the medium of instruction (MOI), with English taught as a subject. From Years 5 to 8 English becomes the medium, with Chichewa a subject. In Zambia, on the other hand, English is the medium from Years 1 to 7 (when primary school ends), and although seven Zambian languages (including Chichewa) are supposed to be taught as subjects, in practice they are often ignored, as local languages are not taken into account for promotion to secondary school.

Rwanda provides a rather different research context. It is atypical in that, unlike most countries in Africa, the overwhelming majority of its inhabitants speak the same language, Kinyarwanda, and most are effectively monolingual in that language. According to Samuelson and Freedman (2010), 'As high as 99.4% of the population can speak Kinyarwanda (Rosendal, 2009), and approximately 90% of Rwandans speak only Kinyarwanda' (LeClerc, 2008; Munyankesha, 2004). Immediately before the 1994 massacres, Kinyarwanda was used as the sole medium of education at primary level, with French used as the medium from secondary upwards. As of January 2009, English was instituted as the medium of instruction from the beginning of primary onwards, with the intention of raising a generation of Rwandans fluent in English. The problems inherent in achieving this are considerable, not least the matter of teaching English to the thousands of teachers who have hitherto only used French or Kinyarwanda as MOI. However, the policy of privileging English is one strongly promoted by the present Tutsi-dominated government, who are themselves largely 'Anglophone' with many having been educated in English in neighbouring Uganda. In February 2011, however, there was a further change to policy when the Minister for Primary and Secondary Education announced that, with immediate effect, the medium of instruction for the first three years of primary school would be Kinyarwanda, with English and French taught as subjects (reported in *The New Times,* 16 February, 2011). English would be the medium thereafter.

'Safetalk' in classroom procedure

In terms of classroom procedures, English teaching in primary schools in Malawi, Zambia and Rwanda is remarkably similar (based on observation of over 100 lessons in each country from 1992 to 2004). As we shall see in the following extract, lessons are highly text based: this reduces demands on the English of both teachers and students, and the students' lack of English proficiency is masked by this type of discourse. Lessons typically follow the following three-phase pattern:

(1) The teacher writes various words on the blackboard; the words are read aloud by the teacher, and repeated by the class as a whole and/or in various combinations (boys, girls, front row, back row, etc.), or by individuals. Alternatively, and less frequently, the teacher may generate words from a picture.

(2) The text is read out from the book or from the blackboard by the teacher (or by students known to be competent), sentence by sentence, and each sentence is repeated by the class or individuals. The whole text may then be read again by the teacher from beginning to end, and sections of it again repeated by students. This phase usually takes up the greatest amount of lesson time.
(3) Oral questions may then be asked by the teacher. These are normally direct reference questions, which usually follow the sequence of sentences in the text, in which case the questions can be answered by students reading the sentences in sequence. (Occasionally as a fourth phase the students may be asked to write the answers in their exercise books.)

By way of example, an extract follows from a transcript (corresponding to Phase 2) of a Year 3 lesson, with a class of 45 students from a Zambian school. The text for the lesson had been written on the blackboard:

Teacher: OK. Paragraph four. The first sentence.
Student: Chuma and his father walked away from the river.
Teacher: Again.
Student: Chuma and his father walked away from the river.
Teacher: Yes, that is the sentence. Chuma and his father walked away from the river. Read.
Class: Chuma and his father walked away from the river.
Teacher: Walked.
Class: Walked.
Teacher: Walked.
Class: Walked.
Teacher: Read the sentence.
Class: Chuma and his father walked away from the river.
Teacher: Next sentence? Then …
Student: They … they walked away from the crocodiles.
Teacher: Yes. They walked away from the crocodiles. Read.
Class: They walked away from the crocodiles.
Teacher: Read this word as 'walked.' Say 'walked.'
Class: Walked.
Teacher: Now read the sentence.
Class: They walked away from the crocodiles.
Teacher: Now this.
Student: They walked away from the hippos.
Teacher: Again.

Student: They walked away from the hippos.
Teacher: They walked away from the hippos. Read.
Class: They walked away from the hippos.
Teacher: Next sentence.
(Extract from Appendix B in Williams, 1998: 79)

Noteworthy here is that no attention is paid to the presentation or checking of meaning, and that the activity is largely a 'reading-like' activity whereby students simply repeat the teacher's words while looking at the blackboard. These relatively undemanding behaviourist-based 'look-and-say' practices have been described as 'safetalk' by Chick (1996), to refer to a similar situation in South African schools where the 'co-ordinated chorusing prompts and responses enabled the teacher and students [...] to hide their poor command of English; to obscure their inadequate understanding of academic content; and to maintain a façade of effective learning taking place' (Chick, 1996: 238). Such pedagogic procedures, which do not engage with meaning but require only accurate repetition, are unlikely to enhance language learning. However, these classroom discourses are not confined to English language lessons, but are also evident across the curriculum. Williams (2006: 41) describes similar procedures in social science lessons in Malawi. It is hard to see how these practices can engage learners, and years spent at school attending lessons that consist of such 'safetalk' arguably do not constitute effective education. As Hornberger and Chick (1998) conclude from classroom observation in Peru and South Africa, the result of 'safetalk' is that 'teachers and learners know more or less what to expect and how to behave in class, but where a high price is paid in terms of (a lack of) learning, e.g. [...] chorusing, reading as repeating, writing as copying'. I would highlight that the above reference by Chick to 'safetalk' enabling teachers and students to 'hide their poor command of English' is crucial: the policy of using English as the MOI has favoured 'safetalk' – a mode of classroom discourse that is highly text-based and puts few demands on participants' language ability. (It should be noted that there is ample justification for these practices, which have certain advantages in their context, see Williams, 2006: 39-43 for a fuller discussion. However, they are widely agreed to have failed students in that years of attending school results in very little learning for the majority.)

Testing Language Proficiency

In order to provide evidence for the effect of 'safetalk' procedures in the context of exoglossic languages as media of instruction, this section reports on investigations of reading proficiency in Malawi, Zambia and Rwanda.

In the interests of brevity, the research reported here is confined to discussions of the reading tests, rather than analyses of classroom observations or one-on-one reading sessions (for these, see Williams, 2006: chaps 5-7). The research in Malawi and Zambia was carried out from 1992 to 1996; that in Rwanda in 2003 and 2004. Subsequent visits to these and five other African countries, most recently in 2010, confirms that teaching in almost all government primary schools continues to consist of 'safetalk' procedures.

In Malawi and Zambia, modified cloze tests of reading in English and Chichewa[3] were devised (30 items per test), and administered in Chichewa-speaking areas in both Malawi and Zambia. It was decided to test at Year 5 since that is the year at which schools in Malawi switch to English as a medium, and testing at that point therefore maximizes the differential proportion of exposure to English that the two groups have had. In both countries two urban schools and four rural schools were selected. A total of 290 pupils were tested in Malawi and 227 in Zambia. Tests were complemented by individual reading sessions in English and Chichewa/Nyanja conducted with 24 students in each country. All the children in Malawi and Zambia claimed to speak Chichewa/Nyanja, and this was supported by teachers and observation.

Table 3.1 shows that Malawian students have a slightly higher mean score than Zambian students on the test results, but this is far from statistically significant ($p > 0.3337$). This result suggests there is no difference in English reading ability between children in Zambia and children in Malawi at Year 5. Contrary to what one might expect, it seems that Year 5 Zambian children who have officially had their first four years of education through the medium of English are not superior to Malawian children who have had Chichewa as a medium of instruction for those years. However, in neither country do the results indicate that students' English levels are adequate for learning entirely through the medium of English, as they are meant to be doing. Even if we accept the generous interpretation that scores of 15 and over (i.e. above 50%) suggest that students can read independently, then we find that 70% of Malawian students and 66% of Zambian students are not capable of such reading.

Table 3.1 Test results in English and Chichewa/Nyanja

Country	*Number of pupils*	*Mean English (out of 30)*	*Mean Chichewa/Nyanja (out of 30)*
Malawi	290	12.8	19.9
Zambia	227	11.7	4.4

However, there is a big and significant difference in Chichewa results: Zambian students score very low, close to the chance score of 4. The reasons are probably (1) they rarely see Nyanja in print since their teachers neglect it (it doesn't feature in the promotional exam to secondary school) and (2) the variety of Nyanja used in the textbooks (on which the test was based) is a conservative variety, whereas many Zambian students speak a 'contact variety', which includes words borrowed from English and other Zambian languages. Malawian students on the other hand score highly (the mean is around 66%). Further analysis of the results for Malawi also reveals that Chichewa discriminates far less than English against rural children, the probable reason being that urban children are more likely to encounter English in their everyday environments than rural children. These findings readily suggest that using known local languages as media of instruction would be far more effective for student learning than using English.

The research in Rwanda involved an investigation into student proficiency in English, French and Kinyarwanda in six primary schools in 2003 (when Kinyarwanda was the MOI). Four of the schools were categorized as rural, and two as urban. The tests employed a modified cloze format, and were administered at Year 4; items were based on material taken from the Years 1 to 3. A total of 261 primary school students were tested in all three languages. Results overall in percentages can be seen in Table 3.2.

Although test equivalence cannot be established, expert judgement concurred that in terms of language proficiency required for the tests, the English test was the most accessible in terms of the lexis and grammar and thus made fewest demands on the students, while the test in Kinyarwanda made the most. Table 3.2 suggests that proficiency in English is extremely weak, while that in Kinyarwanda is by far the strongest.

The interpretation for the scores was carried out in terms of three scoring levels:

- 0-49% Poor readers: Candidates in this range are judged as unlikely to be able to read, even at minimal comprehension level, the texts in the course books intended for their Year.

Table 3.2 Results in percentages for Primary 4 tests in English, French and Kinyarwanda

	English	*French*	*Kinyarwanda*
Mean	18.62	25.90	74.43
Minimum score	0.00	3.33	13.33
Maximum score	53.33	63.33	100.00

Table 3.3 Categorisation of Year 4 Students by test results in English, French and Kinyarwanda

	Poor readers (below 49%)	*Dependent readers (50–65%)*	*Independent readers (66–100%)*	*Total*
English	259 (99.23%)	2 (0.77%)	0 (0%)	261 (100%)
French	252 (96.55%)	9 (3.45%)	0 (0%)	261 (100%)
Kinyarwanda	32 (12.26%)	41 (15.71%)	188 (72.03%)	261 (100%)

- 50-65% Dependent readers: Candidates in this range are judged as unlikely to be able to read independently, at adequate comprehension levels, the texts in the course books intended for their Year.
- 66-100% Independent readers: Candidates in this range are judged as likely to be able to read independently, and with adequate comprehension, the texts in the course books intended for their Year.

The numbers and percentages of student scores in the three levels can be seen in Table 3.3.

Clearly many students are independent readers in Kinyarwanda, while in French and English there are none at this level. The effect of the recent change to Kinyarwanda as MOI for the first three years of primary school is likely to consolidate literacy skills in the language, but the early switch to English suggests that this is a transitional policy and not a sincere attempt to enhance bilingualism, and that the main thrust of schooling is to inculcate English language skills. In all but élite urban schools, it is likely to fail in this aim (as it has in Malawi).

Research Findings and Political Perspectives

Previous findings and recommendations

The conclusions that may be readily drawn from the above findings for all three countries are that proficiency in English is extremely weak among primary students in Malawi, Zambia and Rwanda. There is no doubt that the majority of students are not able to adequately read their textbooks for either English or other curriculum subjects. Such findings support other research done in these and other African countries. The SACMEQ studies,[4] for example, concluded that 74.2% of Zambian students and 78.4% of Malawian pupils at Year 6 did not reach a minimum 'level of mastery' in reading English (see Nkamba & Kanyika, 1998; Milner *et al.*, 2001, respectively).

Similar low levels of reading have been documented by SACMEQ for other countries in southern Africa. It is also apparent that the 'straight for English' policy of Zambia has not given their students any significant advantage in English over the Malawian students who simply studied English as a subject for their first four years. Further, it is highly unlikely that the majority of students in Rwanda will cope academically with English, especially in view of the fact that very few teachers at primary level are proficient in the language.

Such gloomy findings have been a consistent result of research into language proficiency in African countries, and are no doubt one of the reasons why a succession of declarations have been made over the last century, advocating a more central role for African languages in African education. These include:

- 1909: United Missionary Conference, Kenya
- 1922: The Phelps-Stokes Commission of West Africa
- 1924: The Phelps-Stokes Commission of East Africa
- 1953: UNESCO Report on the Use of the Vernacular Languages in Education
- 1976: Lagos Conference of Education Ministers of African Member States
- 1982: Harare Declaration of Ministers of Education of African Member States
- 1986: OAU's Language Plan of Action for Africa
- 1994: Pan African Colloquium on Educational Innovation in Post Colonial Africa
- 1997: Intergovernmental Conference on African Language Policies in Africa
- 2010: African Conference on Integration of African Languages and Cultures into Education, Burkina Faso

Declarations from such bodies have been almost entirely ignored by African governments. It would appear that these governments are unaware of the fact that learning a language to a level of proficiency that renders one academically proficient takes some five to seven years, even in situations which are much better resourced than those pertaining in African government schools. Crossover of academic skills from first to second language is only possible if the skills have already been adequately acquired in the first language.[5] Immersion education in Canada is sometimes cited by Africans who wish to advance the cause of English as MOI from the early years. But Canadian and African contexts are entirely different in terms of available material, teacher expertise, and parental support, added to which students who struggle with immersion schooling in Canada may be (and are) withdrawn and transferred to first language education.

Given the consistency and clarity of the research on this matter, and the strong probability that no improvement can be effected for several decades, the obvious question is why do African governments persist with these fruitless educational language policies? An immediate answer is that two prime motivations for African governments' language policies hitherto have been unification and development,[6] both of which will be discussed below.

English and unification

In the years immediately following independence, unification of the country was a prime concern for countries that usually encompassed several ethnolinguistic groups, many of whom had aspirations for separation (e.g. the Biafrans in Nigeria, and the Lozi in Zambia, neither of whom were successful; the southern Sudanese in Sudan, however, after 30 years of civil war, voted in January 2011 for separation, with implementation due in the latter half of the year).

If we take the case of Zambia, no group has an absolute majority in population terms, and maintaining unity was a prime concern for Kenneth Kaunda (president at independence in 1964), whose political slogan was 'One Zambia, one nation'. That English was to serve an important role in unification was made quite clear by John Mwanakatwe, Minister of Education at the time: 'Even the most ardent nationalists of our time have accepted the inevitable fact that English – ironically a foreign language and also the language of our former colonial master – has definitely a unifying role in Zambia' (Mwanakatwe, 1968). The Ministry also made clear that the primary school was intended to be the prime agent in bringing about such linguistic unity: 'for the sake of communication between Zambians whose mother tongues differ and in order to promote the unity of the nation, it is necessary for all Zambian children to learn the national language as early as possible, and to use it confidently' (MOE [Zambia], 1976: paragraph 47). The 'national language' referred to here is, in fact, English.

In Malawi, however, English was not regarded as the sole linguistic means of unification. From 1969, it was the indigenous Chichewa that was imposed by President Banda as the medium of instruction in the first four years of primary education. This was 'in the interests of national unity' (Kayambazinthu, 1999: 49). However, it is clear that English was intended to play a communicatively unifying role at the 'upper levels' of state institutions. Thus English was the MOI in Kamuzu Academy, the elite secondary school set up and funded by Banda, and English was also made compulsory in parliament, with all MPs 'required to pass a stringent test' in it (Schmied, 1991: 24). Although this test was abolished in 1995, the parliament still operates in English.

In Rwanda, given that almost the entire population is fluent in Kinyarwanda, there is no need for an exoglossic language to serve the purpose of unification. The stress on English is rather for reasons of political alignment: the USA and UK both support the current régime, which has since 1994 distanced itself from France and the French language. In 2009 Rwanda joined the (ex-British) Commonwealth, although it was never a British colony. The United Kingdom is also Rwanda's largest bilateral donor, having given around £380m between 1994 and 2010 (Macintyre, 2010).

However, one of the consequences in each of these three countries of using English as the MOI (and as an official language) is that, far from uniting the nation, it has created two nations: the rich who can afford to send their children to private schools where reasonable standards of proficiency in English are available, and the poor majority have no such possibility. Thus English is ultimately counterproductive in terms of unification. As Kayambazinthu (1999: 52) says, with respect to Malawi:

> The dominance and limited access to English [...] has created an élite group, [whose] proficiency in English is near-native [...] these élites maintain and regularly use their knowledge of English in their professional environments, where they typically occupy the middle ranks of the political, administrative and academic institutions.

English and development

Development would appear to be the justification provided by Yisa Claver, the then Director of Policy Planning at the Ministry of Education in Rwanda, for the 2009 decision to use only English as MOI from Year 1. In a press conference in early 2009 he said:

> English is now a world language, especially in trade and commerce. Rwanda is trying to attract foreign investors – most of these people are speaking English. [...] It's choosing English as a medium of instruction so we Rwandans of today, and tomorrow, will benefit. If Spanish or any

> other language could get us to that, no problem. If Kinyarwanda could get us to that, that would be marvellous. It is not English for its own sake. (Claver quoted in McGreal, 2009)

However, other countries in Africa that have long ago gone down the route of English as MOI provide little inspiration for Rwanda. The Rwandan government's claims that their language policy will lead to greater prosperity and improved human development for all Rwandans are, as Samuelson and Freedman (2010: 192) point out, 'misleading in several ways'. There is no reason to believe that the dominance of English in education will lead to any more favourable conclusions in Rwanda than it has in Malawi and Zambia. Indeed, English-medium education in Africa generally has often lacked impact on human development especially as concerns women. In Malawi, for example, an unexpected finding from Fotso (2006: 10) is that the infant mortality rate of children up to the age of one year, per 1000 live births, for children born to women in Malawi with no education is 98.6 compared to 104.0 for children born to women with eight years of primary education. Fotso's speculative explanation for this higher rate is 'that the mortality pattern whereby children from mothers with some primary education stand greater risk to die than those whose mother have no formal education, reflect, at least in part, the differentials in under-reporting of deaths by education (sic)'. A more plausible explanation, however, is that the education that the women received was not effective, simply because they were not proficient in the language of instruction, English, and that the eight years of schooling had actually been counterproductive. Moreover, research in the previous decade had also revealed that maternal education in Africa lacked benefit: Hobcraft (1993), in a review of major studies, noted that the length of mothers' education has far less effect on child survival for African countries than for countries elsewhere. Hobcraft's method was to calculate the odds ratio for the 'maternal education contrast' (an odds ratio of 0.5 means that the child of a mother with seven or more years of education has a 50% probability of dying before age two, compared with the child of a mother with no education). In all nine Latin American countries reviewed, the ratio was below 0.5. On the other hand, ratios in Mali, Zimbabwe, Botswana and Uganda were 0.75-0.8, and in Ghana, 0.95. In short, seven years of mothers' education in Ghana made little difference to a child's survival chances.

Although the last decade has seen improvements, UNICEF's latest statistics, extracted in Table 3.4, suggest that in terms of both human and economic development, Malawi, Zambia and Rwanda are struggling. Malaysia, which had roughly the same GDP as Zambia in the 1960s, is included for comparison:

Table 3.4 Indicators of development for Malawi, Zambia, Rwanda and Malaysia (UNICEF, 2010)

	Malawi	*Zambia*	*Rwanda*	*Malaysia*
Under-5 mortality rate per 1000 live births (2008)	100	148	112	11 (2007)
Population below US$1.25 per day poverty line (%) (1992–2007)	74	64	77	2
GDP per capita average annual growth rate (%) (1990–2008)	0.6	0	1.5	2.4
Life expectancy at birth in years (2008)	53	45	50	74
HIV/AIDS: 15–49-year-old population (%) (2007)	11.9	15.2	2.8	0.5

Hobcraft could find no convincing explanation for the weak effect of education in Africa. Similarly, the work of Cochrane and Farid (1989) also concluded that in Sub-Saharan Africa there are smaller differentials in birth rates between the rural uneducated and the urban educated than in other regions (particularly Latin America). I would suggest again that the explanation lies partly in the fact that the education that the women in Africa received was not effective, and that the use of English as MOI was a major contributory reason. Likewise Malaysia, which in the 1960s had roughly the same GDP as Zambia, has, as Table 3.4 indicates, become an Asian economic 'tiger' (Edwards, 1999: 49-50). It is surely not irrelevant that Malaysia has educated the bulk of its primary school students through the first language of the majority, Bahasa Malaysia.

In sum, the evidence of the past decades is that the use of English as MOI in Sub-Saharan African countries has not contributed to either unification or development, for the simple reason that most students have acquired very little competence in it. Their education has thus not been effective, and ineffective education cannot contribute to development. African politicians, however, do not seem to have fully appreciated the problems that students face in learning through a language in which, through no fault of their own, they have little proficiency.

Social Capital

It is of course obvious that effective education does not rely solely on the choice of MOI. Likewise an effective education does not guarantee national development. While effective education can contribute to the human capital of a country, human capital is not the only form of capital necessary for national development: economic capital is clearly important, and here international terms of trade combined with debt repayments have often put African countries at a disadvantage. Recent massive Chinese investments across Africa, together with ongoing and significant Chinese immigration (see Addis Fortune, 2010; Foster *et al.*, 2008) are too recent for long-term effects on economic capital to be clear. In the last section of the chapter, however, I will focus on a third capital, namely social capital, which has been identified as making a crucial contribution to the well-being of a country.

Social capital is defined as a critical mass of trust and a sense of obligation between members of a state, with governments committed to the welfare of their fellow citizens. Individuals 'buy in' to a shared morality, which both draws on and stimulates a sense of national solidarity. Since its use by Hanifan (1920), the term has been developed in education (e.g. Coleman, 1988) and above all in sociology, especially by Putnam (e.g. Putnam, 1995). In recent decades it has been widely appropriated by development specialists, many of whom (e.g. Edwards, 1999) claim that it is differing degrees of social capital that distinguishes the East Asian experience from that of most of Africa. Large-scale financial corruption, together with manipulation of democratic processes (Zimbabwe, Kenya), chronic low-level insurgency (Burundi, Nigeria, Somalia) and civil war (Rwanda, Democratic Republic of Congo, Liberia) are all indicators of a lack of social capital.

The lack of social capital in Africa is highlighted by Bayart (especially Bayart, 1993), who claims that in Africa the rulers (the 'big men') will amass wealth through the abuse and manipulation of power; this wealth is then retained, although a certain amount may be redistributed among family members and allies. Bayart terms this system 'the politics of the belly'. Such behaviour may be widely identified in Africa: Kamuzu Banda in Malawi; Idi Amin in Uganda; Bokassa in the Central African Republic; Mobutu in Zaire – now the Democratic Republic of Congo – are among the very many examples. Many rulers too have come to power claiming they would eliminate corruption, only to perpetuate the system. Thus Finlayson (2005: 48) notes that although Bakili Muluzi, who took over democratically as president of Malawi from Kamuzu Banda, claimed to be a reformer, in due course 'Bad habits cultivated under the dictatorship of Kamuzu Banda started to reassert themselves ... [T]he slide into autocracy and corruption became inexorable'.

Bayart, however, is at pains to point out that such behaviour is not to be regarded as simple 'corruption'. He stresses that 'Anyone seeking to dismiss this form of politics as no more than a symptom of corruption is making a grave mistake. These representations can be institutional' (Bayart, 1993: xvii). He claims that such institutionalization and normalization of 'the politics of the belly' is apparent in the Nigerian draft constitution in 1976, the authors of which defined political power as 'the opportunity to acquire riches and prestige, to be in a position to hand out benefits in the form of jobs, contracts, gifts of money etc. to relations and political allies' (Bayart, 1993: xvii). The Nigerian authors' readiness to commit this wording to print in the national constitution suggests that they regarded the definition as unexceptional, and the associated behaviour as the norm. Such an attitude is unlikely to take to heart the failure of the public education system, or the malign effect of this failure upon the well-being of the mass of the population. Djité (2008: 165) relates this to 'élite closure' (Myers-Scotton, 1990) and furthermore sees an element of conspiracy at play, claiming that African élites 'manipulate language policy to maintain their positions of power in society, thereby denying the majority access to knowledge and know-how, and full and active participation in the exercise of power, hence depriving them of the benefits generated by all'.

Conclusion

A paradox in education is that poor African countries operate relatively expensive and complex language policies involving home-school language switches for most of their school population, whereas rich countries typically operate relatively cheap and simple language policies, which do not involve home-school language switches for the majority. The classroom and test data that have been described above indicate beyond doubt that the policy of using exoglossic languages as media of instruction penalizes African students by turning the primary school classroom experience, which should be one of illumination and growth, into one of mystification. Furthermore, the political rhetoric of unification and development buttresses this policy, while the lack of social capital means that the powerful political and commercial classes disregard its malign effects, or even connive at them.

The conclusion that one draws from this depends on whether one has a 'glass half full' or 'glass half empty' outlook on Africa. The pessimistic conclusion is that the continued use of English as MOI means that government schools are destined to remain sites of mystification, and largely ineffective. At best these schools play a screening role, whereby they identify the most apt students, whom the powerful will then recruit, and who will, in personal terms, probably benefit considerably. (The number of such students is minute, but they join the phalanx of privately educated students who will form the bulk of the élite.) The use of English as a medium of instruction offers a convenient screening method, and one which, ironically, is generally approved of by its victims and their parents, irrespective of research conclusions that, for the vast majority of African students, English is a barrier rather than a bridge to their human development (see, for example, Djité, 2008; Heugh, 1999; Webb, 1999; Williams, 2006).

The optimistic interpretation is that the weaknesses in African schooling, due to the dominance of English, are the unintended consequences of an overambitious, but essentially benevolent, policy, originally intended to unify and modernize the country in question. Such a view holds that these weaknesses can be remedied over time; this optimistic interpretation generates a great deal of in-service educational provision, and internationally funded projects to ameliorate education by providing materials, teacher training courses and the like.

Whichever perspective is taken, I would suggest the way forward lies in an incremental approach towards more effective education in Africa, involving change on two fronts: first a greater role for African languages, especially in literacy skills at primary level; second, more efficacious teaching of English as a subject at primary level and beyond. While there have been a number of successful initiatives involving the use of African languages for initial literacy and as MOI – for example, the Yoruba project in Nigeria (Afolayan, 1999) and the Molteno project in Zambia (Tambulukani *et al.*, 1999) – they do not hitherto seem to have taken root and flourished nationally. Lack of will on the part of governments and the psychic disbelief of many Africans in the suitability of African languages as MOIs are major reasons. There is no current evidence that Sub-Saharan African governments are about to change their negative attitudes towards their own languages, while their citizens largely connive at language education policies that perpetuate schooling as a process of mystification for the majority of students. It may be some time before a critical mass of better-educated African populations is capable of playing a stronger role in bringing about its own human and economic development.

Notes

(1) However, Rosling holds that although stable government contributes to human development, democracy does not do so, although it may be valuable in its own right.

(2) The particle *Chi-* denotes 'language of': thus Chichewa is the language of the Chewa people. It is not employed consistently in English; many Zambians drop it, while Malawians tend to retain it. Elsewhere in the Bantu language continuum it may occur as *Si-*, *Ici-* or *Ki-* with or without capitalization in writing.

(3) Identical Chichewa/Nyanja tests were used in both countries, with the exception of a few orthographic differences.

(4) Large-scale pieces of research carried out on behalf of UNESCO by the Southern Africa Consortium for Monitoring Educational Quality.
(5) For example, British students are not 'taught to read' again when they begin to study French although the pronunciation of some letters, typically 'u' and 'r' may be taught.
(6) This term has largely supplanted the previously common 'modernization'.

References

Addis Fortune (2010) *Africa: China's complex view of Africa. All Africa.com*, accessed 8 June 2010. http://allafrica.com/stories/201006100397.html

Afolayan, A. (1999) The alienated role of the mother tongue in literacy education for sustainable national development: The western Nigerian Yoruba example. In S. Manaka (ed.) *Proceedings of the 1st Pan-African Conference on Reading for All* (pp. 70-88). Pretoria: International Reading Association, READ, & UNESCO/DANIDA.

Anderson, C.A. (1966) Literacy and schooling on the development threshold: Some historical cases. In C.A. Anderson and M.J. Bowman (eds) *Education and Economic Development* (pp. 347-362). London: Frank Cass.

Arndt, H.W. (1987) *Economic Development: The History of an Idea*. Chicago, IL: University of Chicago Press.

Azariadis, C. and Drazen, A. (1990) Threshold externalities in economic development. *The Quarterly Journal of Economics* 105 (2) 501-526.

Bayart, J-F. (1993) *The State in Africa: The Politics of the Belly*. London: Longman.

Chick, J.K. (1996) Safe-talk: Collusion in apartheid education. In C. Candlin and N. Mercer (eds) *English Language Teaching in Its Social Context* (pp. 227-242). London: Open University & Routledge.

Cochrane, S.H. and Farid, S.M. (1989) *Fertility in Sub-Saharan Africa: Analysis and Explanation*. World Bank Discussion Paper 43. Washington, DC: World Bank.

Coleman, J.C. (1988) Social capital in the creation of human capital. *American Journal of Sociology* 94, S95-S120.

Crystal, D. (1987) *The Cambridge Encyclopedia of Language.* Cambridge: Cambridge University Press.

Djité, P.G. (2008) *The Sociolinguistics of Development in Africa.* Clevedon: Multilingual Matters.

Edwards, M. (1999) *Future Positive: International Cooperation in the Twenty First Century.* London: Earthscan/Kogan Page.

Finlayson, G. (2005) Malawi: A suitable case for treatment? *NORRAG News* 36, 48-49.

Foster, V., Butterfield, W., Chen, C. and Pushak, N. (2008) *Building Bridges: China's Growing Role as Infrastructure Financier for Sub-Saharan Africa*. Washington, DC: World Bank.

Fotso, J.-C. (2006) *Malawi's Future Human Capital: Is the Country on Track to Meeting the MDGs in Education?* Laxenburg: International Institute for Applied Systems Analysis.

Hanifan, L.J. (1920) *The Community Center*. Boston, MA: Silver Burdett.

Heugh, K. (1999) Languages, development and reconstructing education in South Africa. *International Journal of Educational Development* 19, 301-313.

Hicks, N.L. (1980) Is there a trade-off between growth and basic needs? *Finance and Development* 17 (2), 17-20.

Hobcraft, J. (1993) Women's education, child welfare and child survival: A review of the evidence. *Health Transition Review* 3 (2), 159-175.

Hornberger, N.H. and Chick, K. (1998) *Co-constructing Safetime in Peruvian and South African Classrooms.* Handout for paper given at Sociolinguistic Symposium 12, Roehampton, 12 March, 1998.

Kayambazinthu, E. (1999) The language planning situation in Malawi. In B. Kaplan and R.B. Baldauf (eds) *Language Planning in Malawi, Mozambique and the Philippines* (pp. 15-85). Clevedon: Multilingual Matters.

Knight, J.B. and Sabot, R.H. (1990) *Education, Productivity and Inequality: The East African Natural Experiment*. Oxford: Oxford University Press for the World Bank.

LeClerc, J. (2008) *Rwanda. L'aménagement linguistique dans le monde.* http://www.tlfq.ca/axl/afrique/rwanda.htm

Lewis, M.P. (ed.) (2009) *Ethnologue: Languages of the World* (16th edn). Dallas, TX: SIL International. http://www.ethnologue.com

Lockheed, M.E., Jamison, D.T. and Lau, L.J. (1980) Farmer education and farm efficiency: A survey. *Economic Development and Cultural Change* 29, 37-76.

Macintyre, J. (2010) Charity must not stop at home. *New Statesman,* accessed 16 July 2010. http://www.newstatesman.com/international-politics/2010/08/mitchell-development-aid

McGreal, C. (2009) Why Rwanda said adieu to French. *Guardian Weekly*, accessed 16 January 2009. www.guardian.co.uk/education/2009/jan/16/rwanda-english-genocide

Milner, G., Chimombo, J., Banda, T. and Mchikoma, C. (2001) *The Quality of Primary Education in Malawi.* Interim Report for the Southern African Consortium for Measuring Educational Quality. Paris: International Institute for Educational Planning, UNESCO.

Ministry of Education (MOE Zambia) (1976) *Education for Development: Draft Statement on Educational Reform*. Lusaka: MOE.

Moock, P.R. and Addou, H. (1994) Agricultural productivity and education. In *International Encyclopedia of Education* (Vol. I, pp. 244-254). Oxford: Pergamon Press.

Munyankesha, P. (2004) Les defis du plurilinguisme officiel au Rwanda. Analyse sociolinguistique. Unpublished PhD thesis, The University of Western Ontario.

Mwanakatwe, J.M. (1968) *The Growth of Education in Zambia since Independence*. Lusaka: Oxford University Press.

Myers-Scotton, C. (1990) Elite closure as boundary maintenance: The evidence from Africa. In B. Weinstein (ed.) *Language Policy and Political Development* (pp. 25-41). Norwood, NJ: Ablex.

Nkamba, M. and Kanyika, J. (1998) The quality of education: some policy suggestions based on a survey of schools: Zambia. (Southern Africa Consortium for Monitoring Educational Quality (SACMEQ) Policy Research: Report No. 5) Paris: International Institute for Educational Planning, UNESCO.

Putnam, R.D. (1995) Bowling alone: America's declining social capital. *Journal of Democracy* 6 (1), 65-78.

Rogers, A. (1990) Background to the seminar. In B.V. Street (ed.) *Literacy in Development* (pp. 2-4). London: Education for Development and the Commonwealth Institute.

Rosendal, T. (2009) Linguistic markets in Rwanda: Language use in advertisements and on signs. *Journal of Multilingual and Multicultural Development* 30 (1), 19-39.

Rosling, H. (2009) *Human Rights and Democracy Statistics.* Presentation for Oslo Freedom Forum 2009. http://www.youtube.com/watch?v=QNX31t7Cees

Samuelson, B.L. and Freedman S.W. (2010) Language policy, multilingual education, and power in Rwanda. *Language Policy* 9, 191-215.

Schmied, J. (1991) *English in Africa*. London: Longman.

Tambulukani, G., Sampa, F., Musuku, R. and Linehan, S. (1999) Reading in Zambia: A quiet revolution through the primary reading programme. In S. Manaka (ed.), *Proceedings of the 1st Pan-African Conference on Reading for All* (pp. 170-175). Pretoria: International Reading Association, READ, & UNESCO/DANIDA.

Thomas, A. and Potter, D. (1992) Development, capitalism, and the nation state. In T. Allen and A. Thomas (eds) *Poverty and Development in the 1990s* (pp. 116-141). Oxford: Oxford University Press/The Open University.

United Nations Childrens' Fund (UNICEF) (2010) *Info by Country: Eastern and Southern Africa*. New York: UNICEF. http://www.unicef.org/infobycountry/esaro.html

United Nations Development Programme (UNDP) (2010) *The Real Wealth of Nations: Pathways to Human Development*. Human Development Report 2010, 20th Anniversary Edition. Basingstoke: Palgrave Macmillan for UNDP. http://hdr.undp.org/en

Webb, V. (1999) Multilingualism in democratic South Africa: The overestimation of language policy. *International Journal of Educational Development* 19, 351-366.

Wheeler, D. (1980) *Human Resources Development and Economic Growth in Developing Countries: A Simultaneous Model*. World Bank Staff Working Paper 407. Washington, DC: World Bank.

Williams, E. (1998) *Investigating Bilingual Literacy: Evidence from Malawi and Zambia*. Education Research Paper No. 24. DFID. London. http://www.dfid.gov.uk/r4d/SearchResearchDatabase.asp

Williams, E. (2006) Bridges and Barriers: Language in African Education and Development. Manchester: St Jerome.

4 Grassroots Attitudes to English as a Language for International Development in Bangladesh

Elizabeth J. Erling, M. Obaidul Hamid and Philip Seargeant

Introduction

This chapter examines grassroots attitudes towards the role played by English-language education in international development, looking specifically at the context of Bangladesh. While there have been significant improvements in the general socio-economic situation of Bangladesh through various development projects over the last 30 years, the country still ranks 146th out of 187 in the UNDP Human Development Index, and 50% of the population live below the international poverty line, measured at US$1.25 per day (UNDP, 2011; UNICEF, 2010). The country is described as having high levels of unemployment, rapid population growth, frequently occurring natural disasters and high illiteracy rates (the adult literacy rate is reported to be 41.6%) (Ahmed & Nath, 2003: 4). As a result, several development projects have been and continue to be carried out in the country, focusing upon economic and social development, health, education, human rights and legal services (cf. BRAC Annual Report, 2008). One such project is English in Action (EIA), a nine-year, £50 million English-language development programme, funded by the UK's Department of International Development (DFID), which specifically targets English-language teaching skills as a means of development. This was a follow-up to the earlier DFID-funded 'English Language Teaching Improvement Project' (ELTIP), which ran between 1997 and 2008. In a context such as Bangladesh, where there continue to be cases of acute poverty, a question faced by such projects is *whether* and *how* English-language teaching is likely to benefit those in need of international aid, and what influence it has on the lives of those in most need of support. Much recent research (discussed below) has been exploring the relationship between English-language learning and economic gain, and the extent to which this relationship can underpin development initiatives. Another important aspect to the equation, however, is what those from poor socio-economic backgrounds *think* about English-language learning, and whether they feel that it can benefit them and their prospects. In this respect, local language ideologies can have an influential effect on the manner in which development initiatives are viewed and adopted by a local community, and as such they function as an important part of the overall success of such projects.

The aim of the chapter is to provide a survey and description of the language attitudes held by people who are the subject of international development initiatives of this sort, which specifically promote English-language education. Drawing on both quantitative and qualitative data collected in Bangladesh, the chapter explores grassroots discourses in order to better understand issues around the need and desire for English as a language for international development as these exist within local communities. It also looks at whether, and how, these local attitudes echo the discourse of English constructed in official policies (i.e. those produced by government organizations, funding bodies and academic institutions), and how they can be used to inform debates about the content of international development projects.

'English in action' and economic development

The analysis in the chapter draws on two data sets: one compiled as part of the research for the English in Action (EIA) project; the other from a questionnaire survey involving local community members. As one of the sources for the data, and as a major development initiative of the sort our later discussion focuses upon, it is worth firstly providing some background information about the English in Action project, its structure and aims, and how it responds to language-educational concerns in the region. EIA is expected to run from 2008 to 2017. The goal of the project is to contribute to the economic growth of Bangladesh by providing language education, which will help 'increase significantly the number of people able to communicate in English, to levels that enable them to participate fully in economic and social activity and opportunities' (EIA, 2010). One of the ways in which EIA is implementing change is by supporting the teaching of English in primary and secondary schools across the country. This is in response to a situation in which, despite the fact that English is a compulsory subject in the curriculum from Class 1 in primary school, and despite a number of recent educational reforms intended to improve the provision of English-language teaching, a low quality of English-language education persists, as does a shortage of skilled English teachers (Hamid, 2010). High scores in English are required for both school-leaving certificates and university entry; and yet English is the most commonly failed examination subject at the secondary certificate level. Likewise, for a career as either a civil servant or an academic, English is required, and low levels of competence are thus thought to be keeping people from effective participation in international opportunities. For instance, Shahidullah (2002, n. p.) quotes a Ministry of Public Administration order, which reads:

> It is noted that due to weaknesses in English many candidates selected for foreign training/higher studies are not acceptable to funding countries or agencies. Such a situation is embarrassing both for the selected candidates and for the government.

Besides dealing with English in the school system, another focus of EIA is to provide better access to English learning materials for adult learners. In order to do this, BBC Janala, a supported programme of EIA, has created a media platform that harnesses technology to provide affordable education to the Bangla-speaking community. The programme allows people to learn English easily and affordably through their mobile phones, the internet, television programming and print media. In addition, this aspect of EIA aims to alter people's perceptions of language learning in Bangladesh in order to reduce barriers to learning English and to address the lack of educational opportunities faced by the majority of people in the country (EIA, 2009: 3-7).

EIA project documents state that in Bangladesh there is a 'national bilingual deficit', which is 'a constraint to economic development', and that EIA has been designed specifically to address this (EIA, 2008). In a statement supporting the project, the former UK Minister for International Development, Douglas Alexander, wrote that the programme intends to 'make a valuable and lasting contribution to economic and social development' in the country (Alexander, 2008).

As can be seen from these quotes, the focus of the EIA project is on *economic development*, which generally means:

> raising the productive capacities of societies, in terms of their technologies (more efficient tools and machines), technical cultures (knowledge of nature, research and capacity to develop improved technologies), and

> the physical, technical and organization capacities and skills of those engaged in production. (Bernstein, 1983: 59)

The project seeks to promote competence in English as a central factor in this process. As such, English (along with ICT skills) is deemed to be part of a 'basic education' or 'functional literacy', as it is needed for successful engagement in higher education and the global economy (cf. Graddol, 2010). It is thus framed as a skill that, like literacy, can expand the real freedoms that people enjoy (Sen, 2001).

Until recently, however, little has been known about whether the acquisition of English operates as a causal factor for economic development. Because of the increasing importance being placed on English-language teaching in development, a number of scholars have started to investigate this issue empirically (e.g. Arcand & Grin, this volume; Azam *et al.*, 2010; Chakraborty & Kapur, 2008; Coleman, 2010; Grin, 2001; Levinsohn, 2007), and evidence is beginning to emerge that supports the existence of some form of causal relationship between English-language ability and economic reward. However, in all the cases researched so far, it has been found that the local social environment works to complexify any simplistic relationship between the two, while other environmental factors also play a significant part in the equation. For example, while evidence from West Bengal shows a positive causal correlation between English learning and economic gain, as was found by Chakraborty and Kapur (2008), a similar conclusion cannot be inferred for other localities where different economic and linguistic realities exist (variations such as those in education policies, in language ecologies, in pockets of industry that attract English speakers) (cf. Azam *et al.*, 2010).

Another issue of importance for the success of any development project is local attitudes, and the role they play in people's relationship to English. Peoples' attitudes to English can be influenced by the effects of globalization processes (cf. Kubota & McKay, 2009), and can reflect the global discourses of English and development. They are also often of relevance for issues of motivation for learning the language, and can explain something about expectations for development projects. A deeper understanding of attitudes can thus assist with the managing of those expectations. Again, until recently little has been known in Bangladesh about popular beliefs about English and the associations that may exist in people's minds with regard to English and development. There is little recorded evidence about the attitudes and desires of the people at whom development initiatives are targeted, and the extent to which they themselves consider English learning an important means to achieving their own development (although see Erling *et al.*, 2012). It is this particular aspect of the equation which this chapter therefore focuses upon.

Methods and Methodology

In order to provide empirical evidence about the local beliefs and ideologies that Bangladeshis have towards English and language education, the chapter draws on insights from two different studies conducted in Bangladesh: one quantitative in nature and the other qualitative. The quantitative data set was compiled in 2009 as part of the media baseline research conducted as part of the English in Action project, while the qualitative research stems from a small-scale questionnaire conducted independently from this in 2010, involving local community members. While the data were collected in slightly different contexts and for different initial purposes, they complement each other in a number of productive ways and together provide valuable insights into how people perceive the role of English both in their own personal development and in the development of Bangladesh. The quantitative data provide a wide breadth of information, and allow for the comparison of attitudes from participants from different socio-economic backgrounds and those living in both urban and rural areas. The qualitative study, meanwhile, gives more nuanced data on perceptions of English and the (potential) role that the language plays in development issues. Although only sampling a small number of people, these qualitative results provide rich insights into people's personal experiences of learning English and offer detailed stories about their beliefs about the role that the language can play in achieving their success. Taken together, therefore, these two data sets give a rounded picture of local attitudes towards English and the associations often made with respect to the language. The details of the design and circumstance of collection of this data are outlined in the two sections below.

Quantitative study

The quantitative data analyzed in this study were initially collected by BBC Janala, which aims to provide affordable English-language education to the Bangla-speaking community through mobile phones, the internet and television. As part of the baseline studies for this initiative, a national survey of 8300 Bangladeshis was conducted orally, in Bangla, in January 2009 (EIA, 2009). The original purpose of the study was to capture data from a sample of targeted groups as part of the BBC's media and audience research; however, the data also provide interesting sociolinguistic insights.

The sampling followed a randomized process of selection, and was distributed across four socio-geographic levels in Bangladesh: cities, large towns, small towns and villages (cf. EIA, 2009: 15). The sample is made up of two groups: The first group consists of 6000 15-45-year-olds (50/50 male to female) who were classified to be in the top four socio-economic categories of the study (SEC A-D); this group represents the BBC's main target audience. The second group consists of 1000 15-45-year-olds (60/40 male to female) who were classified to be in the lowest socio-economic category (SEC E). Socio-economic classification (SEC) was measured by using a well-recognized system of calculating data on head of household occupation and education level. 'High' socio-economic classes refers to SEC A&B, 'mid' socio-economic class refers to SEC C and 'low' socio-economic classes refers to SEC D&E. For the BBC's study, SEC E participants were not considered to be likely users of media and were therefore not included in their main analysis, but for the purposes of this study, their data provide useful insights into language attitudes of the very poor.

Regarding the characteristics of the sample, 46% of the first group and all of the second had a personal income below 3000 Bangladeshi taka per month (less than £23/$36), which is below the international poverty line at 2012 rates of exchange, and roughly comparable to the number of people living at this level nationally. Around 35% of the first group were working, while 22% were students. Nine percent of this group had achieved a 5th grade education or less (around age 10), while 22% had been educated up to secondary level and 22% up to higher secondary. Around 13% held a tertiary qualification.

The survey collected a variety of different data by means of an orally conducted questionnaire in order to assist with building a contextualised picture of the language education situation in Bangladesh. The most relevant aspects of this questionnaire for the issues analyzed in this chapter were:

- Perceptions of English and learning English
- Motivations for learning and using English
- Work and English

The data were analyzed in terms of the participants' perceptions of the need for English learning, the use of English at work and for career development, and the role of English in personal and national development. These themes also provided a basis for the analysis of the qualitative data. For the quantitative analysis we present the results from both groups (SEC A-D and SEC E), and also compare any differences between the attitudes of those who come from a more privileged socio-economic background and the least advantaged of the participants. All differences of opinion between the two groups were calculated using one-way ANOVA tests at a 99% confidence interval. In many cases, little variation could be detected, but we have highlighted differences when they arise. It should be noted too that since the data from the quantitative study were originally collected for the purpose of media research, certain assumptions may have been made in framing the questions. It is for that reason that we interpret the results with caution and draw any distinctions between the two groups carefully.

Qualitative study

The qualitative data were collected from a sample of individuals who were born not only in one of the poorest regions of Bangladesh, but also into adverse or particularly deprived family and social circumstances. Although we do not have details about their families' socio-economic status growing up, we can assume from their own descriptions of their background that they are comparable to SEC D or E. Despite the socio-economic and cultural barriers they faced, all were able to establish themselves professionally as government bureaucrats and were working in high-level jobs in different parts of the country (detailed information on these participants is included below). The data were elicited through an open-ended written questionnaire administered in February–April 2010 to 16 individuals (13 males and 3 females[1]), all of whom were born in the same district. In selecting the participants, previous social disadvantage was considered as a criterion with the expectation that this would allow us to understand their perceptions of the role of English in their social transformation. The majority of these people were personally known to one of the chapter authors (Hamid), who was also born in the same region, and they were all widely known throughout the rural community that they came from because of the status of their jobs (known as 'class one'). Hamid spoke to each of the 16 participants (the unknown minority being recommended and introduced by those who were known) on the phone and requested their participation in the study. Of the 16, 10 (all males) returned the questionnaires. Despite initial assurances of participation, the three female officials could not return their questionnaires, for whatever reasons, by the deadline.

The questionnaire was offered in both Bangla and English, and respondents were invited to reply in either language, according to their preference. The majority of the participants responded in English, and their replies have been left unaltered, and thus reflect the local dialects and idiolects of English of the participants. Responses in Bangla were translated by Hamid. In order to generate as rich data as possible, participants were encouraged to make their responses to the questions as long as they wished. The result was that most of them provided precise but substantial autobiographical sketches, along with reflections on the role of English in relation to their career goals, and the extent of English use in their everyday professional routines.

As will been seen from the analysis, one salient aspect of the data is the participants' reports on their subjective perceptions of the role of English in their social development and career progression. While perception data clearly cannot indicate any causal relationship between English knowledge and socio-economic development, they do provide an important perspective on the complex relationships between language learning and development, most notably in terms of issues of motivation. Analysis proceeded by means of categorizing the content of the participants' responses into four different themes so that they were comparable to the data from the quantitative study:

- English and career goals
- English and job benefits
- The use of English at work
- Prestige

Findings

In this section, the results from the quantitative study are presented first in order to provide an overall picture of the situation. This is followed by results from the qualitative analysis, which offer more detail on people's attitudes towards English and its role in personal and national development.

Quantitative findings

As was noted above, the evidence from the quantitative study focuses on perceptions about the need for English learning, the use of English at work and for career development, and the role of English in personal and national development. The results from this survey also hint at certain societal beliefs connecting English with economic value, professional success and feelings of respect. The analysis will draw out these different threads, which will then be contrasted with the findings from the qualitative study in the next section.

Desire for English

As can be seen in Table 4.1 below, a large majority of people in the quantitative sample have learnt English at some point in their lives (97%). That a large number (30%) of the respondents in the lower socio-economic category have never learnt English suggests they may not have attended school, or dropped out at an early age, since English has been a part of the government school curriculum from Class 1 since 1991 (when the youngest in the sample

Table 4.1 Learning English (EIA, 2009: 23)

	15-45 yrs SEC A-D	*15-45 yrs SEC E*
n	6000	1000
Have you ever learnt English?	97%	70%
Want to learn English?	79%	54%
Currently learning English?	23%	7%

would have started primary school). Despite the fact that a large proportion of the respondents have learnt English, many of them still want to learn more. The survey indicates that the main reasons that the respondents want to learn English are to get a job or to teach their children. Why they do not consider that the English they have learned so far sufficient to do this is not covered by the survey, but it is perhaps because the English they have learned at school has not provided them with the skills in the language that they want or need (cf. Hamid & Baldauf, 2008 for an account of the Bangladeshi educational system's failure to mediate students' English proficiency).

The number of those in the higher socio-economic categories wanting to learn English is significantly higher than those in the lower socio-economic category (79% compared to 54%) (see Table 4.1).[2] Although the data do not indicate why this should be the case, it may be that those in lower categories see less of a need for knowledge of English. One can only speculate on the reasons for this, but it could stem from there being less of a presence of English in their communities, or it could be that their jobs are less likely to demand English, or there may be other skills that this group sees as more valuable than learning English. While just over half of the respondents in the lowest socio-economic category still have a desire to learn English (54%), only 7% are currently doing so (compared to 23% in the higher socio-economic categories), a difference which is highly significant. Thus, while 29% of those in the higher categories who want to learn the language are currently doing so, only 13% of the lower socio-economic category are (see Table 4.1). This indicates that this group is less likely to (be able to) act on their wishes, which might be a result of financial (or time) constraints.

English and career development

One issue that the data clearly illustrate is that respondents associate English learning with better pay and better employment, as can be seen in Table 4.2. While 87% of the respondents in the higher socio-economic categories believe that learning English will help them earn more money, there is

Table 4.2 English and career development

	15-45 yrs SEC A-D	*15-45 yrs SEC E*
n	6000	1000
Learning English will help me to earn more money	87%	76%
It will enable me to get a good job	54%	31%
It will enable me to get a better job	68%	52%
It will enable me to develop my career	65%	34%

a weaker belief in the relationship between English and career development. Only 54% believe it will enable them to secure 'a good job', 68% believe that it will assist them with getting 'a better job', and 65% that it will enable them to develop their career in some form. The percentages are significantly lower for the respondents in the lower socio-economic grouping, who perceive less benefit for English education with respect to its relation to career development. It is not clear from the questions asked what the differences are between 'better pay', 'better employment' and 'career development', or how these differences were perceived by participants – and these are issues that could be explored in further research – but it is interesting that English-language ability is perceived to bring economic gain, though not necessarily also career development. This appears to suggest that the notion of economic value is more salient in the discourse than associations with job prospects.

The use of English at work

While many respondents felt that learning English would help them get a better job (65%), only a small number suggested that they were currently using English for work (9.4%). This number is significantly higher for the group in the higher socio-economic category (12%) than for the second group (1.2%). But the number is still quite low, and suggests that many people work in jobs where there is no immediate need for English. This calls into question why there is such a strongly expressed general desire to learn the language, and suggests that this stems not from immediate need but from more abstract beliefs about the value of the language, some of which are discussed in the following sections.

English and national development

It is interesting that a very high 92% of respondents believe that a better understanding of English amongst the population in general can accelerate the process of development in Bangladesh. This statistic clearly shows that the majority of the sampled population, across the socio-economic categories, agrees with the assumptions about the value of English upon which EIA is based. Despite the fact that, from questions about uses of English, many respondents seem not to experience an immediate current need for the language, these perceptions are very strong. Furthermore, 91% of respondents agree that 'to succeed, Bangladesh needs to communicate more effectively with other countries'. This perceived need to take part in global dialogue, which presumably is not (yet) felt to be happening on a wide scale, may partially explain the strong desire for English, with its status as the pre-eminent language of international communication in today's world.

English and notions of 'success'

Another possible explanation for the positive attitudes towards English may be found in beliefs about the language's associations with notions of success and respect. Sixty-nine percent of respondents, for example, agree with the statement that 'you cannot be successful without speaking English'. What precisely is meant by 'success' here is not specified in the question, but given the strong links between English and economic gain in the responses discussed above, one can perhaps assume that it is *economic* success that is implied by the respondents. Furthermore, 86% of all respondents agree that learning English will give them a feeling of success. Additionally, 82% agree with the statement that 'if you learn English people respect you more'. Clearly, therefore, there is a sense that the learning of English can alter a person's sense of 'success' and feeling of being respected in society, along with their financial standing. However, what is meant by 'success' or 'respect' in such contexts needs further explanation.

In summary, the quantitative findings point to a generally very positive attitude to the idea of English and the beneficial role it can play in the lives both of individuals and the country as a whole. The issue of economic value – and its pivotal role in the process of development – is particularly salient, though it should be noted that this could be attributed, at least in part, to the way the questionnaire framed the issue. Questions of what motivates this positive attitude, and how these beliefs relate to the biographies of those expressing them, cannot, however, be definitively explained from statistical data of this sort, although we have attempted some speculation. To offer a more nuanced account of the perceptions of English amongst the local community and the language's (potential) role in development, we now turn to the qualitative data.

Qualitative Findings

The results reported in this section are intended both to survey the actual role that English plays in the experiences of this particular sample of people (as this is reported by the participants themselves), and to provide more detailed accounts of individuals' beliefs about the role that English has played in achieving the success they have. As previously indicated, all of the participants chosen for the questionnaire had moved from economic and social disadvantage to positions of status within the social establishment and, as will be shown, they all perceive knowledge of English as having played a vital role in the development both of their lives in general, and specifically in their careers.

The socio-economic background of the participants

As is presented in Table 4.3, the majority of the participants in this study were born into low-income families. For instance, Sahir, who now works as a magistrate, recollects in his autobiographical sketch:

> My father was a primary school teacher. But he did not continue with his job and he became jobless. As a result, he could not maintain our family well. We with my other brothers and my mother would have to go without food sometimes.

Similarly, Dinar, who now works as a lecturer in English in a government college in Faridpur, notes: 'I have come of an impoverished family. My father was a landless farmer who used to work as a day labourer to support the family'. Zaber states that his parents did not have 'institutional education' and were 'illiterate'. He recollects that 'his hope of getting higher education was about to nip in the bud' due to family poverty. Jahir likewise shares his experience of growing up in circumstances of socio-economic constraint, from which only he was able to escape:

> I come from a farmer's family [...] Because my father was dependent on agricultural cultivation, it was not possible for him to educate my siblings. Consequently, of my seven siblings, I am the only one to have received higher education. (translated)

And in his autobiographical notes, Joynal writes that it was hard for his father who was a carpenter to arrange 'two meals a day' for them in some months of the year.

Table 4.3 Participants in the qualitative study

*Participants**	*Family and social background*	*Current profession and location*	*Location at the time of study (district)*
Alamin	Low-income farmer family with little parental education	Assistant Director, Bangladesh Rural Development Board	Dhaka
Chand	Modest-income family; father completed eighth grade	Lecturer in Political Science	Kurigram
Dinar	Impoverished family; no parental education	Lecturer in English	Faridpur
Forman	Rural middle-class family; father had postgraduate qualifications	Lecturer in English	Kurigram
Ibrahim	Low-income farmer family; no parental education	Lecturer in Political Science	Kurigram
Jahir	Low-income farmer family; no parental education	Lecturer in Arabic and Islamic Studies	Dhaka
Joynal	Low-income family; father had primary school education	Lecturer in Chemistry	Kurigram
Sahir	Low-income family; father had secondary school education	Magistrate	Barisal
Wahid	Low-income family	Lecturer in Chemistry	Kurigram
Zaber	Low-income family; no parental education	Lecturer in English	Kurigram

*The identities of these participants have been protected by the use of pseudonyms.

For many of the participants socio-economic disadvantage was accompanied by geographic isolation and, consequently, sociocultural disadvantage. They mention that they were born in a remote region in Bangladesh, which was far behind other regions in terms of opportunities for education, employment and information technology. For instance, Alamin, now an assistant director of Bangladesh Rural Development Board in Dhaka, recollects: 'I was so rustic that everybody, even a child in this modern world, will be surprised to know that I did not see any bus [until] I was 14 years old'.

Forman was an exception, being born into favourable family situations and therefore destined to be educated and employed:

> Though I was born in a remote village of [name] district, I saw the light of education from the beginning of my life; and it has brought me to my present profession.

His family background and education were two factors that, by his own account, determined his career success. As he explains:

> I didn't have any scope to slip from the path of education because in my family there's no member who doesn't have graduation [bachelor's degree]. So to be born in such a family, it was a matter of time that I would be a postgraduate one day.

Yet Forman's supportive family situation only serves to highlight the social disadvantages of the other participants, and to magnify the level of their professional achievements.

English and career goals

All the participants observed that English played a significant role in reaching these career goals. One reason for this is that most of them had to pass through a lengthy and competitive public service recruitment process centrally organized by the Bangladesh Public Service Commission (BPSC). This process has three stages: (1) a preliminary multiple-choice test; (2) written exams in 11 papers including Bangla, English, and domestic and international affairs; and (3) a viva voce. In all three stages, English constitutes an important part of the process. Sahir comments on this as one of the key ways in which knowledge of English has been pivotal in his employment biography:

> Without knowing English, one cannot succeed in life. From my boyhood, I tried to know English language. In my student life, I maintain myself earning money by tuition [in English]. After getting my honours and masters degree, I face competitive exam to get job. I got the job doing better in English portion. In BCS [Bangladesh Civil Service] exam, there is a subject, English, of 100 marks. I did better in that subject. I believe, doing better in English I have passed in BCS exam well. In viva-voce, I did better in English. The exam board asked questions in English. I did better in English. Thus English language has played a vital role in reaching this career goal.

This assessment is echoed by Dinar who reports similar details on how the BCS recruitment process appears to favour English-proficient candidates:

> English has played the key role in reaching this career goal of mine. Persons who have little or poor knowledge in English cannot qualify the preliminary test of this job. Even if they do, they face the real problems

> in the secondary test (written). Viva-voce is another step to succeed in getting this job. And viva voce is conducted in English. So candidates who have good command over English can successfully come out.

Alamin was an exception who did not take the BCS examination. Instead he was recruited by a different agency, yet the process was no less rigorous or competitive, and English played an equally pivotal role:

> My proficiency in English language was very important in reaching this career. If I did not have enough skill in English language, I would not have succeeded in reaching this career. Because, I had to answer the questions of 200 marks in English language and qualify the test conducted by IBA of the University of Dhaka to get the job.

Wahid sees an even broader scope of influence of English in his career as a chemistry lecturer:

> English has played a considerable role in reaching my current career. First, it is my English proficiency that attracted me to education and learning, which in turn led me to my current profession. Second, my English language skills helped me in reading chemistry books written in English. Consequently, I was able to stick to chemistry as the field of my interest. Third, my English skills helped me in a practical way in obtaining jobs. Fourthly, I still apply my English language skills in reading books and research work in my current profession. In fact, English is so important in the contemporary global context that everybody needs it for his/her career. (translated)

However, it may be worth noting that all the comments here are predominantly descriptive in nature, and although the role of English is evaluated in general terms, a critical understanding of exactly how and to what extent English has contributed to their career success was not available. As such, the participants' views of the role of English in career success can be interpreted as predominantly social beliefs about the instrumental value of English which are prevalent in society (cf. Hamid, 2009).

The use of English at work

The next theme that the participants comment on was the actual use of English for their work. In the quantitative data, there was a relatively low percentage of people using English in their current jobs, despite a desire to learn it. In the qualitative data, responses to this question were varied. Some significant English use can be taken for granted for those who are lecturers in English, because they teach mainly through the medium of English. Dinar describes a typical set of activities performed by a lecturer in English in government-funded colleges:

> In my current job I have to deliver lectures to my students in English. Sometimes I use English to communicate with my colleagues. I have to conduct my office work in English (written English). To prepare myself to teach my students, I read books, journals, and related materials in English. I read English dailies to be in contact with the everyday world.

This requirement for English can be expected to be less extensive for lecturers in other subjects, such as political science or chemistry. Wahid offers an assessment of the use of English in his job, which is representative of these other disciplines:

> As a lecturer in a government college the scope of my work is not very wide. We have to speak Bangla with our students in the class because they have limited ability to receive lectures in English. Occasionally I use English terminology. However, I have to study non-local books for the sake of my students as well as my professional development. Here I can see the application of my English reading skills. I also use English for activities related to information technology. Finally, I use English alongside Bangla when I talk to my colleagues. (translated)

Sahir, who works as a magistrate at the district level, notes the need for English to perform his administrative and judicial duties. He often discusses judicial and revenue issues with lawyers and other colleagues and occasionally uses English with them for this:

> I have to read some verdict of the Honourable High Court on civil matters i.e., land litigation between Government and public, Govt. and other organization. Sometimes I have to answer some queries of the High Court in English. Maximum of laws, rules, orders are in English. I have to read that sort of laws to maintain my office.

Alamin reports an extensive use of English in his job, mostly in terms of written communication. He works at the Head Office of the Bangladesh Rural Development Board in Dhaka and, along with a support staff, is responsible for 'keeping contact with different divisions of BRDB apart from different ministries, departments, agencies of home and abroad, electronic media, print media etc.'.

English and job benefits

In order to better understand the participants' perceptions of the role of English in career success, the questionnaire also included a hypothetical question: if their English proficiency had been at a higher level than it currently is, would that have helped them in their career? The participants' responses are consistent with their answers to the previous question, and there is a strong consensus that better English would almost certainly have brought better prospects for them in their career. Joynal's comments are representative in this respect:

> If my English proficiency had been better, I would have received better outcomes in my career. I could have entered the job market immediately after my studies at the university. This is because I was not considered for many lucrative jobs simply because my English was considered inadequate, although there was no question about my content knowledge [chemistry]. Also better English would have placed me in a better institution in my current job. More English would have enhanced my prestige in my workplace. (translated)

Sahir also points out the benefits associated with higher levels of English:

> In my present career we have to attend many training [programmes]. In that training the medium of language is English. If a trainee knows English well, he will do better in that training. He who does better get[s] prizes and honours. This brings him close to the senior authorities and get better chances for [better] posting and promotion. So it is clear that English proficiency is necessary to have been more successful in my career ...

And while Alamin does not mention the benefits that accrue because of English proficiency, he suggests that he would be able to perform his duties more effectively: 'I think [that] if the level of my English proficiency had been higher than what it is now, I would have been more creative and analytic in my career'.

These perceptions can thus offer a certain insight into why some of the participants in the quantitative study expressed a desire to learn English despite the fact they currently had no need for it at work. If the respondents in the quantitative study share the views articulated by the participants in the qualitative study, they may feel that such proficiency would give them access to opportunities for career advancement and prestige, which they would not have without knowledge of the language.

Prestige

One of the most interesting categories of comment is the one related to the psychological impact of possession of English skills. The question of social prestige associated with English, mentioned by Joynal above ('More English would have enhanced my prestige in my workplace'), is noteworthy and reflects popular perceptions of the language in the society (see also Erling *et al.*, 2012). Chand also touched on this point in one of his responses:

> If I had had better proficiency in English, I would have done much better in the exams related to my promotion. English would have allowed me to participate more in different social and educational programs such as seminars, symposiums and discussions. This would have helped me in being promoted to a higher position on the one hand and enhanced my prestige with my colleagues on the other. (translated)

Likewise, Forman refers to the possibility of increasing one's professional prestige by means of higher levels of English:

> No doubt English proficiency works as a[n] extra qualification in any job. To the present context of the world it's a must. So the more proficiency you gather, the better. A man can develop his level or rank among the colleagues by dint of it. May be, the better proficiency would show me to a higher level than now.

Similar associations between English and 'success' and 'respect' are found in the quantitative data, and attitudes of this sort appear to highlight the internalized belief that English is essential not only for success, but also for issues related to self-perception and the standing one has amongst one's peers.

In summary, then, in the qualitative data, although all participants observe that English has played a vital role in reaching their career goals, the actual use of English in their jobs varies, depending on the duties involved (e.g. teaching English versus mathematics) and their location (e.g. the capital city versus rural districts). In all cases, however, they mention at least some need for English, and in their particular situations, there is a relationship between the use of English as part of a gate-keeping mechanism (i.e. in the recruitment procedure), and the actual need for it in the workplace. They also see their knowledge of English as enhancing their prestige amongst their colleagues. Finally, all of these participants achieved career success in their field, despite the fact that they come from disadvantaged backgrounds, and they all seem to perceive their knowledge of English as an important factor in having made this leap.

Discussion and Conclusion

Taken together, the results from the quantitative and qualitative studies suggest strong beliefs about the importance of English for a variety of development-related issues. The majority of respondents in both studies see a strong association between English and personal development, English and career success (at least in particular contexts), and, in the quantitative data, English and national development. Both studies also indicate an internalized belief that English is essential not only for economic success, but also for issues related to self-perception, respect and prestige, an area worthy of further exploration.

The English language plays an important gate-keeping role in Bangladesh society, and the qualitative data show that for a career as either a civil servant or academic, English is required, regardless of whether it is needed on the job or not. For those who do have some skills in English, there is a sense that better English would almost certainly have brought better prospects for them in their career. Similarly, in the quantitative data, it is clear that English is strongly associated with economic gain and career development.

Both the quantitative and qualitative data indicate people's positive attitudes towards English and a strong belief in both the linguistic and cultural capital that can accrue from English-language education and that, they believe, can be transferred into career success and, consequently, individual and social development. We can thus see a parallel between the discourses of English and development at two opposite ends of the scale – the top-down, policy level (cf. Seargeant & Erling, 2011 for discussion) and the bottom-up, grassroots level. While such parallelism is welcome for development projects such as EIA because it suggests that the rationale by which they are working matches the beliefs and aspirations of the local community, it should be reiterated that the associations made for the language are in both cases at the level of language ideologies – that is, deeply held attitudes and beliefs within the society (Blommaert, 2005), which do not necessarily reflect an imminent and practical need for the language. Furthermore, one may wish to suggest that the convergence of top-down and bottom-up beliefs about

English and development makes the task of development projects the more challenging because they are working in contexts in which specific beliefs about the language pre-exist. Such agencies thus have to demonstrate that there is indeed a link between English proficiency and socio-economic development; their 'theory of action' must then be based on the supposition that the promised outcomes be delivered.

While these data can indicate something about how beliefs about learning English are related to assumptions about the economic gain and personal development that will result, they cannot shed light on any causal relationship between English proficiency and its actual social benefits. Indeed, Imam (2005: 480) goes as far as to argue that it is 'unethical' to sustain unsupported and overly general illusions about the relationship between English and economic gain; as she notes, 'by no means everyone who acquires English will join the local or global elite'. For a better understanding of the exact nature of the relationship we need further research and evidence. Detailed empirical studies (of the sort that are starting to be conducted for other contexts, e.g. Arcand & Grin, this volume; Azam *et al.*, 2010; Chakraborty & Kapur, 2008; Coleman, 2010; Grin, 2001; Levinsohn, 2007) would be able to show how English proficiency correlates with economic value in the Bangladeshi context, and the extent to which such correlations are causally linked. Further insight into the role of English from smaller-scale studies, where local development contexts can be investigated, would therefore also be of interest to see how the specific mechanisms operate to improve individual and social development.

Another necessary limitation of this research is that it does not address other forms of cultural or social capital that may be needed to gain resources and positions of esteem and authority in these communities. While the participants *perceive* English as strongly associated with better quality of life and more prestigious positions in society, the studies reported on here do not in any significant way take into account other factors (gender, family background, educational history, etc.) that may (also) play a role in personal and national development. This would also be worthy of further analysis.

The data reported on in this chapter do, however, give an indication of the self-perceived needs of people living in the communities, which development projects such as EIA are targeting. They also highlight how the language is being used, both institutionally and by individuals. Information of this sort can provide ELT professionals and policy makers with a better idea of why and how English is needed in ELT programmes and what type of skills learners need to have in order to engage in the activities that would benefit them. As is also being shown in other studies (e.g. Tembe & Norton, 2011), ELT programmes in development contexts clearly need to be based in local needs and values, while also building on literacy in local languages, not taking resources away from general education programmes, and valuing multilingualism (see, for example, McIlwraith, 2013; MTB-MLE, 2012).

Finally, without further evidence about the relationship between English-language learning and economic gain, overly simplistic notions of English being an essential (or exclusive) tool for personal and national development are clearly best avoided. However, the data from the two studies reported here remind us that we need to recognize the strong sense of hope and aspiration that is often associated with English learning, and to which development agencies need to respond. While English-language skills alone are unlikely to provide a fast-track to development, if people strongly feel that learning English will improve their status in life and offer them greater opportunity, beliefs about the role of English as a language for international development can be part of the envisioned success that is required in order for actual development to occur. After all, achieving success despite the odds is clearly possible in some cases, as can be seen from the narratives related in the qualitative study. Moreover, Vavrus (2002: 373) found that economic hardship among the students in her study in Tanzania 'was tempered by their optimism that their knowledge of English would eventually help them find employment or opportunities for further education'. The participants felt that English was valuable as a means of connecting them to the wider world and providing access to better jobs – if not now, then perhaps in the future.

Programmes that are thus able to harness these positive associations with English, and that combine them with practical insights from the experiences of people living in these circumstances, can hopefully assist in creating realistic policies and practices for the use of the English as one of the (many) tools that can assist in international development.

Acknowledgements

We would like to thank the 'English in Action' project team and our funders, the UK Department for International Development, for supporting this research. In particular, we would like to thank BBC Janala for making available their Baseline study data with us (and particular thanks go to Tim Cooper, Sonia Whitehead and Md. Abu Sayed for their facilitation of this). We are also grateful to Tanvir Ahmed for his support in the analysis of the data, and to Bob McCormick, Jan Rae and Marc van der Stouwe for their critical readings of this paper. Finally, we would like to thank the participants for sharing their time and insights with us.

Notes

(1) Although Bangladeshi women have increasingly entered the workforce over the past couple of decades, they are still underrepresented in government bureaucracy, particularly in class one jobs.

(2) Here the difference of opinion is also significant: 88% of the core group and 74% of the second group agree ($F = 12.687$ at a 99% confidence interval).

References

Ahmed, S. and Nath, S.R. (2003) *Public Service Delivery in Education: The BRAC Experience*. Paper for Annual Bank Conference on Development Economics. The World Bank, Bangalore, India, 21-23 May.

Alexander, D. (2008) English language skills, Bangladesh. *Written Ministerial Statements*, 18 March. http://www.theyworkforyou.com/wms/?id=2008-03-18b.61WS.1

Azam, M., Chin, A. and Prakash, N. (2010) *The Returns to English-language Skills in India*. Discussion Paper Series. Bonn: Institute for the Study of Labor. http://www.econ.ucl.ac.uk/cream/pages/CDP/CDP_02_10.pdf

Bernstein, H. (1983) Development. In A. Thomas and H. Bernstein (eds) *The 'Third World' and 'Development'*, Block 1 of the Open University course U204 *Third World Studies*, The Open University, Milton Keynes.

Blommaert, J. (2005) *Discourse: A Critical Introduction*. Cambridge: Cambridge University Press.

BRAC (2008) BRAC Annual Report. Dhaka: BRAC Centre.

Chakraborty, T. and Kapur, S. (2008) *English language premium: Evidence from a policy experiment in India*. Washington University St. Louis. www.isid.ac.in/~pu/conference/dec_08_conf/Papers/ShilpiKapur.pdf

Coleman, H. (2010) *The English language in development*. British Council: Teaching English. http://www.teachingenglish.org.uk/transform/books/english-language-development

English in Action (EIA) (2008) *Implementation phase, Bangladesh*. BMB Mott MacDonald. www.bmb.mottmac.nl/projectsintro/southasiaprojects

English in Action (EIA) (2009) *Baseline Research Synthesis, Research and Learning Group Bangladesh*. BBC Janala. Dhaka: EIA.

English in Action (EIA) (2010) *English in action: About us*. http://EIAbd.com

Erling, E.J., Seargeant, P., Solly, M., Chowdhury, Q.H. and Rahman, S. (2012) *Attitudes to English as a Language for International Development in Rural Bangladesh*. London: British Council.http://www.teachingenglish.org.uk/publications/attitudes-english-a-language-international-development-rural-bangladesh

Graddol, D. (2010) *English Next India*. London: British Council.

Grin, F. (2001) English as economic value: Facts and fallacies. *World Englishes* 20 (1), 65-78.

Hamid, M.O. (2009) Sociology of language learning: Social biographies and school English achievement in rural Bangladesh. Unpublished PhD dissertation, the University of Queensland.

Hamid, M.O. (2010) Globalisation, English for everyone and English teacher capacity: Language policy discourses and realities in Bangladesh. *Current Issues in Language Planning* 11 (4), 289-310.

Hamid, M.O. and Baldauf, R.B.J. (2008) Will CLT bail out the bogged down ELT in Bangladesh? *English Today* 24 (3), 16-24.

Imam, S.R. (2005) English as a global language and the question of nation-building education in Bangladesh. *Comparative Education* 41 (4), 471-486.

Kubota, R. and McKay, S. (2009) Globalization and language learning in rural Japan: The role of English in the local linguistic ecology. *TESOL Quarterly* 43 (4), 593-619.

Levinsohn, J. (2007) Globalization and the returns to speaking English in South Africa. In A. Harrison (ed.) *Globalization and Poverty* (pp. 629-646). Chicago, IL: The University of Chicago Press. http://www.nber.org/chapters/c10714.pdf

McIlwraith, H. (2013) *Multilingual Education in Africa: Lessons from the Juba Language-in-Education Conference*. London: British Council.

Mother Tongue Based–MultiLingual Education Network (MTB-MLE) (2012) *The Juba Conference in Language-in-Education in South Sudan: Concluding Statement of Principles.* Statement developed at the Language-in-Education policy conference, Juba, South Sudan. http://www.mlenetwork.org/content/juba-conference-conclusions

Seargeant, P. and Erling, E.J. (2011) The discourse of 'English as a language for international development'. In H. Coleman (ed.) *Dreams and Realities: Developing Countries and the English Language* (pp. 248-267). London: British Council.

Sen, A. (2001) *Development as Freedom*. Oxford: Oxford University Press.

Shahidullah, M. (2002) The present state of English teaching and learning in Bangladesh. *The Holiday* [Internet edition], n. p. accessed 9 August 2002. http://www.weeklyholiday.net/090802/mis.html

Tembe, J. and Norton, B. (2011) English education, local languages and community perspectives in Uganda. In H. Coleman (ed.) *Dreams and Realities: Developing Countries and the English Language* (pp. 117-140). London: British Council.

United Nations Children's Fund (UNICEF) (2010) *Bangladesh: Statistics*. www.unicef.org/infobycountry/bangladesh_bangladesh_statistics.html; *The human development index-going beyond income*. http://hdrstats.undp.org/en/countries/profiles/BGD.html

United Nations Development Programme (UNDP) (2011) *International human development indicators: Bangladesh*. http://hdrstats.undp.org/en/countries/profiles/BGD.html

Vavrus, F. (2002) Postcoloniality and English: Exploring language policy and the politics of development in Tanzania. *TESOL Quarterly* 36 (3), 373-397.

5 The Relationship between English-Medium Instruction and Examining and Social and Economic Development: A Sub-Saharan African Case Study

Pauline Rea-Dickins, Zuleikha Kombo Khamis and Federica Olivero

Introduction

Education, and being successful at school, has an economic value as it opens doors to employment and has the potential to stem the tide of intergenerational transfer of poverty. As such, improving access to education has been a central focus of development targets such as Education for All and the Millennium Development Goals (2000). But the harsh reality is that school is still failing millions of children in Sub-Saharan Africa who, for a wide variety of reasons, do not complete their schooling or fail their national examinations, and leave school with poor levels of literacy and numeracy. When such students drop out of school, the overwhelming option is to participate in smallholder subsistence farming, 'the least remunerative sector in the economy' (Research and Analysis Working Group, 2009: xxii). In Tanzania, for example, the majority of the population are still smallholder farmers, with 12.9 million estimated to live below the poverty line in 2007. According to the UK's Department for International Development, this pattern is repeated across many Sub-Saharan African countries, which have a predominately rural population with 51% of the total population

(388 million) living below the international poverty line, with 32 million children of primary school age alone not in school – representing '45% of the global out of school total' (DFID, 2010). Issues of quality in education, attendance and completion rates are not, however, restricted to those living in rural communities and may apply equally to those in urban settings, in particular those in urban poverty and deprivation.

Although there has been increased access across all phases of education, and a recognition that '[p]oor rural children especially have benefitted from improved access to primary and secondary education' (Research and Analysis Working Group, 2009: xxiii), quality (as opposed to quantity) of educational provision remains an enduring challenge, an issue reinforced by the World Bank Group Education Strategy 2020 (2011). Failure to achieve success at school carries the consequence that many individuals do not achieve their potential. They remain on the periphery of society, unable to contribute economically in the labour market which, in turn, impacts on their own capabilities and well-being, as well as those of their immediate community.

Success at school is also crucial to the socio-economic development of a country. This success is usually associated exclusively with the capacity to access higher education as the means to achieve socio-economic transformation, rather than also successfully equipping young people to gain Basic and upper secondary education qualifications as a legitimate goal in itself. Leaving school fully literate and numerate would then open up a wealth of different opportunities thus enabling significantly more school leavers to progress onto some form of vocational or technical training or achieve 'diversity in household economic engagement' and 'diversification of income generating activities' (Research and Analysis Working Group, 2009: xxvi).

Engagement in many of these activities is not tied to a degree but requires a sound grasp of basic life skills in, for example, numeracy and literacy; but for such transformations to take place, current standards need to be significantly raised both at the end of Basic Education (which comprises primary and lower secondary education) and upper secondary education. However, with reference to Tanzania, '[k]ey indicators – including examination pass rates and primary to secondary transition rates – have deteriorated recently, highlighting the persistent challenges of achieving educational quality' (Research and Analysis Working Group, 2009: xxiii).

Whilst teacher shortages, lack of qualified teachers, inadequate resources, school indiscipline and so forth are frequently mentioned as the root causes of these low standards, policy analyses make infrequent mention of language as one of the possible impediments to school achievement. Examination Councils, likewise, deplore poor standards and the abysmal levels of English in schools but we have yet to read a nuanced discussion of the impacts that working through an unfamiliar language might have on students' ability to be taught and examined through a language of wider communication. This chapter addresses some of these issues, in particular how the use of English as the medium of formal national examinations impacts on school (under) achievement. It does so through two principal lenses: the first is that of test construct validity and the extent to which national examining processes within this research context have consequential validity (McNamara, 2008; Messick, 1989) for the fair and equitable assessment of school-age learners. The second, related to the first, interprets the empirical findings presented in this chapter with reference to dimensions of social justice (Ellwood & Lundy, 2010; Fraser, 2007) and national development.

Background and Context

In Sub-Saharan Africa, a significant number of children demonstrate their school achievement through formal examinations administered through a second (L2) or even a third language, with English predominating as the medium of instruction and examining in much of the region. The role of an unfamiliar language as a mediating tool for subject learning is the focus of increasing controversy, and a considerable amount of research has focused on the impact of this on the quality of classroom interaction and subject learning (e.g. Brock-Utne & Skattum, 2009; Brock-Utne, 2001, 2005; Mlama & Matteru, 1978; Qorro, 2003; Rubagumya, 1991, 1994, 1997). One important dimension that has been far less researched is the impact that a language that is not the first language of the majority might have in determining student progression within an education system. The media in East Africa abounds with tales of national examination failures and significant increases in failure rates, explained by a variety of causes (e.g. Lwaitama, 2011). These are seldom attributed to the impact that the language medium might have on school achievement as operationalized through examination standards (but see Cooper & Dunne, 2000, who have done considerable work in the United Kingdom to show the impact of social class on student participation and achievement in mathematics).[1]

Furthermore, issues of the impact of 'language in education' are not restricted to concerns of educational successes and failures, as there are more serious outcomes in terms of the ultimate consequences upon the social and economic lives of individuals and their overall well being, issues that are taken further in the discussion below.

An additional key facet within the context is that the switch of medium from a heritage language or a *lingua franca* to English occurs at different phases in schooling in Sub-Saharan Africa. In public (state) schools in Kenya, for example, the heritage language (L1) is the medium for the first three years of primary school when a switch is then made to English medium, with the exception of conurbations that are linguistically very diverse; here Kiswahili – as *lingua franca* – is used from Primary 1-3. In Tanzania, the abrupt switch from a familiar to an unfamiliar language takes place at the transition between primary and secondary education. However, research has shown that the reality on the ground, irrespective of policy, is that the language actually used for instruction is frequently the L1 or the dominant language of the region, and that teachers may also move seamlessly from one language to another in their lessons (e.g. Probyn, 2009; Rea-Dickins, 2011). Thus, many children are examined through the 'new' medium of schooling after relatively little exposure to this language in their subject learning. This calls into serious question the validity of testing school knowledge in English and whether these school-age learners are in fact sufficiently equipped linguistically to demonstrate their subject learning through the unfamiliar language. Have they, for example, actually been taught their subjects through English? Have they been supported in developing their language skills in the international language that is the official medium of instruction?

Irrespective of the language transition stage, as well as the other diverse factors inhibiting the provision of quality education more generally (e.g. availability of qualified teachers), the prevailing 'language in education' policies appear oblivious to the fact that many children and their teachers do not have the requisite language skills to engage with the curriculum and the examinations as they are currently configured. Levels of achievement at the end of Basic Education are alarmingly low in Sub-Saharan Africa, where over 50% of school-aged children do not pass their school examinations at the end of primary or Basic Education and, thus, leave school as unsuccessful learners (Alidou & Brock, 2006). There are reports of devastating failures of whole schools even to register passes in some subjects (Lwaitama, 2011). Whilst the enduring educational problems facing low income countries and the sectoral reform plans to address these are well rehearsed, there is a need to probe further into why so many children underachieve, and language ought to be one among the variables investigated. For the reasons outlined above, it therefore becomes critical to begin to problematize issues surrounding the dynamics that languages might play in enabling or hindering individuals to demonstrate their scholastic achievement. What, if any, is the role of language in the underachievement of school-age learners? To what extent can underachievement be attributed to language factors?

With this background in place, our chapter explores the dynamics of languages within the examining process at the end of Basic Education in one Sub-Saharan African context and considers the extent to which language might be a (key) factor in school underachievement. The data come from empirical studies undertaken with the SPINE research project – Student Performance in National Examinations: The dynamics of language in school achievement.[2] This research took place in an educational setting in which there are high-stakes national examinations at the end of the second year of secondary school, that is at the end of Basic Education and only two years after the switch of medium to English. These examinations aim to measure student achievement in all school subjects and, with the exception of Kiswahili, Arabic and Civics, the medium of examining is English. They also function as a gatekeeper to educational progression, as only those who perform at or above a specified threshold level can be assured access to upper secondary education. In terms of language proficiency levels, it cannot be assumed, as our own and other research amply evidences (see for example Rubagumya, 2003, 2004), that teachers and their students have a strong command of English, thus assuring effective subject learning through English as the medium of instruction. The language policy prevailing in this country is very similar to many other countries and not unique to Sub-Saharan Africa. Reasons for such a policy relate to the view that an international language is essential to a country's social, economic and industrial development. In turn, this implies that any employment opportunities based on English language proficiency are determined by the quality of an individual's examination performance through and in English (Crispin Wandera Ojwang'a, personal communication). This chapter, however, questions this policy view as the reality on the ground runs counter to aspiration: The majority of school children simply cannot cope with being taught and tested in a foreign language as huge numbers fail their school examinations, drop out of school and fail to complete successfully their Basic or upper secondary education.

The aim of the research reported here was to investigate the dynamics of two languages – English and Kiswahili – in the formal examining of subject content in the achievement of learners at the end of Basic Education. Details of the research and some findings are presented next, followed by a discussion of the consequences of these findings for the lives of huge numbers of the school-age population in Sub-Saharan Africa.

The Research

The research comprised a series of progressively focused studies to uncover the dynamics of language in student performance at the end of Basic Education. We focus on two studies here.

Study 1

Exploratory in design, the aim of the first study was to investigate *whether* achievement in formal Form II Examinations might be inhibited through language factors. It focused on four core subject areas – English, Mathematics, Biology and Chemistry – and was implemented as follows:

Phase 1: Original examination items

This involved the administration of selected items from past examination papers (original items) to six targeted learners in one Form II class in each of eight research schools, followed by individual interviews that were audio-recorded. These took place between June and August 2008. Each student was interviewed by two researchers, to ensure both content coverage and use of both Kiswahili and English; a total number of 48 students took part.

From the interviews with the students on these original items, a host of different factors emerged as proving problematic and potentially inhibiting to student examination performance (see below) and it was therefore decided to probe further, as follows:

Phase 2: Modified examination items

A few of the original items that were found to be particularly challenging were selected as the basis for follow-up with the students to explore further their specific difficulties. Learner Workshops were held in January 2009 and included the same but a smaller number of students who had participated in Phase 1. These workshops were video-recorded and some audio recording during small group learner discussions also took place.

We present one example from a Maths paper to illustrate some of the difficulties that students experienced.[3] Figure 5.1 and Appendix 1 provide the text for the original and the modified examination items respectively. In the original item (Figure 5.1), we note that the use of the word 'below' carries two different meanings: (1) in the instruction to mean 'underneath'; whereas (2) the meaning of 'below 14 years' in Part 1a is 'younger than'. The modified item has five parts, as shown in Appendix 1. Student performance on these two examination items is summarized in Table 5.1, for the original and the modified items Tasks 1 a-c.

From Table 5.1, we observe that on the original item, there were no correct answers, with 30% of the learners not even attempting to answer the items. By way of contrast (see Figure 5.2), all modified tasks achieved some correct or partially correct answers, with only a very small percentage of learners failing to answer the question at all, as follows:

- Modified Task 1a: all learners attempted the task, with 10% correct answers, 30% partially correct, 60% incorrect responses.
- Modified Tasks 1b and 1c accounted for the largest number of partially correct answers, 40%, but no fully correct answers.

Further, the linguistic modifications in changing the word 'below' to 'under' and 'younger than' in the instructions appear to have had a significant impact on the way in which the learners processed the item mathematically (compare Figure 5.1 and Appendix 1). In the original task the

Question 7 The table below shows the age group of children in a class

Age	**10**	**11**	**12**	**13**	**14**	**15**
F	3	2	5	4	2	4

Use the table to find out:

a) the number of children below 14 years

____

____

b) the % of children who are 12 years old in a class

____

____

Figure 5.1 Original item

Table 5.1 Student performance on original and modified mathematics item

	Original task	*Modified Task 1a*	*Modified Task 1b*	*Modified Task 1c*
Wrong answer	70% (7)	60% (6)	50% (5)	60% (6)
Partially correct answer	0% (0)	30% (3)	40% (4)	40% (4)
Correct answer	0% (0)	10% (1)	0% (0)	0% (0)
No answer	30% (3)	0% (0)	10% (1)	0% (0)

Original: $N = 48$; Modified: $N = 10$

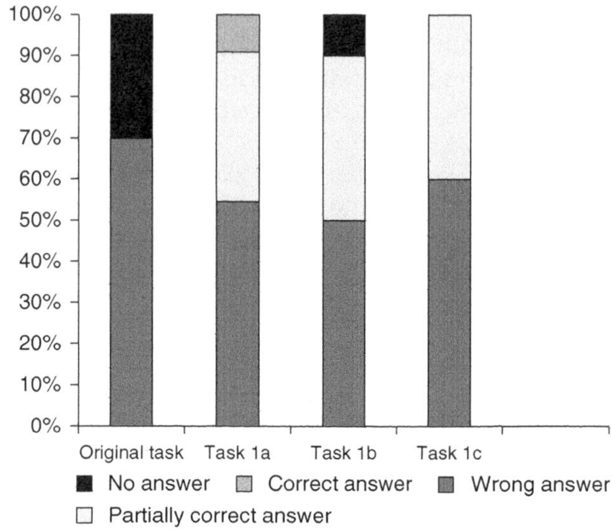

Figure 5.2 Student performance on original and modified mathematics item

word 'below 14 years' was interpreted in three different ways, with students including:

- the 14-year-olds (3 + 2 + 5 + 4 + 2 = 16)
- the cells on the left of the cell containing 14 (10,11,12,13)
- the cell below the cell containing 14 (which says 2).

However, in the modified task, only one student made a mistake in interpreting this item.

A fourth part (1d, Appendix 1) was added, requesting the students to provide a translation of the item into Kiswahili. An analysis of the learners' performance on the item in relation to their ability to translate the instructions revealed that:

For Part 1a:

- All six learners who were able to provide a fully or partially correct translation got the correct answer for 1a.

- Three out of four who did not provide a translation at all got 1a wrong, which suggests that they were unable to engage with the task because they did not understand the instruction/item requirements in the first place. However, the fact that one student who provided the correct translation got the wrong answer also evidences that the problem was not one of language – shown through the correct translation – but one of inadequate relevant subject (mathematical) knowledge to solve the task.

For Part 1b:

- Four out of five learners who did not provide a translation either did not respond to part a, b and c or got the wrong answer, thus suggesting that the English language presented them with an initial hurdle in the processing of this item and therefore they did not attempt to answer the question as they did not understand the instruction in the first place.
- One out of the five who got the correct answer was able to give the correct translation. The other four learners got the task partially correct suggesting that they lacked mathematical knowledge rather than experiencing difficulties with understanding the language of the task.

The conclusions drawn from the above analyses, which were replicated several times over in the other school subjects, are that students *do* have problems in answering examination questions on account of English language issues, either in processing the instructions or in their ability to provide responses in English. Restructuring and modifying the original items (e.g. the use of visuals, context, simplifying the wording of items) generally impacted positively on learner performance with an increase in overall response rates and/or the number of correct or partially correct responses to the examination questions. There also appeared to be a trend that those learners who were able to provide the Kiswahili translation were able to provide either the correct or partially correct answers to questions. It was also found that students failed on the examinations through a lack of subject knowledge (Rea-Dickins *et al.*, 2009a, 2009b).

Study 2

The above findings led us to conduct a wider scale administration of examination items in core school subjects, namely Maths, Chemistry and Biology. These papers were prepared by the language and subject specialists on the research team[4] based on an analysis of past examination papers, the textbooks in use in schools, and the syllabus for each of the school subjects. In drafting the papers, the research team also consulted with each of the research schools to check that the topic areas selected were aligned not only with the syllabus but that they had also actually been taught in that year in their schools.

Each of these three different subject papers was presented in three different language modes: English only, Kiswahili and bilingual (English and Kiswahili). Students in their second year of secondary school (Form II) from eight schools participated in this study. The schools themselves were selected to represent the prevailing diversity across the sector. Two sets of findings are provided in this section. The first presents results from the examination administration in the three school subject areas (Maths, Chemistry, Biology) and the three language versions. This is followed by a qualitative analysis of learner responses in the Biology paper.

The different versions of the examination papers were randomly allocated within each Form II class (one-third Kiswahili, one-third English, one-third bilingual). Table 5.2 summarizes the sampling for the rest of the analyses presented in this chapter.

Table 5.2 Sample size – large-scale examination study in eight schools

Language version	*Biology*	*Chemistry*	*Maths*
Kiswahili	184	183	184
Bilingual(Kiswahili and English)	152	152	152
English	171	171	171
Total	507	506	507

In presenting the findings below, we highlight some of the differences that have emerged in the data that signal the complexity of the issues involved. In other words, in analysing the data there is no simple conclusion to be drawn about which language best enables students to demonstrate their school learning and, hence, no easy policy solutions. The first analysis compares the performance of students across the eight schools by both school subject area (Maths, Chemistry and Biology) and language version (English only, Kiswahili only, bilingual version).

Table 5.3 compares the performance of all the students who took the school subject examinations in the eight schools participating in the research (see Table 5.2). What this analysis shows is that irrespective of which version of the examination they sat (subject or language version), no significant difference in the levels of student performance was observed for Chemistry

Table 5.3 Comparison of student performance – three school subjects and three language versions in eight schools (ANOVA)

		Sum of squares	*df*	*Mean Square*	*F*	*Sig*
Biology	Between groups	684.872	2	342.436	4.633	0.010
	Within groups	38,949.845	527	73,909		
	Total	39,634.717	529			
Chemistry	Between groups	299.157	2	149.579	1.949	0.143
	Within groups	40,442.067	527	76.740		
	Total	40,741.225	529			
Maths	Between groups	70.108	2	35.054	0.351	0.704
	Within groups	52,603.725	527	99.817		
	Total	52,673.832	529			

and Maths, that is, they performed equally well or poorly on the different versions. However, in the case of the Biology examination, the findings are different, as a statistically significant difference between the three language versions (English, Kiswahili and bilingual) was observed in the results across all the schools ($p < 0.01$), which means that the particular language version of the examination that the students took impacted on their overall scores achieved. Further probing revealed additional dimensions.

Given the school diversity represented across the eight schools, an analysis was undertaken by clusters of schools. Table 5.4 presents the findings across school subjects and language versions for schools in contexts where

Table 5.4 Comparison of student performance, schools with limited exposure to English (A-F): Three subjects and three language versions (ANOVA)

		Sum of squares	*df*	*Mean square*	*F*	*Sig*
Biology score	Between groups	4044.315	2	2022.157	44.244	0.000
	Within groups	18,099.208	396	45.705		
	Total	22,143.523	398			
Chemistry score	Between groups	126.386	2	63.193	1.301	0.273
	Within groups	19,234.837	396	48.573		
	Total	19,361.223	398			
Mathsscore	Between groups	11.126	2	5.563	0.186	0.831
	Within groups	11,875.660	396	29.989		
	Total	11,886.787	398			

Table 5.5 Schools with limited exposure to English (A-F): Biology scores

Language version	*N*	*Subset for alpha = 0.05* 1	2
English	130	10.1731	
Bilingual (Kiswahili and English)	135	12.1944	
Kiswahili	134		17.7146
Sig.		0.052	1.000

Means for groups in homogeneous subsets are displayed

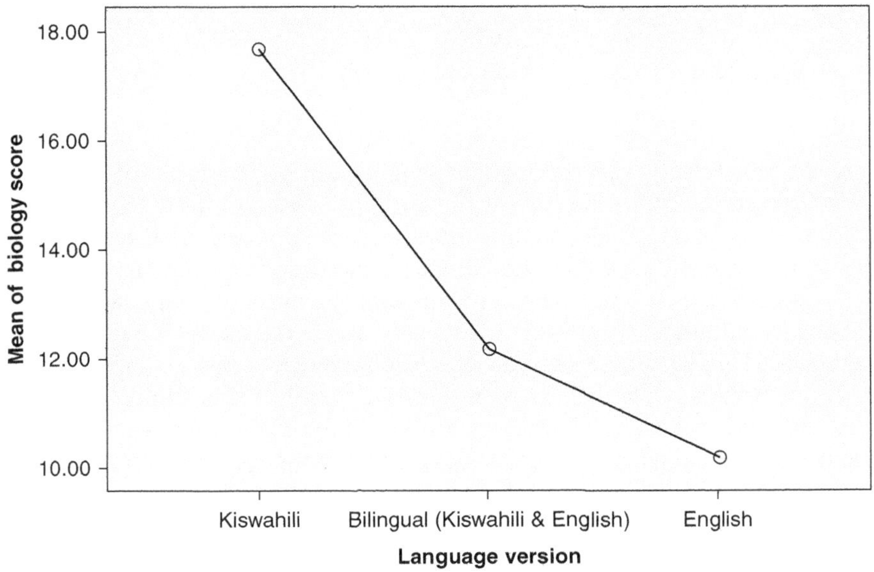

Figure 5.3 Schools with limited exposure to English (A-F): Biology scores

their students would be expected to have limited or no exposure to English outside of the classroom, identified as schools A-F.

The pattern observed above in Table 5.3 is repeated with this specific cluster of schools (A-F), with a highly statistically significant difference between the three versions emerging in Biology ($p < 0.001$). Further analyses revealed in Table 5.5 and Figure 5.3 above begin to identify further the relationships between the two languages, as reflected in the different language versions of the examination papers.

As shown in Table 5.5, a majority of students found the English version of the Biology examination the most difficult, as evidenced by the lowest mean score for the English version (10.2). In part, this finding could be said to reflect the view that the Biology paper was the most linguistically challenging, given the nature of the questions and responses required, e.g. explanations requiring spontaneous English language use on the part of the students. The bilingual version in this analysis only achieved a slightly higher mean score than English, but a statistically significant difference is observed between these two language versions and the Kiswahili-only examination. A graphical representation of this appears in Figure 5.3.

Figure 5.3 illustrates that students in schools and contexts where they are least likely to have exposure to English do significantly better on the Kiswahili version of the examinations than the bilingual or the English-only versions. The question raised here is whether this same result or trend would be obtained for the two schools in the research sample whose students had increased likelihood of exposure to English, through in-class and/or out-of-class opportunities. The findings in Table 5.6 below show that for this next school cluster (schools G-H), there is a significant difference across all three subjects and the three language examination versions – the L1, L2 and bilingual versions.

Table 5.6 Comparison of student performance, schools with likelihood of increased exposure to English (G-H): Three subjects and three language versions (ANOVA)

		Sum of squares	*df*	*Mean square*	*F*	*Sig*
Biology score	Between groups	6214.229	2	3107.115	86.008	0.000
	Within groups	4624.130	128	36.126		
	Total	10,838.359	130			
Chemistry score	Between groups	511.439	2	255.719	5.065	0.008
	Within groups	6462.989	128	50.492		
	Total	6974.427	130			
Maths score	Between groups	587.337	2	293.669	3.207	0.044
	Within groups	11,721.079	128	91.571		
	Total	12,308.416	130			

Investigating subject by subject, it is observed that for Biology (Table 5.7) there is a significant difference between the Kiswahili version on the one hand (subset 1, lowest mean score: 12.6) and both the English and bilingual versions on the other (subset 2), with the highest means attained in the bilingual version (27.7).

Table 5.7 Schools with likelihood of increased exposure to English (G-H): Biology scores

		Subset for alpha = 0.05	
Language version	*N*	*1*	*2*
Kiswahili	48	12.6042	
English	39		25.7692
Bilingual (Kiswahili and English)	44		27.7273
Sig.		1.000	0.320

Means for groups in homogeneous subsets are displayed

A comparison of the means for groups in homogeneous subsets above suggests that students in these two schools would be highly disadvantaged in an examination where the medium was Kiswahili only, as they achieve significantly better on both the bilingual and the English versions. The results for Chemistry are presented next (Table 5.8).

Table 5.8 Schools with increased exposure to English (G-H): Chemistry scores

		Subset for alpha = 0.05	
Language version	*N*	*1*	*2*
Kiswahili	48	22.583	
Bilingual (Kiswahili and English)	44	24.159	24.159
English	39		27.410
Sig.		0.588	0.108

Means for groups in homogeneous subsets are displayed

Here we observe that the highest mean is observed in the English-only version. Given that the bilingual version loads on both factors 1 and 2, this suggests that the bilingual version (as in the Biology examination, Table 5.7) might actually scaffold the performance of students even though they do better overall on the English-only version of this Chemistry paper. For Mathematics (Table 5.9), too, the students in schools G-H perform significantly better on the English version.

The highest mean score observed for the English-only version (25.5) further evidences that students in these two schools (G-H) would be disadvantaged by having to do their examinations through Kiswahili only. In this analysis, we also observe the existence of a 'scaffolding factor', this time

Table 5.9 Increased exposure to English (G-H): Mathematics scores

		Subset for alpha = 0.05	
Language version	*N*	*1*	*2*
Bilingual (Kiswahili and English)	44	20.4091	
Kiswahili	48	21.6250	21.6250
English	39		25.5385
Sig.		0.840	0.167

Means for groups in homogeneous subsets are displayed

with the Kiswahili version of the Mathematics paper playing a potentially facilitating role for enhancing student performance.

In complete contrast, however, if we consider the means for groups in homogeneous subsets for schools A-F, that is, schools with minimal exposure to English (see Figure 5.3, Table 5.10), these students perform significantly better on the Kiswahili version.

Table 5.10 Schools with minimal exposure to English (A-F): Biology scores

		Subset for alpha = 0.05	
Language version	*N*	*1*	*2*
English	130	10.1731	
Bilingual (Kiswahili and English)	135	12.1944	
Kiswahili	134		17.7146
Sig.		0.052	1.000

Means for groups in homogeneous subsets are displayed

In summary of our findings, whilst children's exposure to hearing and using English in and out of school appears to influence their ability to engage and do well in an examination, there was also evidence to show that these same children may do equally as well on the bilingual version of the examination. Our data also suggest that those children with less likelihood of exposure to English in and out of school are less likely to do well on examinations through the medium of English and perform significantly better on the Kiswahili or bilingual versions. We suggest that this affirms that the interplay between the two languages differs within the student population across school clusters with divergent profiles and that a switch in language medium would not resolve the inequalities surrounding the medium of examinations.

We turn next to the qualitative analysis of the responses written by students to one of the questions in the Biology paper. This item had five parts, as follows:

Question 5: Write about an animal you have studied.
Name of the animal.
What does the animal look like?
Where does the animal live?
Describe how the animal eats.

Given the findings above, that some learners performed better in either the Kiswahili or the bilingual versions with others performing better in the English version, a qualitative analysis of examination responses was undertaken. Thirty scripts from the Kiswahili-only and the English-only versions of the examinations were analysed, comprising for each language version: (1) the best 10 papers, (2) 10 papers from the average performance range, and (3) 10 of the weakest papers. What follows are exemplar answers provided by the learners in the top-performing groups. Those for the English-only version are presented first (Table 5.11), followed by those for the Kiswahili-only version (Table 5.12).

In the responses from the highest performing group on the English version, we note that the answers are correct in terms of subject content, as per the scoring rubric. Although they broadly convey the requisite meanings, the writers exhibit a very limited command of grammar and a lack of ease in their overall ability to communicate their ideas, with a tendency to string together a list of lexical items in their responses. By way of contrast, the answers from the highest performing group on the Kiswahili version are qualitatively very different. The translation for the Kiswahili is provided in italics in Table 5.12.

There are a number of differences that emerge in these responses. Overall, they display features of a good writer, exhibiting a fluency and ease in their writing, a command of grammar and register such that nuanced subject-specific answers are articulated (e.g. 'It also uses its front teeth (canines) …', paper 255; 'A cow is among the animals known as herbivores', paper 263), together with a richer set of lexis. What we conclude from this analysis is that the top-performing students in the Kiswahili-only versions of the Biology examination were not only able to convey their meanings better in Kiswahili through providing more detail in their explanations but they also wrote 'better Science', that is, demonstrating better conceptual understanding in their detailed responses, in comparison to the answers provided by the top-performing students who had to write their answers in the L2, that is, English.

Table 5.11 Higher performing learners: Responses on English only version

Paper *No*	*Gender*	*Name of the animal*	*Marks*	*What does the animal look like?*	*Marks*	*Where does the animal live?*	*Marks*	*Describe how the animal eats*	*Marks*	*Total*
				Question 5: [11 marks] Write about an animal you have studied.						
89	M	cat	1	Cat is small and is the perfect animal, cat don't bites person but it can bite insects and others animal. Cat also have four legs	3	Cat lives at home or some place where it can get food	2	Cat a lot of thing or food, cat can east fish, meat, rice, bread, rat so cat can eat many things	2	8
33	M	lions	1	Its look like cennine animals which has for four (4) legs and one tails	3	Its live in big forest in Tanzinia its live in Serengeti Ngorogoro e.t.c.	2	Its eat flesh meat; this flesh meats:-sheep, goats, cow, deer, e.t.c. and it have cennine teeth in order to bit them clearly	3	9
24	F	the name of animal is monkey	1	The animal is hard, hand tooth, mouth, toes, sholder, noes, eyes, ears	3	The animal live in the plants and bushes	2	The animal eats the cassavas, maizes, white cocnuts and mangoes	2	8

Table 5.12 Higher performing learners: Responses on Kiswahili only version

Nam. .ya karatasi	*Jinsia*	*Jina la mnyama:*	*Alama*	*Myama huyo yuko vipi?*	*Alama*	*Anaishi wapi?*	*Alama*	*Anakula vipi?*	*Alama*	*Jumla*
				Higher performing students						
				Swali la 5: [alama 11] Andika kuhusu mnyama ambaye umemsoma.						
87	M	Ng'ombe *Cow*	1	Huyu ni mnyama wa kundi la mamalia, ana miguu mine, ngozi yenye manyoya mengi ili kumzuia na baridi anazaa pamoja na kunyonyesha watoto wake. *This animal belongs to the class of Mamalia, it has four legs, skin covered with fur to protect it from cold. It produces off springs and lactates them.*	3	Anaishi katika mazingira yetu ya kawaida kwani mnyama huyu mara nyingi hufugwa na watu. *It lives in our common environment because it is normally a domestic animal.*	2	Mnyama huyu anakula majani na yana yana meng'enywa ndani ya tumbo lake, kwa kuwa mmeng'enyo wa majani ni mgumu kutokana na cell za miti kuwa na ukuta wa seli (cell wall) mnyama huyu hula majani kasha akayacheua kasha akayameza tena hadi yatakaporainika. *This animal eats leaves and they are digested in its stomach, but the process of digesting the leaves is hard because the cells of leaves have cell membranes, the animal has to chew the cud and then take it in again repeating the process until they become properly digested/ soft.*	3	9

255	F	Simba *Lion*	1	Ana manyoya mengi yaliyo-tokaliana mwili mzima lakini yamezidi kuwa mengi sehemu ya shingoni na ana miguu mine na ana kawaida ya kunguruma lakini anakula watu pamoja na wanyama wengine. *It has thick fur all over the body and gets even thicker along the neck, it has four legs it normally roars but eats human beings and other animals.*	4	Anaishi mwituni au kwenye mbuga zenye hifa-dhi maalum. *It lives in the forest or in special game reserves.*	2	Anakula nyama. Hutumia meno yake ya mbele (chonge) kwa kurarua mawindo na kuyakamata vizuri ili yasimtoroke na baadae kuyala. Vile vile hutumia magego yake ya mbele ili kusagia mifupa. *It eats meat and flesh. It uses its front teeth (canines) to tear up its prey and holds the prey firmly so that it does not escape and then eats it up, it also uses its molars to break up the bones.*	4	11
263	M	Ng'ombe *Cow*	1	Ng'ombe ana miguu mine (4), ana mkia mrefu pia vilevile ana-cho kichwa kwenye kichwa chake kuna pembe mbili na masikio mawili ana macho na mdomo wa kiasi pia ng'ombe ana tunungu karibu na mgongo *A cow has got four legs (4), a long tail and also has got a head and on his head there are two horns two ears, it has got eyes and a mouth it also has got a hump near its back.*	4	Ng'ombe anaishi mwituni na majumbani, mwituni hupelekwa kwa malisho, nyumbani anaishi. *A cow lives in the forest as well as in homes, it is taken to the forest for pasture, and lives in homes.*	3	Ng'ombe anakula majani na ulaji wake anatumia meno ya aina tatu yaani insiza, magoge ya mbele na magoge ya nyuma. Ng'ombe ni miongoni mwa wanyama wajulikanao kama habivaras. *A cow eats grass and when eating it uses three types of teeth, incisors, molars and premolars. A cow is among the animals known as herbivorous.*	2	10

Discussion

The findings presented above provide a snapshot of the complexities in attempting to understand the role of the L1 and L2 in formal examining processes. In the results presented here, and our analyses elsewhere (e.g. Rea-Dickins *et al.*, 2009a, 2009b), we observe differential student performance: across schools and clusters of schools, across higher performing learners in content subjects (see the Biology qualitative analysis above) in English and Kiswahili. In other words, some students in some schools do better on the English versions, others on the Kiswahili versions, still others on the bilingual (Kiswahili/English) examination version. In addition, there is significant variation according to subject area. However, it appears that overall many students do better on either the Kiswahili or the bilingual versions, in particular in the more rural regions, which has considerable significance from the perspective of urban/rural equity. These findings when reviewed together with other critical factors relating to the provision of quality education are significant, with potentially influential implications for policy makers and the fair and equitable assessment of school-age children in English L2 or L3 contexts. Three such factors are discussed below.

Preparedness for English-medium instruction

Whilst there may be very favourable statistics in relation to achieving some development targets, such as increasing school enrolments and access to education for marginalized communities as in the case of Tanzania (e.g. Research and Analysis Working Group, 2009), standards of achievement in numeracy and literacy remain very poor. For example, the Uwezo Report for Tanzania (2010: 2) states that half the children who complete primary school cannot read in English: 'English is by far the hardest subject for children ... By the time they complete primary school, half of all children (49.1%) still cannot read a Standard 2 level English story, and far fewer are likely to be able to read at the Standard 7 level'.

What this also means is that of those who do manage to secure a pass on the Primary School Leaving Examination, many will enter secondary school with a very low level of English language proficiency. Given the official policy that the language of instruction at secondary school will be English, it is not surprising that this abrupt switch to English medium presents problems for teachers and students alike. We need to question how realistic the expectation is that children will be able to engage productively in learning their school subjects through English-medium instruction, an unfamiliar language. Our view is that only a minority will be able to transition this hurdle successfully, and those that do are most likely to be in school in urban areas where their potential exposure to the language of wider communication is greater. If we recall the facts presented at the outset of the chapter, and the urgent need in particular to develop the basic skills of rural-based children, the fact that these students perform lower than their urban counterparts should be of great concern to educationists and policy makers alike. Indeed, Uwezo further reports that rural children 'seem to catch up the Standard 2 level eventually by the time they are in Standards 6 and 7, but in fact may be falling further behind at being able to read at their *own* level' (Uwezo, 2010: 3). It should be recognized, too, that English and literacy are not the only problematic areas, with similar results reported for early numeracy learning. Nonetheless, the fact remains that expecting children with exceedingly low levels of literacy and English to progress successfully in their content learning through the medium of English at secondary level is a hugely problematic assumption, and this has to be one of the reasons why teachers will use more than one language in subject classrooms. An additional reality is that teachers' own English may be weak, also accounting for their use of the L1 or both languages in instruction. Thus, *de facto*, the majority of children receive their schooling through two languages. With reference to examining processes, therefore, and not unique to the context of the research reported here, our evidence shows that formal high-stakes school examinations are not aligned to teaching and learning language use in school, see Rea-Dickins and Yu (2012), Rea-Dickins (2011). The linguistic construct underpinning actual classroom learning and language(s) use involves two languages but the examinations are administered entirely through the medium of one language only, namely English, and learners are penalized if they use their L1 in their written responses. The ultimate consequence of this state of affairs is that those communities who are most marginalized will in all likelihood largely remain so on account of unequal exposure to the language of instruction, unless they have privileged access to quality educational opportunities. This raises concerns about justice in education.

Justice for all children

In their article about the consequences of assessment and children's rights, Ellwood and Lundy (2010) draw our attention to the explicit rights and access to education that children should have. From a purely numerical perspective, a number of Sub-Saharan African countries have made significant improvements in terms of school enrolments, especially in remote regions and areas of deprivation and, thus, from the perspective of Fraser's framework (2007), access to education – one of the Millennium Development Goals (2000) – has been distributed (re-distributed) more widely.

However, recognition of differentiated needs and therefore participation is problematic. We should ask whether and to what extent children are able to benefit from the education on offer and whether, as raised earlier in this chapter, this actually enables them to develop the basic skills required to be participating members of civil society. According to Ellwood and Lundy, the United Nations Conventions on the Rights of the Child, Article 28 sets out Children's Rights Principles in terms of 'best interests', 'non discrimination' and 'participation' (Ellwood & Lundy, 2010). Recalling the research findings in this chapter, there are data that evidence that English-medium examinations are discriminatory for some children, as English may not be the medium through which they are best able to demonstrate their understandings. On the other hand, switching the medium of the examinations to the L1 would not be the answer either, as the data show that some learners would be disadvantaged having to use the L1 to show their levels of school achievement. In terms of learner achievement on the examinations, it is clear that English acts as a major inhibitor for some children to show how much they know, in particular in areas where there are few opportunities to hear English both within and outside school. *De facto*, then, these children are faced with at least two obstacles to full participation in schooling and examining. Firstly, in class they have to struggle to develop conceptual understandings through an unfamiliar language. Secondly, even if they do manage to participate through the bilingual learning opportunities that the classrooms afford, learners are not given a fair chance to show their abilities in their national examinations, as subject area knowledge can only be assessed when the unfamiliar linguistic construct (L2) has been successfully negotiated. In this light, therefore, the human rights of the child, as operationalized in the UN Conventions on the Rights of the Child, are not protected for the majority within the formal examining contexts in many Sub-Saharan African contexts.

The above perspective aligns closely with that of Fraser (2007) in the sense that her framework of social justice can also be employed at the micro-level, such as the classroom, where concern with social justice ensures that all students have access to knowledge to be able to learn effectively and achieve within the school and beyond. In the words of Halai (personal communication):

> recognition at the classroom and school levels requires acknowledgement and acting upon the diverse backgrounds and needs of various individuals and groups, such as urban/rural or linguistic minorities. Participation requires creation of space in classroom processes and schooling for the optimal participation of all learners. However, we see from

the data presented here that bilingualism in classrooms potentially creates the space but examination processes do not do so.

Social and economic inclusion

The third factor we raise, aligned closely with the notion of justice for all, has to do with preparation of the individual school child for civil society. As we saw at the start of this chapter, one of the goals of education in Sub-Saharan Africa is to raise both the economic power and the well-being of rural communities, thus enhancing national development. We have seen from various sources (e.g. SACMEQ, 2011; Yu & Thomas, 2008) correlations between socio-economic status variables and higher levels of school achievement. In the Uwezo study in Tanzania, for example, there were significant effects on literacy performance in relation to a mother's level of education: 'Children, and specifically girls, whose mothers have never been to school, are more likely to be out of school or to perform poorly than those whose mothers have completed at least primary education' (Uwezo, 2010: 32).

What we have here is an example of the vicious cycle of poverty becoming entrenched and thus national development being hindered. When you then reflect on the examination findings presented above, the maintenance of English as the *status quo*, that is, the language of examinations, can only support and perpetuate this scenario. But the 'language' issue here takes on an additional dimension. A widely held assumption is that English is *the* gateway to higher education or to skills and knowledge as the means to participating socially and economically in local, regional and international arenas. These aspirations have been the driving force behind language policies that favour the use of an international language as medium of instruction at both primary and secondary school. Parents and students, too, voice their support for schooling to be through the medium of an international language with a pervasive view of 'the earlier the better' (e.g. Rea-Dickins *et al.*, 2005). But the question to ask here is, what are the languages of communication required for community, rural and light industrial development or small-scale entrepreneurial activity? In reality, economic growth and societal well-being require more than one language for development in multilingual societies. A major challenge for growth and income poverty reduction 'remains to link poor households, particular smallholder farming households, to the national growth strategy by enhancing their capabilities and accessibility to inputs and technological improvements for increased productivity' (Research and Analysis Working Group, 2009: xxiii). But to be a participant in these processes, English and a first or higher degree are not needed for the majority. Neither are degrees required for what the report calls for in terms of diversification of income-generating activities, whether they be inside or outside the home. What is needed for the majority are sound competencies in numeracy, literacy and science, and increasingly ICT, and for these skills to be acquired within formal Basic Education. Ideally, increasing numbers of learners should also be able to progress to secondary and upper secondary education, but where the medium of examinations continues to be exclusively in a foreign language[5] there remains, for many, a glass ceiling that curtails their potential. If children do not acquire the basic skills in school for vocational and lifelong learning then their life chances as a productive member of society are slim.

Our findings therefore carry implications for issues of social justice/injustice with reference to the use of an unfamiliar language for formal examinations and the impact that this has on whether students are actually able to benefit from educational opportunities. Potential disadvantages and consequences are outlined in Table 5.13.

Table 5.13 Examining through an unfamiliar language: Impact and consequences

Context	*Impact and disadvantage*	*Consequences and injustice*
Student achievement in high-stakes examinations is measured through the medium of an L2/L3	Learners do not engage or respond poorly in examinations	Loss of self-esteem and motivation for learning
	Learners are not given a fair chance to show their abilities	Learners do not achieve their potential – glass ceiling effect – or fail altogether
	Subject area knowledge (e.g. Biology, Maths concepts and constructs) can only be assessed where an unfamiliar linguistic construct has been successfully negotiated	Exit a major phase of education as unsuccessful learners, (e.g. at end of primary or basic education)
		Unequal access to available resources, educational experiences and work opportunities
		Unskilled and unable to join the workforce, leading to social and economic deprivation

In summary, in such cases where learners are denied the opportunity to show what they know, these cannot be considered fair assessments and the policy decisions that may be subsequently taken may not be in the best interests of the student population. Language in education has an economic value in that those who are unable to master it and use it to effect in examinations are highly likely to remain on the periphery of society, remain within 'marginalized' communities and be unable to escape from the very poverty that the Millennium Development Goals (2000) are striving to eradicate (see also World Conference on Education for All, 1990).

Conclusion

This chapter has analysed the role of language as a critical factor for effective learning and, specifically, the demonstration of this learning through examination performance. Returning to the title of the chapter, there are both threats and promises that surface from our findings. Against a backdrop of poor outcomes at the end of primary education, the lack of recognition of the realities of language use in many Sub-Saharan African classrooms and the consequent violation of the human rights of children, the threats are numerous. Changing the language medium of examinations will not, however, resolve the inequalities in high-stakes examining described here, as both languages – Kiswahili and English – have been shown to introduce some construct-irrelevant variance in the formal examination of student achievement in their various school subjects. There are also far more linguistically complex contexts across Sub-Saharan Africa than the one presented here, such as in those countries with many more heritage languages or in a country such as Rwanda that has recently undergone a dramatic shift in language policy from French to English as the medium of instruction.

In order to respond to this systemic diversity, what might be the way forward? In our view, it is crucial for policy and professional practice to be aligned, but this would require acknowledging what the underlying language constructs in use in schools are. Should there be more differentiated solutions within contexts, in recognition that in many countries, or in the majority of the regions of a country, English has no place in communities outside of school and that learning in school is not following current language policy? Would it be fairer to celebrate and take account of the multilingual resources that learners have at their disposal to demonstrate their school achievements and implement solutions to match this reality? Ultimately, in the interests of fairness, more students should be enabled to show how much they *do* know rather than show what they cannot do and/or what they cannot express even when they have the knowledge.

It is a basic human right to aspire to a better life, for richer opportunities for the next generation than the current one. But how can this be achieved if children are disenfranchised on account of language medium issues? Broadfoot (2000) makes two important observations that are relevant to this analysis about the nature and role of assessment. She highlights 'the potential for assessment to be a powerful positive force in supporting lifelong learning, provided its role as part of the process of teaching and learning is properly understood' (Broadfoot, 2000: xii) and that we need assessment that 'is employed in liberalising the power of learning to change lives' (Broadfoot, 2000: 23).

In our view, then, the promise lies in the hands of policy makers to develop language polices and strategies that will minimize disadvantage and ensure that *all* learners and teachers have a more equal share of resources and opportunities that are available. Recognizing and celebrating the linguistic diversity and resources that students and teachers have through the formulation of a multilingual or bilingual education policy would be one suggestion. More concretely, providing students with an opportunity to be tested through more than one language and giving them a choice as to which language they can use to write their examinations would be another option. Parents and guardians, too, will need to be mobilized as they represent an extremely powerful force in wanting 'more English and the earlier the better'. The use of the media such as radio and newspapers in particular, as well as television in areas where this is available, proves to be a very effective way of communicating with the wider public.

Quality education is fundamental to quality of life and social well-being, and significant underachievement in schools means slower progress towards a well-educated and learning society. Unless there is an increase in the pool of citizens with skills for engagement in productive economic activity, socio-economic transformation for all will not be attained and those living in poverty will continue to remain on the periphery in national growth processes.

Acknowledgements

We gratefully acknowledge the contributions of all colleagues in the SPINE research team: Mohammed Abeid, Oksana Afitska, Sibel Erduran, Harvey Goldstein, Neil Ingram, Amour Khamis, Abdulla Mohammed, Haji Mwevura, Rosamund Sutherland and Guoxing Yu. For this chapter, special thanks to Guoxing Yu and Oksana Afitska.

Notes

(1) We are very grateful to Dr Anjum Halai, a colleague of the first author, for providing us with this reference but more importantly for her very valuable suggestions on an earlier draft of this chapter. The chapter is all the better for her insightful comments.

(2) ESRC/DFID Major Research Grant, RES-167-25-0263. See www.bristol.ac.uk/spine; http://www.esrc.ac.uk/funding-and-guidance/funding-opportunities/international-funding/esrc-dfid/growth.aspx.
(3) The full report is available at www.bristol.ac.uk/spine/publication%20and%20 reports.
(4) Oksana Afitska, Mohammed Abeid, Sibel Erduran, Neil Ingram, Federica Olivero, Pauline Rea-Dickins and Guoxing Yu.
(5) In this context, English has the status of a foreign language as many students will have little to no exposure to English outside of their classrooms, that is, English will not be spoken within their communities. This contrasts with contexts where English is taught and used in school as an additional (or second) language, with English as the predominant language outside of school.

Appendix 1: Modified maths items

Mathematics

Task 1a: This table shows the age of children in a class

Age	10 years	11 years	12 years	13 years	14 years	15 years
Number of children	3	2	5	4	2	4

Find out:

i) The total number of children under 14 years old
ii) The % of children who are 12 years old in the class

Answer:

Task 1b: This table shows the age of children in a class

Age	10 years	11 years	12 years	13 years	14 years	15 years
Number of children	3 children	2 children	5 children	4 children	2 children	4 children

Find out:

i) The total number of children younger than 14 years old
ii) The percentage (%) of children who are 12 years old in the class

Answer:

Task 1c: This table shows the age of children in a class

Age	10 years	11 years	12 years	13 years	14 years	15 years
Number of children	3 children	2 children	5 children	4 children	2 children	4 children

Use the card from the envelope to help you find out:

i) The total number of children younger than 14 years old

ii) The percentage (%) of children who are 12 years old in the class

Answer:

Task 1d: Translate into Kiswahili (Tafsiri kwa Kiswahili)

This table shows the age of children in a class

Age	10 years	11 years	12 years	13 years	14 years	15 years
Number of children	3	2	5	4	2	4

Find out:

i) The total number of children younger than 14 years old

ii) The percentage (%) of children who are 12 years old in the class

Your translation:

Task 1e: Jadweli hii inaonesha umri wa wanafunzi katika darasa

Age	10 years	11 years	12 years	13 years	14 years	15 years
Number of children	3	2	5	4	2	4

Tafuta:

i) Jumla ya watoto walio chini ya umri wa miaka 14

ii) Asimilia ya watoto walio na umri wa miaka 12 katika darasa

References

Alidou, H. and Brock-Utne, B. (2006) Experience I – Teaching practices – Teaching in a familiar language. In H. Alidou, A. Boly, B. Brock-Utne, Y.S. Diallo, K. Heugh, H.E. Wolff (eds) *Optimizing Learning and Education in Africa – The Language Factor: A Stock-taking Research on Mother Tongue and Bilingual Education in Sub-Saharan Africa*. Paris: ADEA.

Broadfoot, P. (2000) Preface. In A. Filer (ed.) *Assessment: Social Practice and Social Product* (pp. ix-xii). London: Routledge.

Brock-Utne, B. (2001) Education for all – In whose language? *Oxford Review of Education* 27 (1), 115-134.

Brock-Utne, B. (2005) Language-in-education policies and practices in Africa with a special focus on Tanzania and South Africa – Insights from research in progress. In A.M.Y. Lin and P.W. Martin (eds) *Decolonisation, Globalisation: Language-in-education Policy and Practice* (pp. 173-193). Clevedon: Multilingual Matters.

Brock-Utne, B. and Skattum, I. (eds) (2009) *Languages and Education in Africa: A Comparative and Transdisciplinary Analysis*. Oxford: Symposium. Cooper, B. and Dunne, M. (2000) *Assessing Children's Mathematical Knowledge: Social Class, Sex and Problem-Solving*. Buckingham: Open University Press.

Department for International Development (DFID) (2010) *World statistics day*. www.dfid.gov.uk/Media-Room/Features/2010/World-Statistics-Day-2010

Ellwood, J. and Lundy, J. (2010) Revisioning assessment through a children's rights approach: Implications for policy, process and practice. *Research Papers in Education* 25 (3), 335-353.

Fraser, N. (2007) Reframing justice in a globalizing world. In D. Held and A. Kaya (eds) *Global Inequality* (pp. 252-271). Cambridge: Polity Press.

Lwaitama, A.F. (2011) Tanzania: Wanted – Commission on education. *The Citizen*. 5 July. http://allafrica.com/stories/201107060147.htmlMcNamara, T. (2008) The socio-political and power dimensions of language testing. In E. Shohamy (ed.) *Language Testing and Assessment* (Vol. 7, pp. 2542-2554). Encyclopedia of Language and Education. New York: Kluwer Springer.

Messick, S. (1989) Validity. In R.L. Linn (ed.) *Educational Measurement* (pp. 13-103). New York: Macmillan.

Mlama, P. and Matteru, M. (1978) *Haji ya Kutumia Kiswahili Kufundishia Katika Elimu ya Juu [The Need to Use Kiswahili as a Medium of Instruction in Higher Education]*. Dar es Salaam: BAKITA.

Probyn, M. (2009) 'Smuggling the vernacular into the classroom': Conflicts and tensions in classroom code-switching in township/rural schools in South Africa. *International Journal of Bilingual Education and Bilingualism* 12 (2), 123-136.

Qorro, M. (2003) Unlocking language forts: The language of instruction in post-primary education in Africa with special reference to Tanzania. In B. Brock-Utne, Z. Desai and M. Qorro (eds) *Researching the Language of Instruction in Tanzania and South Africa* (pp. 93-116). Cape Town: African Minds.

Rea-Dickins, P. (2011) *Challenges for Assessment Policy on Formative Assessment: A Multilingual Classroom Perspective*. Paper presented in the Invited Colloquium Formative Assessment: Uncharted Territories for Applied Linguistics. American Association for Applied Linguistics Annual Conference (AAAL), March 26-29, Chicago.

Rea-Dickins, P., Clegg, J. and Rubagumya, C. (2005) *Evaluation of the Orientation Secondary Class Zanzibar, a Consultancy Report*. Bristol: Centre for Research on Language and Education, Graduate School of Education, University of Bristol.

Rea-Dickins, P. and Yu, G. (2012) English medium instruction and examining in Zanzibar: Ambitions, pipe dreams and realities. In C. Benson and K. Kosonen (eds) *Language Issues in Comparative Education*. Rotterdam: Sense Publishers.

Rea-Dickins, P., Yu, G. and Afitska, A. (2009a) The consequences of examining through an unfamiliar language of instruction and its impact for school-age learners in Sub-Saharan African school systems. In L. Taylor and C.J. Weir (eds) *Language Testing Matters: Investigating the Wider Social and Educational Impact of Assessment, Studies in Language Testing 31* (pp. 190-214). Cambridge: Cambridge University Press.

Rea-Dickins, P., Yu, G., Afitska, O., Olivero, F., Ingram, N., Erduran, S., Khamis, Z., Mohamed, A., Mbaraok, M., Mwevura, H. and Said, S. (2009b) *Investigating the Language Factor in School Examinations: Exploratory Studies*. SPINE Working Papers (2). Bristol: University of Bristol. www.bristol.ac.uk/spine/publication%20and%20reportsResearch and Analysis Working Group (RAWG) (2009) *Poverty and Human Development Report*. Dar es Salaam: United Republic of Tanzania.

Rubagumya, C. (1991) Language promotion for educational purposes: The example of Tanzania. *International Review of Education/Internationale Zeitschrift für Erziehungswissenschaft/Revue internationale l'éducation* 37 (1), 67-85.

Rubagumya, C. (ed.) (1994) *Teaching and Researching Language in African Classrooms*. Clevedon: Multilingual Matters.

Rubagumya, C. (1997) Disconnecting education: Language as a determinant of the quality of education in Tanzania. *Journal of Linguistics and Language in Education* 3, 81-93.

Rubagumya, C. (2003) English medium primary schools in Tanzania: A new 'linguistic market' in education? In B. Brock-Utne, Z. Desai and M. Qorro (eds) *Languages of Instruction in Tanzania and South Africa* (pp. 149-169). Dar es Salaam: E & D Limited.

Rubagumya, C. (2004) English in Africa and the emergence of Afro-Saxons: Globalization or marginalization? In M. Baynham, A. Deignan and G. White (eds) *Applied Linguistics at the Interface* (pp. 133-144). London: BAAL/Equinox.

Southern and Eastern Africa Consortium for Monitoring Educational Quality (SACMEQ) (2011) *Reports on the quality of education*. www.sacmeq.org/reports.htm

United Nations (UN) (2000) United Nations Millennium Development Goals (UNMDG). www.un.org/millenniumgoals

Uwezo (2010) *Are Our Children Learning?* (Annual Learning Assessment Report Tanzania 2010). Dar es Salaam: Uwezo.

World Bank Education Strategy 2020 (WBES) (2011) *Learning for All: Investing in People's Knowledge and Skills to Promote Development*. Wasington, DC: World Bank.

World Conference on Education for All (WCEA) (1990) *World Declaration on Education for All and Framework for Action to Meet Basic Learning Needs*. Paris: UNESCO, EFA Forum Secretariat.

Yu, G. and Thomas, S. (2008) Exploring school effects across southern and eastern African school systems and in Tanzania. *Assessment in Education* 15 (3), 283-305.

6 Proficiency in English as a Key to Development? Helping Teachers to Help Learners to Succeed

Martin Wedell

Introduction

Much of the impetus for this volume, as noted in many of the other chapters, is a critical questioning of a current belief among individuals and policy makers worldwide that citizens' proficiency in English will enhance the value of the national 'pool' of human capital, on which continued economic development and also political power are thought to depend. At present there is little or no hard evidence directly supporting this belief (Coleman, 2010). However, whether policy makers' impetus for the provision of English classes stems from a view that widespread English proficiency is essential for ongoing national development (see, for example, Smotrova, 2009), or is a response to parental and societal pressure (see, for example, Brock-Utne, 2010: 642; National Council of Educational Research and Training, 2006), English is now a core curriculum subject within the majority of state education systems worldwide.

Indeed its perceived importance seems to be growing. In recent decades English teaching has been introduced at ever-earlier levels of formal schooling (for example, in China, Chile, Turkey, parts of India, Oman), proposals have been made (and sometimes abandoned) to use English to teach other core curriculum subjects (for example, to teach maths and science in Malaysia and Oman) and the role of English as the medium of instruction in schools in Sub-Saharan Africa is currently being extended to a previously Francophone setting such as Rwanda. As its presence within state education systems grows, so too does the pressure on learners to 'succeed' in English, especially in the many contexts where passing high-stakes English exams determines entry to 'good' secondary schools and/or higher education.

The literature has responded to the spread of English and the educational change initiatives that have accompanied it from at least two points of view. Firstly a growing number of researchers (Canagarajah, 1999; Holliday, 1994; Pennycook, 1994; Tabulawa, 2003; Williams, 2011) have pointed out the need to critically question the influence of the increasing importance of English within national school curricula, the effects of choosing English as medium of instruction on learners' general educational development and the sense of exporting (language) teaching approaches without concern for local contextual realities. A further body of work (Kennedy, 1988; Markee, 1997; Wedell, 2009) has questioned the efficacy of purely top-down, power-coercive, rational approaches to the planning and implementation of national English Language Teaching (ELT) change initiatives. Such calls for caution seem to have gone largely unheard. Most national ELT change policies remain resolutely Ministry initiated and controlled. Official English curriculum documents continue to express the hoped-for outcome of school English teaching in terms of learners' communication skills and continue to recommend teaching approaches that are stated to be some version of 'communicative' or 'task based' language teaching. In addition, many such documents explicitly emphasise the desirability of a pedagogical shift across the education system as a whole from teacher centred, to more learner or child-centred classrooms (Altinyelken, 2010; Carney, 2008; MoE Oman, 2001; Tabulawa, 2009). Such a shift is in turn often explicitly linked to a changed role for (English) teachers. The 'traditional' transmitter of (language) knowledge is expected to become a facilitator of (language) learning (De Segovia & Hardison, 2009; Vavrus, 2009). There is no sign that these trends will change in the near future.

The expansion of English teaching worldwide and the frequent curriculum reforms that have accompanied it come at a price. Grin (2002) has pointed out how difficult it is to discover what the price is, since exact data about the cost of English language teaching is

> almost non existent, or at least extremely rare, because current education accounting practices generally fall short of analytical counting and so do not yield figures of expenditure by subject. (Grin, 2002: 26)

Graddol (2006) predicted that there would be some two billion people learning English by 2010, a majority in state education systems. Even if this figure is only approximate, the annual global financial and human investment in English Language Teaching (ELT) must be substantial. Reports from contexts around the world suggest a poor return on this investment, with hoped-for outcomes, in state education systems especially, rarely being achieved (for example, see Bohn, 2003 for Brazil; De Segovia & Hardison, 2009 for Thailand; Nunan, 2003 for East Asia; Ong'ondo, 2009 for Kenya; Wu & Fang, 2002 for China). It is likely that this substantial investment will continue in the medium term. If current and future state sector ELT initiatives are to be justifiable in development terms, they need to begin to achieve at least some of their hoped-for outcomes. One way in which such achievement might be supported is by reconsidering existing approaches to how such initiatives are planned and implemented.

This chapter takes the view that for most existing education systems, the transition from teaching a 'traditional', teacher-led, form-focused, English curriculum to teaching a curriculum that aims to develop learners' communication skills represents a complex, large-scale educational change (Fullan, 2007). This view is supported by the Organization for Economic Co-operation and Development (OECD, 2009) preliminary report on their Teaching and Learning International Survey (TALIS). This states the following, based on responses from 4000 teachers in 23 countries (19 in central and western Europe plus Mexico, Brazil, Korea and Malaysia):

> In the classroom, teachers in all countries put greater emphasis on ensuring that learning is well structured than on student-oriented activities which give them more autonomy. Both of these teaching practices are emphasized more than enhanced learning activities such as project work. This pattern is true in every country. (OECD, 2009: 90)

The report goes on to say that the above tendency to emphasize teacher-controlled and structured learning is particularly strong in mathematics, science and foreign language classrooms (OECD, 2009: 102).

If such an emphasis on 'structured learning' (which the TALIS report equates with a direct transmission view of student learning) is true for foreign language teachers in relatively 'developed' countries, it is also likely to be true elsewhere. Policy makers' unwillingness to acknowledge this baseline reality, and so to recognise the scale of change implied by introducing curricula that expect English teachers to become facilitators of language learning, is one important reason for the lack of success of most recent ELT initiatives (and also of many attempts to introduce learner or child centred learning initiatives in other subjects).

In the next section I expand on this assertion by considering what such a transition entails for English teachers' most basic day-to-day classroom practices and behaviours. I then consider a small set of key factors from the wider educational change literature, which are thought to influence implementation success, and discuss what they imply for the manner in which ELT development initiatives would ideally be conceived and implemented.

Clearly such ideal circumstances do not exist anywhere, within ELT or education more generally. However, I believe that discussion of these factors is nonetheless a useful means of beginning to imagine how ELT initiatives might be planned more effectively. The last part of the chapter briefly presents two different ELT initiatives that I have had familiarity with over the past 20 years. They both aimed to introduce more communicative and learner-centred curricula to school English classrooms. After outlining them I then analyse the extent to which their relative success or failure can be accounted for by the degree to which they did (or did not) take these change-planning and implementation factors into account.

Developing Learners' English Communication Skills: Challenges and Changes for English Teachers

Despite widespread rhetoric recommending and/or claiming to employ sociocultural or constructivist approaches to supporting classroom learning, the OECD report mentioned above suggests that there are few state education systems anywhere in which these are, in practice, the primary approaches that are used. In the great majority of state system (English) classrooms, teachers continue to teach 'the textbook' in a teacher-fronted manner emphasising factual learning of language knowledge. The 'overly formal teaching methods' that Smotrova (2009: 729) reports from the Ukraine, are also widely reported, using different words, in a range of other contexts, for example Uganda (Altinyelken, 2010), China (Dello-Iacovo, 2009), Kiribati (Liyanage, 2009), the Middle East (Mahrous & Ahmed, 2010) and Kenya (Ong'ondo, 2009). English curricula, whose rhetoric presupposes that teachers will be able to make an easy transition from their familiar role as 'transmitters' of knowledge about English, to a new role as 'facilitators' of learners' development of communication skills, underestimate the degree of challenge that such a transition entails. A successful change of role requires significant professional adjustments to almost every aspect of teachers' daily classroom practice and behaviour. Table 6.1 outlines some of the most obvious of these in broad terms.

As Table 6.1 makes clear, even when considering only some of the most common linguistic and pedagogic skills and understandings that English teachers need to have to be able to deal with common aspects of their professional role, the challenges that such transitions pose are substantial. I suggest that it is planners' reluctance to recognise the complexity of what teachers are being asked to do, and failure to consider how they might experience any transition process in their own classroom context, that is one key reason why there are so few examples of successful English teaching in large-scale state education systems. The importance of understanding how teachers experience change has been highlighted in the educational change literature for almost 30 years. Fullan has repeated the quote below in each edition of his book since 1981:

> Neglect of the phenomenology of change – that is how people actually experience change as distinct from how it might have been intended – is at the heart of the spectacular lack of success of most social reforms. (Fullan, 2007: 8)

Table 6.1 From transmitter to facilitator

Teacher as transmitter of knowledge about English	*Teacher as facilitator of learners' English communication skills*
Learners all learn in the same way and have a single set of language needs.	Learners are individuals with different ways of learning and different personal needs and interests.
A teacher can teach the language with only limited personal proficiency in spoken English.	A teacher needs a high level of proficiency in spoken English to deal with a range of materials, activities and classroom management issues.
A teacher usually uses a single textbook that follows a predictable sequence of knowledge inputs/exercises and activities.	A teacher may be expected to use teaching-learning materials from a wider range of sources, and to be able to adapt these to contextual realities and to learners' needs and interests.
A teacher needs mastery of a predictable and limited range of largely whole-class teaching procedures and classroom management skills.	A teacher needs to develop a range of more flexible and complex classroom management skills to cope with a range of varied procedures/techniques/activities entailing varied patterns of classroom interaction, and differing degrees of focus on form.
A teacher can usually focus on summative assessment of specific knowledge that s/he knows has been taught.	A teacher needs to understand how to design/carry out assessment (continuous, formative and summative) of language performance as well as knowledge.

Source: Adapted from Wedell (2009: 33).

The experience of moving from a transmission-based teacher to becoming a confident facilitator entails teachers engaging in what Fullan calls a process of 'reculturing'. Such a process involves adjusting many habitual professional (and probably personal) behaviours, and eventually developing a new concept of a teacher's professional roles and responsibilities. This is a long-term process, and potentially very threatening to existing 'key meanings' (Blackler & Shinmin, 1984). It needs support from many different directions over time.

Factors That Support Educational Change Implementation

The educational change literature from 'developed' contexts also offers few examples of large-scale, state-system, educational change initiatives that have been unambiguously successful. However, the growing body of research in the field is beginning to develop consensus about some key factors that seem to be supportive of successful educational change in any context. A recent paper outlines three central issues.

> The central lesson of large scale educational change that is now evident is the following: Large scale, sustained improvement in student outcomes requires a (i) *sustained effort to change school and classroom practices, not just structures such as governance and accountability*. The heart of improvement lies in changing teaching and learning practices, (ii) *in thousands and thousands of classrooms,* and this requires (iii) *focused and sustained effort by all parts of the education system and its partners*. (Levin & Fullan, 2008: 291; my italics and numbering)

I interpret these to mean:

(i) In order to change what actually happens in school classrooms, rather than just the language or appearance of a curriculum or materials, or the manner in which schools are evaluated, takes sustained effort over time. Provision of funding and policy makers' commitment to ongoing leadership and management of change implementation needs to reflect the timescale. The time needed will depend on the degree of 'reculturing' that the change entails for those whom implementation affects. Suggested timescales range from 5 to 10 years (Fullan, 2007), to a generation or more (Polyoi *et al*., 2003).

(ii) Implementation of national educational change takes place in numerous classrooms. Schools in different parts of a city, region or country are different. The classrooms within them are different. Implementation will never look identical across the whole of any education system anywhere. Any evaluation of success will need to bear this in mind.

(iii) Teachers' behaviours in classrooms will of course be a visible sign of whether or not anything actually changes. However, if policy makers introduce a complex educational change, teachers are not the only ones who need to make the sustained effort needed to 'reculture'. Other components of, and actors in, the existing education system, together with members of the wider society, can also critically influence how teacher experience implementation, and so will also need to (be) adjust(ed), if teachers' reculturing efforts are to be supported.

While bearing in mind that (i) to (iii) above are of course interdependent, in this chapter I intend to focus on (iii), since I believe that it is the failure to understand *the need for sustained effort by all parts of the education system and its partners* when planning ELT initiatives that is largely responsible for so many unsatisfactory outcomes.

What and who then are the *parts of the education system and its partners* that need to be considered if teachers are to be supported as they try to make the transition from transmitter to facilitator? They are introduced separately here, although in truth it is only through the sustained efforts of the 'partners' that the 'parts' can ever be consistent. Table 6.2 below illustrates important 'parts'.

It seems self-evident that teacher training, assessment, materials and syllabuses should be consistent with the goals and rhetoric of the curriculum

Table 6.2 Some important 'parts' of any English teaching system

The content and emphases within English teacher education and training (initial and in-service) for teachers of different levels		The format and content of the high-stakes English tests at different levels
	The English curriculum (with 'communication skills' as its hoped for outcome) that the teachers are expected to introduce	
The content and structure of, the most widely used English teaching materials at each level		The content and emphases of the English syllabus at different levels

that teachers are being expected to teach. However, experience suggests that in the case of teacher education and high-stakes assessment in particular, this is often not the case.

One reason for such frequent inconsistency is that the organisational cultures of most education systems remain very top-down. Policy makers within such cultures, often using power coercive (Chin & Benne, 1970) and overly rational (Hatch, 1997) change planning strategies, ignore the need to develop and maintain shared understanding of curriculum change among the 'partners', who critically influence how the above 'parts' are conceived. Some of the most influential 'partners' appear in Table 6.3.

Table 6.3 Some main partners in any educational change process

English teacher educators need to understand the rationale for and classroom implications of curriculum change, before they can be expected to successfully help teachers to implement change in their own classrooms.		*English test and materials writers* need to understand what the curriculum changes imply for their professional specialisms, if they are to become able to make tests/materials supportive of what teachers are trying to achieve.
	Teachers need to learn to adjust their own practices in order to become able to introduce (a locally appropriate version of) change in their classrooms.	
Educational leaders, administrators and inspectors at local levels need to understand what change means for classroom practice, if they are to become able to plan to provide appropriate professional, resource and moral support for teachers.		*Learners' parents and members of the wider society* need help to understand how their expectations of what teachers and learners should 'do' in English classrooms will need to be adjusted, if children are to develop communication skills in English.

Here again it seems self-evident that national policy makers and their local representatives should work to ensure that the messages that teachers get (directly or indirectly) from all of the above are more or less consistent. However, the substantial literature reporting on ELT initiatives (see above and Li, 1998; Wedell, 2003, 2005; Hyde, 1994; Orafi, 2008; Al Hazmi, 2003) again suggests that this is often not the case.

Policy makers' approaches to the strategic initiation and implementation planning of new (English) curricula seem in most contexts to remain firmly 'rational' (Hatch, 1997), or 'technological' (Blenkin *et al.*, 1992), even where what is planned introduces new ways of thinking about teaching and learning and is thus clearly culturally challenging. Such rational planning approaches stereotypically view education systems as consisting of stable and unchanging institutions, populated by people (leaders, teachers and learners) whose behaviour is rational and predictable, and whose attitudes and behaviours when confronted by change remain unaffected by contextual realities or by the norms and behaviours of the world beyond the institutional environment.

McGrath (2010) suggests that such rational views of educational planning remain influential at the top levels of contemporary development discourse. He quotes Sachs (the former director of the UN's Millennium project) as saying, 'Of all of the MDGs [Millennium Development Goals], universal access to basic education is surely the easiest to achieve. The technology is the best understood and most straightforward' (Sachs, 2008: 301-302 in McGrath, 2010: 246). The scarcity of successful examples of large scale ELT initiatives (in basic or post-basic education) suggests that for these initiatives at least, the 'existing technology' is not working. If the provision of English for everyone studying in state education systems continues to be considered to be an important element of development, it seems necessary to reconsider how the parts and partners outlined above might work together to better support the reculturing processes of all those who need it, including (but not exclusively) English teachers.

To become able to facilitate learners' communication skills development, English teachers need direct and indirect support. An obvious starting point is for implementation planning to try to support teachers by maximising consistency between all parts of the system in Table 6.2, through early involvement of many of the partners in Table 6.3. Further direct support would ideally be through cycles of formal training and less formal development over sufficient time to enable (many) teachers to become confident enough in their own language proficiency and pedagogical skills to begin to adjust their teaching practices and classroom management styles in desired ways.

Curriculum documents often complexify teachers' reculturing further by including statements that urge them not only to change their teaching approach but also to develop the ability to, for example, *creatively design learning activities that are relevant to the students' real lives* (MoE China, 2003). This represents a further dimension of professional change, especially where teachers work in educational cultures which, until the curriculum changes, allowed

> little autonomy and agency to teachers, who are forced to submit to a highly prescriptive and authoritarian system, and where perhaps as a result of generations-old authoritarian practices and culture, teachers themselves seem to have lost any belief in their autonomy and agency. (Padwad & Dixit, 2011: 14)

An education system that genuinely wants more autonomous classroom teachers needs head teachers, teacher educators and school inspectors who understand the rationale for, have positive attitudes to, and know how to support teachers' attempts to take personal pedagogic initiatives. In such circumstances implementation planning needs to include time, funding and expertise to support the reculturing of many of the partners in Table 6.3. In addition in many contexts learners' parents hold views of teaching and learning similar to those below:

> Every day they (parents) would usually expect their children to learn some specific things at school and show them at home. Otherwise they would question the teaching quality of the teachers or the school. (Zeng, 2005: 20)

In such contexts (as Case Study 1 below suggests), the far less visible daily outcomes of language teaching that focuses on the development of learners' communication skills may lead parents to question the value of such teaching, and the conscientiousness of English teachers. Where this is so, teachers will not feel encouraged to adapt their teaching approaches.

The introduction of complex changes (and I am saying that most ELT initiatives represent such changes) means policy makers need to make plans that maximise the consistency and coherence between all parts of, and all partners in, the change process over time. Where ELT initiatives have the development of learners' communicative proficiency as their goal, successful change implementation involves a degree of professional reculturing throughout the education system and beyond. If classroom English teachers are to feel supported in their professional reculturing, the following will also need (to differing degrees) to adjust how they view their roles and responsibilities:

- National educational planners and their regional/local representatives
- Institutional leaders at all levels
- Teacher educators
- School inspectors
- National testing bodies
- National materials design/writing organisations and/or publishers
- Learners and their parents

What appears to be a simple matter of introducing a new English curriculum, with a new set of expected outcomes for learners, is in fact a very complex process. If all of the above partners are to be at least open to, and at best actively supportive of, the adjustments that teachers will need to make to become able to develop learners' communication skills, policy makers and planners need to consider what needs to happen, and in what sequence, at every stage of the process. Given the lengthy timescales involved, and the complex political relationships and negotiations that such an integrated planning process may have to deal with, it becomes clearer why so few examples of successful initiatives can be cited. The two case studies that follow are examples of ELT change initiatives. Each case could, of course, be a chapter in itself. Here therefore I present only a brief overview of each, focusing on the extent to which it took what has been discussed above into consideration.

Case Study 1: China

Case study 1 dates from the early 1990s towards the end of a decade of collaborative ELT initiatives between the British Overseas Development Administration (ODA) and the Chinese Ministry of Education. The collaboration covered a period during which the Chinese government was keen to expand its international engagement after several decades of relative isolation. Increasing levels of English proficiency was seen as one means of enabling such greater engagement. What follows is anecdotal since I did not personally work on this project. However, at the time of the project I lived and worked in China at two universities offering this programme (including the one referred to below), with British and Chinese colleagues who did so. My analysis is informed by interactions at the time, discussions with the author of the quoted paper and personal experience of working in different capacities within the Chinese ELT context since the mid 1980s. The case provides an example of what 'reculturing' might actually feel like for a teacher and also illustrates how focusing on teachers alone does not lead to widespread change.

During the late 1980s, the Ministry of Education introduced a new English curriculum for secondary learners into an existing transmission-based system. It aimed to enable learners to develop communication skills in English. The curricula for other subjects were not changed and at this point no adjustments were made to existing high-stakes English examinations or to the national secondary textbooks. As in many contexts there were considerable disparities in levels of socio-economic development between large cities (especially those nearer to the coast) and small towns and cities in more remote and rural areas of the country. In order to try to promote greater equality of opportunity for learners in such settings, the Ministry planned to establish English training programmes, lasting full-time for two years, for teachers from remote areas, to enable them to develop the linguistic and methodological skills needed to be able to introduce the new curriculum to their learners. This training programme ran in various forms for approximately 10 years, and thus represented a significant resource investment.

Local educational leaders in the selected areas were asked to choose 'good teachers' for admission to the programme. Those considered as 'good' teachers in the educational culture of the time were usually those who had been the most successful at enabling their learners to pass the high-stakes English examinations that determined entry to tertiary education. Teachers accepted onto the programmes were then sent, often great distances, to study at some of the most prestigious language education institutions in the country.

The teachers arrived at the universities with the assumptions about language teaching and about teacher and learner roles that they had developed through their prior teaching-learning experiences. As teachers who had been using the grammar translation method in their classrooms for at least five years and who had been granted the in-service training opportunity as a result of their success in doing so, they expected to be taught more or less as they had been teaching. They expected the university trainers to take charge of what was to be learned in the classroom, and to teach both English and the theories and practices of communicative teaching approaches in the same manner and with the same detail and thoroughness as they had previously taught English in their own classrooms. As learners they expected to be told what to do, to have new language points or professional ideas fully explained, in their mother tongue if necessary, and to receive a clear correct answer to any question that they might pose. Instead, according to one participant, they found

> a kind of vagueness which confuses me, it's like walking in the air. In the past the teacher explained everything to us, the clear grammatical rules, the explanation of vocabulary and simple memorisation made us feel confident and easy. It seemed I had learned all the knowledge the teacher taught us. (Ouyang, 2000: 405)

In terms of the above expectations, the trainers were not doing their job properly. They were not explaining unknown items in the text, but asking the teachers to infer from context. They were not telling the teachers what the correct answer to each question or the correct outcome to each activity was, suggesting that there could be more than one correct answer or conclusion. They did not give teachers specific items to memorise and learn and so at the end of a class it was not clear what the purpose of the class had been and what had actually been achieved. The trainers conversely felt that the teachers were unwilling to make decisions for themselves, reluctant to participate in classroom language and/or practise teaching activities, unable to approach problems independently and over-reliant on the guidance of the trainer.

Each side's expectations were therefore initially unfulfilled. However, since the teachers perceived themselves as (and were perceived by the trainers to be) students in the university setting, it was they who had, over time, to adjust to the expectations implied by the teaching approaches and culture of the training environment. Over their two years of study they therefore went through a process of personal and professional reculturing as they gradually developed the confidence to start making teaching and learning decisions for themselves, and the ability to independently analyse and develop solutions to teaching and learning problems that they encountered. By the time they had finished one was able to say:

> Now I have learned to judge, to decide, to act, to do everything I should do as soon as possible and all by myself. And I think if I am facing another great change in my life I will certainly be able to make a more active response. For the training has helped me to form an excellent ability in analysing things and solving problems. I have learned to rely on myself, to make full use of my ability, and to seize any opportunity. (Ouyang, 2000: 409)

The teachers returned to their schools in their hometowns. Here they began to try to implement the new communicative curriculum in their classrooms, using the skills they had developed during their programme. They tried to adapt the textbook materials to enable their classrooms to become more interactive and tried to share their new professional skills and knowledge with their English teaching colleagues. However, during their two years of study there had been no systematic attempt to help head teachers, local education administrators, other English teachers or the parents of their learners understand what successful introduction of the new curriculum implied for classroom practices and behaviours. All the above 'partners' in the system thus retained a 'traditional' view of English teaching and learning and found it difficult to understand how the 'new' kind of interactive, activity-focused teaching that the returned teachers were trying to implement could provide learners with any real knowledge. Most importantly they worried whether such teaching was preparing learners properly for the (unchanged) high-stakes exams. Their concerns seemed vindicated when exam results showed that the returning teachers, previously so successful at helping learners to pass, no longer seemed to be so.

Returning teachers had made great efforts to reculture, and change their professional teaching practices and behaviours, but their immediate partners within their professional setting had not changed their expectations of what appropriate English teaching practices and behaviours should be like. Nobody was satisfied with the outcome. School heads, local educational administrators and parents were concerned because English exam results were not as good as they used to be. The teachers who had found it so hard to adjust to the expectations of the new curriculum, felt unappreciated and frustrated that their genuine efforts had been in vain. The outcome was that in many cases teachers left their schools, either setting up as private teachers or returning to schools in more developed parts of the country where their up-to-date teaching skills were more likely to be appreciated. The national investment in trying to increase equity of access to English was not an unqualified success.

Discussion

Support from the 'parts' of the system (Table 6.2)

The teacher training that the teachers had received was consistent with what the new curriculum expected them to do in their classrooms. The second quote above suggests that it had helped them to develop many of the abilities needed to cope with many of the challenges (see the right hand column in Table 6.1) posed by the curriculum expectation that they should establish a more learner-centred, interactive, communication-focused classroom.

The content and focus of the textbooks that they used once back in their schools were not fully in line with the curriculum expectations. However, their training had enabled them to understand how to adapt existing texts and exercises to become more interactive and to act as a basis for activities that encouraged oral and written performance. The content and format of the high-stakes tests had not been changed to be consistent with the goals of the new curriculum. As will be obvious by now it was primarily this lack of 'fit' between what the curriculum claimed to want teachers to do, and what they needed to do in order to help learners pass the test, that ultimately meant that their new pedagogic skills and understandings were under-appreciated when they returned to their original schools.

Support from the partners in the system (Table 6.3)

Although teacher educators at the training institutions were able to provide appropriate support for the teachers' reculturing, there was no parallel effort by policy makers to raise local school leaders', educational administrators' and parents' awareness of the aims of the new English curriculum and what these aims implied for classroom practices and behaviours. These important partners did not therefore support the returning teachers.

Given the unchanged structure and content of the main high-stakes test and its perceived importance among most members of society, it is doubtful whether any awareness-raising efforts among the partners would in fact have made much difference. Within the local community, the competence of English teachers and the effectiveness of school principals and local education administrators continued to be judged mostly by their ability to ensure good results in the high-stakes tests. In such circumstances teaching that was not clearly linked to what was tested was bound to be seen as having little merit. When it became evident that such teaching did indeed do little or nothing to improve test results, it is understandable that partners were unimpressed. In such circumstances teachers were not and could not possibly feel supported.

Case Study 2: Oman

This case summarises an ELT teacher training initiative in Oman, which ran from 1999 to 2008. The University of Leeds worked with the Omani Ministry of Education to develop a three-year bachelor's (BA) programme to upgrade all existing diploma-holding Omani primary English teachers to graduate level. For the first three to four years I was involved in the project as a materials writer and tutor. This case demonstrates the benefits of a more holistic approach to curriculum change planning.

The education system in Oman dates from 1970. For the first 20 years of its development the emphasis was on increasing access to education across the country. By the mid-1990s more or less universal access to education had been achieved, and the focus turned to improving the quality of education to support the long-term strategy of achieving sustainable national development. This entailed reform of the 10-year basic education curriculum for all subjects, through which it was hoped to change the existing traditional transmission based system to one that was characterised by a more learner-centred pedagogy. The implementation of the new curriculum was recognised to be a long-term process from its inception. It was initially introduced at lower primary level and it was planned that it would work its way 'up' through the system over a period of years.

The English BA project was thus one strand of the overall effort to develop an Omani teaching profession that would be able to implement the approaches and practices that the new (English) curriculum implied. New English teaching materials and assessment practices were introduced at the same time. The 1000 or more teachers were grouped into six cohorts over the lifetime of the project. Each cohort was made up of subgroups of about 10-15 teachers representing different parts of the country. They studied mostly in-country, during the summer and winter holidays. For the remainder of the year they continued to work four days a week in their existing schools, and attended weekly day-release sessions with other members of their group at a Regional Centre staffed by Leeds-recruited but Ministry-employed expatriate Regional Tutor. In order to agree day-release terms for teachers it was necessary for local educational administrators and school heads to be consulted. This need, the national spread of the project, and the fact that teachers continued to work in their schools for most of the week helped raise awareness of the goals of the reform and its implications for classroom practice among 'partners' across the country.

Over the three years of the programme, teachers attended six summer/winter schools, staffed by Leeds tutors, at which they studied a range of undergraduate modules that had been expressly designed for the programme context. Modules were continuously redesigned in the light of experience over the life of the project. Extracts from the materials that teachers used in their schools were widely used as the basis for teaching inputs and in-class practice opportunities, and the principles and practices introduced in the project Language Assessment modules closely reflected the assessment practices expected in schools.

For the bulk of the working year teachers taught in their own schools, and so had numerous opportunities to try out new procedures, work with new materials, and use new assessment formats. They were also able to consider and discuss their experiences and the relevance of new ideas and practices for their own working contexts during their weekly meetings with their colleagues and regional tutors. One of the external evaluators (Freeman, 2007) suggested that the opportunities for collaboration and professional learning that the day release sessions provided over the three years of the programme, constituted arguably the most important source of professional and personal support for participants. Over repeated cycles of learning, trying out, and discussing the experiences of doing so with peers and their Regional Tutors, (a more expert 'coach' Joyce & Showers, 1988), the majority developed both an understanding of the main ideas underpinning the reform, and confidence in their ability to incorporate at least some of these in their own classroom practice.

The project was of course not perfect. For example, while the project itself was extensively externally evaluated during its lifespan, there was no opportunity to carry out empirical studies of the effects of teacher change on learner outcomes. In addition, there were initial issues to do with relevance of the content and assessment of some BA modules. But both Oman and UK-based project leadership remained very stable, and over time the project leaders on both sides became better attuned to each other's cultural realities and eccentricities. This, together with long-term experience of working on the project and feedback from students, regional tutors, project evaluators and in-country project leaders, enabled later versions of modules and assignments to better reflect the professional needs of the teachers in their classroom contexts.

Discussion

Support from parts of the system

The educational reform project of which the above case was part covered the whole school curriculum, so to varying degrees all the parts of the system were supporting the changes that were taking place. The teacher education programme that was the core of the above project was clearly designed to support English teachers' reculturing. Similarly the newly designed textbooks that most teachers were using in their schools and the new emphasis on formative assessment also broadly supported the more learner-centred, communicative pedagogy that the formal training programmes introduced.

Support from partners in the system

The fact that the BA project lasted for 10 years and covered the whole country contributed greatly to raising awareness of the educational policy changes of which it was part. An unexpected but useful by-product of the teachers needing to be released from some of their teaching in order to attend the programme was that head teachers and colleagues in all their schools, together with some of those responsible for evaluating teachers, were alerted to the existence of the programme and the reform of which it was part. The 10-year timescale also meant that more informal bottom-up awareness-raising about the programme and the reform of which it was part also played an important role.

> As cohort followed cohort, graduates from earlier cohorts were available to provide information and advice for head teachers and for their colleagues in later cohorts about what participation on the programme entailed and what degree of adjustment to established working patterns was needed. Anecdotal evidence suggests that these informal contributions were often highly influential, given the nature of Omani society and the tendency to share experience orally in social gatherings. (Wedell & Atkins, 2009: 205)

The very existence of a nationwide programme over such a long time span thus helped to raise awareness nationally of many ideas that the educational reform was trying to introduce. With head teachers, local administrators, supervisors and parents all at least broadly aware that the reform was taking place, and that this would result in new teaching behaviours and practices in (English) classrooms, teachers were at worst tolerated and at best supported by most partners within the system.

The project timescale had further benefits. Most project leaders in both the United Kingdom and Oman remained in place throughout the whole 10 years of the programme. Many of the regional tutors worked with more than one cohort of teachers.

> Almost all staff involved with both the day to day running of the project and its macro level management worked on the project for far longer than is normally the case. . . . such continuity among those filling key leadership and management roles was a very positive feature. (Wedell & Atkins, 2009: 205)

The ongoing project leadership over time together with the consistent national level political and financial commitment to supporting the reculturing of all partners had two connected positive outcomes. Firstly the reality of active national level leadership and management throughout the project time span enabled a really *focused and sustained effort by all parts of the education system and its partners* that Levin and Fullan (2008: 291) consider to be essential for changing teaching and learning practices in real classrooms. Over time the appropriateness of the effort made also increased as awareness of what change meant in practice, and of what this implied for how it could best be supported, in turn developed among the project planners and leaders.

Conclusion

Although resources for education are scarce in most developing contexts, an ever-growing number of national education systems worldwide commit significant resources to enabling their citizens to develop a degree of proficiency in English. The explicit or tacit assumption is that such investment will help develop national (and individual) human capital and so enhance future economic and/or political development. If policy makers are ever to become able to judge whether this assumption is valid, they need to develop approaches to the initiation and implementation of ELT initiatives that result in at least some degree of English proficiency for the majority of school learners.

For learners to attain such proficiency, teachers need to be willing and able to make the major professional adjustments implied by the move from the left to the right hand side of Table 6.1. Such adjustments, in any cultural context, will need support over time. When considering what form such support needs to take and how best to provide it, a starting point for those planning ELT initiatives might be to consider whether their plans make an effort to maximise the consistency between the messages sent by 'parts' of the (English) education system and the 'partners' within it.

As the above discussion and case studies show, if ELT policy planners and implementers fail to maximise the 'common reculturing' of all partners in Table 6.3, the parts in Table 6.2 are almost certain to be in some degree of conflict. As Case 1 above illustrates, where such conflict between the 'parts' (and so probably the 'partners') exists, support for teachers alone will not lead to new practices becoming visible in most classrooms. Instead as Case 2 suggests, if English teachers are to feel able to start introducing teaching approaches and behaviours that will need to become the 'new norms' and if most learners are to leave school with at least some communication skills in English, they need to work within a 'system' whose parts and partners collaborate without major incoherence or contradictions over time. To achieve such harmony within the 'English learning system' a starting point would be for planners of ELT initiatives to:

(a) honestly acknowledge the 'partners' starting point i.e. the existing educational administrators', heads', teacher educators', teachers', learners' and parents' views and expectations of 'education';
(b) honestly assess the gap between these starting points and the approach to teaching and learning that their ELT initiative hopes to introduce;
(c) recognise the complexity of supporting reculturing: accept the need to plan carefully to consider which groups (from (a)) will need what kind of support, when, and for how long?

Honest responses at (a) to (c) will almost certainly mean that implementation plans will extend across a longer period than planners are accustomed to planning for. Thus a final (and probably critical) step will be their willingness to

(d) emphasise national interest over short-term political needs: recognise that they are planning for, funding and leading the implementation of an initiative whose full effects (in terms of citizens' language proficiency) will almost certainly not become evident for a decade or more.

This looks so simple. However, for political, economic, human, cultural and other contextual reasons it seems in practice to be very difficult.

This chapter began by pointing out that, despite the lack of empirical evidence, and a body of literature suggesting caution, policy makers continue to justify the rapid growth in English provision within state sector systems by assuming a positive relationship between their investment in the teaching of English for communication and future national development. Whether this relationship in fact holds true can only become apparent if greater care is taken to carry out the planning and implementation of change initiatives more coherently.

References

Al Hazmi, S. (2003) EFL teacher preparation programmes in Saudi Arabia: Trends and challenges. *TESOL Quarterly* 37 (2), 341-345.

Altinyelken, H.K. (2010) Pedagogical renewal in sub-Saharan Africa: The case of Uganda. *Comparative Education* 46 (2), 151-171.

Blackler, F. and Shinmin, S. (1984) *Applying Psychology in Organisations*. London: Methuen.

Blenkin, G.V., Edwards, G. and Kelly, A.V. (1992) Perspectives on educational change. In A. Harris, N. Bennett and M. Preedy (eds) *Organisational Effectiveness and Improvement in Education* (pp. 216-230). Buckingham: Open University Press.

Bohn, H.I. (2003) The educational role and status of English in Brazil. *World Englishes* 22 (2), 159-172.

Brock-Utne, B. (2010) Research and policy on the language of instruction issue in Africa. *International Journal of Educational Development* 30, 636-645.

Canagarajah, A.S. (1999) *Resisting Linguistic Imperialism in English Teaching*. Cambridge: Cambridge University Press.

Carney, S. (2008) Learner-centred pedagogy in Tibet: International education reform in a local context. *Comparative Education* 44 (1), 39-55.

Chin, R. and Benne, K. (1970) General strategies for effecting changes in human systems. In W. Bennis, K. Benne and R. Chin (eds) *The Planning of Change* (pp. 32-59). London: Holt, Reinhart and Wilson.

Coleman, H. (2010) *The English Language in Development*. London: British Council.

De Segovia, L.P. and Hardison, D.M. (2009) Implementing educational reform: EFL teachers' perspectives. *English Language Teaching Journal* 63 (2), 154-162.

Dello-Iacovo, B. (2009) Curriculum reform and 'Quality Education' in China: An overview. *International Journal of Educational Development* 29, 241-249.

Freeman, D. (2007) *Fourth Independent Evaluation of the Ministry of Education Oman – University of Leeds BA Educational Studies (TESOL) Project*. Muscat: Ministry of Education, Oman.

Fullan, M.G. (2007) *The New Meaning of Educational Change* (4th edn). London & New York: Columbia Teachers Press.

Graddol, D. (2006) *English Next*. London: British Council.

Grin, F. (2002) *The Relevance of Language Economics and Education Economics to Language Education Policies: An Introductory Survey*. Strasbourg: Council of Europe.

Hatch, M.J. (1997) *Organisational Theory*. Oxford: Oxford University Press.

Holliday, A. (1994) *Appropriate Methodology and Social Context*. Cambridge: Cambridge University Press.

Hyde, B. (1994) Albanian babies and bathwater. *Teacher Trainer* 8 (1), 10-13.

Joyce B. and Showers B. (1988) *Student Achievement through Staff Development*. New York: Longman.

Kennedy, C. (1988) Evaluation of the management of change in ELT projects. *Applied Linguistics* 9 (4), 329-342.

Levin, B. and Fullan, M.G. (2008) Learning about systems renewal. *Educational Management Administration and Leadership* 36 (2), 289-303.

Li, D. (1998) It's always more difficult than you plan and imagine: Teachers' perceived difficulties in introducing the communicative approach in South Korea. In D.R. Hall and A. Hewings (eds) *Innovation in English Language Teaching* (pp. 149-166). London: Routledge.

Liyanage, I. (2009) Global donors and English language teaching in Kiribati. *TESOL Quarterly* 43 (4), 732-737.

Mahrous, A.A. and Ahmed, A.A. (2010) A cross-cultural investigation of students' perceptions of the effectiveness of pedagogical tools: The Middle East, the United Kingdom, and the United States. *Journal of Studies in International Education* 14 (3), 289-306.

Markee, N.P.P. (1997) *Managing Curricular Innovation*. New York: Cambridge University Press.

McGrath, S. (2010) The role of education in development: An educationalist's response to some recent work in development economics. *Comparative Education* 46 (2), 237-253.

Ministry of Education (MoE) China (2003) *Putong Gaozhong Yingyu Kecheng Biaozhun [English Language Curriculum Guidelines for Senior Secondary School]*. Beijing: People's Education Press.

Ministry of Education (MoE) Oman: English Language and Curriculum Department (2001) *The Ministry of Education – University of Leeds BA (TESOL) Mission Statement*. Muscat: Sultanate of Oman, Ministry of Education.

National Council of Educational Research and Training (NCERT) (2006) *Position Paper: National Focus Group on Teaching of English.* New Delhi: NCERT. www.ncert.nic.in/html/pdf/schoolcurriculum/position_papers/english.pdf

Nunan, D. (2003) The impact of English as a global language on educational policies and practices in the Asia-Pacific region. *TESOL Quarterly* 37 (4), 589-613.

Ong'ondo, C. (2009) Pedagogical practice and support of English language student teachers during the practicum in Kenya. Unpublished PhD thesis. University of Leeds.

Orafi, S. (2008) Investigating teachers' practices and beliefs in relation to curriculum innovation in ELT in Libya. Unpublished PhD thesis, University of Leeds.

Organisation for Economic Co-operation and Development (OECD) (2009) *Creating Effective Teaching and Learning Environments: First Results from TALIS*. Paris: OECD.

Ouyang, H. (2000) One way ticket: The story of an innovative teacher in mainland China. *Anthropology and Education Quarterly* 31 (4), 397-425.

Padwad, A. and Dixit, K. (2011) Continuing professional development of English teachers in India: The ETCs' experience. In M. Beaumont and T. Wright (eds) *The Experience of Second Language Teacher Education.* Basingstoke: Palgrave.

Pennycook, A. (1994) *The Cultural Politics of English as an International Language*. Longman: Harlow.

Polyoi, E., Fullan, M.G. and Anchan, A.P. (2003) *Change Forces in Post-Communist Eastern Europe: Education in Transition.* London: Routledge-Falmer.

Sachs, J. (2008) *Common Wealth.* London: Penguin.

Smotrova, T. (2009) Globalization and English language teaching in Ukraine. *TESOL Quarterly* 43 (4), 727-732.

Tabulawa, R.J. (2003) International aid agencies, learner-centred pedagogy and political democratization: A critique. *Comparative Education* 39 (1), 7-26.

Tabulawa, R.J. (2009) Education reform in Botswana: Reflections on policy contradictions and paradoxes. *Comparative Education* 45 (1), 87-107.

Vavrus, F. (2009) The cultural politics of constructivist pedagogies: Teacher education reform in the United Republic of Tanzania. *International Journal of Educational Development* 29 (3), 303-311.

Wedell, M. (2003) Giving TESOL change a chance: Supporting key players in the curriculum change process. *System* 31 (4), 439-456.

Wedell, M. (2005) Cascading training down into the classroom: The need for parallel planning. *International Journal of Educational Development* 25 (6), 637-651.

Wedell, M. (2009) *Planning for Educational Change: Putting People and Their Contexts First.* London: Continuum.

Wedell, M. and Atkins, J. (2009) The BA Programme as an example of large-scale educational change. In J. Atkins, M. Lamb and M. Wedell (eds) *International Collaboration for Educational Change: The BA Project* (pp. 201-211). Muscat: Sultanate of Oman, Ministry of Education.

Williams, E. (2011) Language policy, politics and development in Africa. In H. Coleman (ed.) *Dreams and Realities: Developing Countries and the English Language* (pp. 39-56). London: British Council.

Wu, X.D. and Fang, L. (2002) Teaching communicative English in China: A case study of the gap between teachers' views and practice. *Asian Journal of ELT* 12, 143-162.

Zeng, Y.H. (2005) Approaches and contexts in TESOL. Unpublished MA assignment, Module ED 5991, University of Leeds.

7 Constructing Local Voices through English as a Lingua Franca: A Study from Intercultural Development Discourse

Tom Bartlett

Introduction

> *In an era of globalization, the threshold of contextualization in discourse analysis or sociolinguistics can no longer be a single society ... but needs to include the relationship between different societies and the effect of these relationships on repertoires of language users and their potential to construct voice.*
> (Blommaert, 2005: 15)

Globalization and language use are inextricably linked, as borders to international trade and communications have opened up with the concomitant rise of 'transnational languages' functioning as the primary means of communication across a host of domains in the new global community. This has led to claims that languages such as English are no longer the sole exclusive property of native speakers and a call for the recognition of English as a lingua franca that does not adhere to native norms but is always adapting according to the needs of its users and the limitations of comprehensibility. A major aspect of research in this field is the description of the linguistic features used in different social contexts in which English is the common language but not the native language of all speakers, and in this chapter I summarize such a case study from the field of international development. After outlining the history of communications between professionals and local communities in the field I suggest that, while there has been a steady movement towards more participatory approaches, the extent to which local communities are enabled to re-create their social values through transnational languages such as English has not been adequately considered. Drawing on the sociolinguistic concept of *voice* I analyse data from development discourse in Guyana, South America, to demonstrate a case where English has been successfully appropriated as a means of expressing social identity and suggest that the approach adopted could be used to further research on lingua francas in other domains.

Globalization, Language and Development

For some, globalization represents a levelling of the economic terrain, providing less developed countries with access to markets that had previously remained closed and an opportunity to exchange ideas and to challenge ignorance, prejudice and insularism; for others, it represents an extension of the military and financial might of the colonial powers and the imposition of a worldview that underwrites this expansion and stifles alternative voices. Fairclough (2006: 7-8) makes the distinction here between the historical fact of 'globalization', defined by Held *et al.* (1999: 16) as 'the rapidly developing and ever-densening network of interconnections and interdependencies that characterize modern social life' and the politically motivated phenomenon of 'globalism', a one-size-fits-all product that 'interprets "globalization" in a neo-liberal way as primarily the liberalization and global integration of markets, linked to the spread of a particular version of "(western) democracy"'. Rather than levelling the field of play, globalism allows the richer and more powerful nations to exploit their position to increase their economic and political advantage at the expense of smaller and less developed nations, who may thus find themselves not only unable to benefit from the new system but left poorer and weaker than before (e.g. Stiglitz,[1] 2002: 18, 54, 67-73, 153-155). From this latter perspective the 'freedom' offered by the reduction of distance and the opening of borders is the freedom of those who already posses the means to exploit the system.

The same ambiguities can be found in the linguistic sphere. Given its predominance as the international language of politics, economics, technology and academia, the benefits of English to developing nations would appear to be obvious; yet here too there is a danger of 'globalism' through the promotion of a one-size-fits-all product, 'the consumer good called "global English" [which] is understood to be vaguely the same thing in different educational contexts around the world. It is the language of communication in business and leisure settings that everyone needs to know in the age of globalization' (Block, 2010: 294-295). This globalist conception of English allows for superficial variations locally, but to all intents and purposes it is a highly homogenized product promoted as a universal language, a means for communities around the world to communicate on the same terms. But the same terms are not necessarily equal terms, as language use does not take place in abstract isolation but as a range of repertoires and varieties that are embedded in wider social structures. The commodity of standardized 'universal English' is in general tailored to the needs of those whose repertoires can be translated wholesale from the local into the international language and still be accepted as 'legitimate' (Bourdieu & Wacquant, 1996: 76). Unfortunately, by buying into transnational English, marginalized sections of society do not automatically buy competence into the dominant repertoires of the global elite, and the freedom offered by a common language is thus once again the freedom of the already advantaged.

A more progressive approach to the internationalization of English has appeared under the label 'English as a lingua franca' or ELF (though the precepts are equally applicable to all transnational languages). From the lingua franca perspective, a language is not a universally valid product but a resource to be tapped by each person according to their needs. For a global language this would mean that local usage involves a process of 'hybridization', of adapting existing forms and functions to local communicative practices. This approach mirrors what has been labelled the 'glocalization' (Robertson, 1995) of international practices within the economic and political sphere. Studies within ELF have considered the effect of hybridization on English pronunciation and grammatical features as well as on intercultural pragmatics (for overviews see Hülmbauer *et al.*, 2008; Mauranen, 2009; Seidlhofer, 2005). Most of these studies to date are concerned with how variation of such features affects comprehensibility, often with the goal of informing a non-prescriptive approach to teaching English. Within such an approach, however, there remains the danger that, although access to dominant discourses will be facilitated, non-native speakers will still be operating within an alien environment that restricts their capacity to contribute. My goal in this chapter is to extend the underlying egalitarian motivation of ELF to suggest ways in which marginalized groups can appropriate the workings of transnational languages not just to be understood but to recreate the distinctive discursive repertoires of their own cultures and to challenge the orthodoxy of the dominant groups.

My focus is on the field of international development, an area in which the interrelationship between globalization and language is brought into particularly sharp relief through parallel debates over the degree to which developing countries should assimilate to global economic models and the question of promoting English as the means of access to new markets and technologies. These two issues come together in the use of transnational languages within the development organizations themselves and the limitations this imposes on integrating affected communities into the discourses of development and enabling them to offer local alternatives to the globalist model. In the remainder of this chapter I will develop this last point as I trace changing conceptions of participation within international development and suggest that an expanded concept of hybridity can highlight ways in which participation can be qualitatively improved.

Changing Conceptions of Participation in International Development

More than *half* a century ago, in his celebrated 'Fair Deal' speech (Second Inaugural Address, 1949, quoted in Escobar, 1995: 3), President Harry S. Truman of the United States set out an agenda for the development of the poorer nations of the world through the transfer of technical knowledge from the richer, more 'developed', nations:

> More than half the people of the world are living in conditions approaching misery. Their food is inadequate, they are victims of disease. Their economic life is primitive and stagnant. Their poverty is a handicap and a threat to them and to more prosperous areas. For the first time in history humanity possesses the knowledge and the skill to relieve the suffering of these people ... I believe that we should make available to peace-loving peoples the benefits of our store of technical knowledge in order to help them realize their aspirations for a better life ... What we envisage is a program of development based on the concepts of democratic Fair Dealing ... Greater production is the key to prosperity and peace. And the key to greater production is a wider and more vigorous application of modern and scientific technical knowledge.

This extract provides an uncompromisingly negative portrayal of the undeveloped world, with its 'primitive and stagnant' economies, its 'misery', 'disease' and 'suffering'. Whatever elements of truth there are in this depiction of hardship, in focusing only on the negative aspects of the poorer nations and presenting their populations as passively suffering their ill fortune, without reference to their resistance and their achievements in adversity or to their existing capabilities and capacity for action, Truman establishes a scenario in which outside intervention appears logical and laudable while the needs and aspirations of the poor and the means by which these might be satisfied are so self-evident as to require no consultation with the poor themselves. Similarly, this emphasis on the negative suggests that less developed nations have nothing to offer in return for the help they receive, with the result that development is construed as a one-way transfer of skills and experience from the rich to the poor. A further presupposition is contained in the simple assertion that 'greater production is the key to prosperity and peace'. While this assumption is questionable in itself, particularly as there are no alternative paths suggested, such as the redistribution of wealth or the creation of a welfare state, it contains two more problematic and enduring assumptions: that achieving greater productivity is simply a matter of applying the new science and following the path of the developed world; and that the benefits from this development will be passed on to the poorest. These assumptions reveal a failure to distinguish between the poorer nations, to treat them all as in need of the same remedy without taking into account the geographical, economic and cultural differences that exist between them and which make different development strategies more or less viable (Stiglitz, 2002: 36). In Fairclough's terms, Truman's speech represents a 'globalist' approach to development.

If Truman's speech is notable for its assumptions regarding the 'aspirations for a better life' of those it purports to help and the self-evident logic of economic growth in meeting these aspirations, the following extract from an influential report by the UN Department of Social and Economic Affairs in 1951 (quoted in Escobar, 1995: 4) is guilty of raising economic growth to the end rather than the means of development, with the aspirations of the poor put on hold as the new world order is established:

> There is a sense in which rapid economic growth is impossible without painful adjustments. Ancient philosophies have to be scrapped; old social institutions have to disintegrate; bonds of cast, creed and race have to burst; and large numbers of persons who cannot keep up with progress have to have their expectations of a comfortable life frustrated. Very few communities are willing to pay the full price of economic progress.

This extract not only demonstrates a reversal in priorities but also sets the tone for future justifications of globalist models in the face of manifest failures, suggesting that it is the unrealistic expectations of the poor and their backward social organizations that are to blame for the failures to make the predicted economic progress (Fairclough, 2006: 42-47; Stiglitz, 2002: 85, 90). Escobar (1995: 40-41) suggests that this reversal of priorities is the result of policy-makers becoming increasingly removed from the material conditions that they originally surveyed and increasingly absorbed with the theoretical and ideological discussions that have come to surround development. In this way development texts, once a second-order representation of concrete realities, become objects of analysis in their own right and, as these texts multiply, their discourse becomes increasingly self-referential and self-enclosed and so ever less accessible to local understanding and participation.

By the late 1980s, however, there were many professional development workers who were dissatisfied with this state of affairs and the entrenchment of policy makers in discourses in which development was inextricably tied to a one-way flow of knowledge and expertise from the rich to the poor, or from the 'uppers' to the 'lowers' in Chambers' (1997: 58) terms. Professionals on the ground became increasingly aware not only of the failures of this version of development to deliver the goods but also of the need to radically alter the foundations upon which it rested, to question from the perspective of those for whom they were working the very 'realities' that sustained the model. In particular these new methods rejected 'Model-T' approaches, 'top-down, centre-outwards' paradigms in which 'the technology is uniform: mass-produced as a standard package, a single variety of tree or crop, a standard practice to be applied everywhere, or a mass-produced piece of hardware' (Chambers, 1997: 67). As a reaction to this standardized approach and in order to understand the complexities of specific contexts better, radical methods of communication were developed that enabled grassroots development workers to gather the knowledge and experience of local communities that offered alternatives to the uniform application of technology and the 'top-down, centre outwards' paradigm.

The idea that it was appropriate for the recipients of aid to contribute to the discourse of development reached as far as the World Bank, who used their own participatory methods to carry out a large scale enquiry into how the poor themselves perceive of 'poverty' and how their lives have been affected by institutional efforts to alter their condition. This project culminated in a series of three books under the general title *Voices of the Poor*. The foreword to the first of these, *Can Anyone Hear Us?* (Narayan *et al.*, 2000), draws on the central metaphor of 'voice' to describe its achievements:

> *Can Anyone Hear Us?* brings together the voices of over 40,000 poor people from 50 countries. The two books that follow, *Crying Out for Change* and *From Many Lands*, pull together new fieldwork conducted in 1999 in 23 countries. The Voices of the Poor project is different from all other large-scale poverty studies. Using participatory and qualitative research methods, the studies present very directly, through poor people's own voices, the realities of their lives. How do poor people view poverty and well-being? What are their problems and priorities?

> What is their experience with the institutions of the state, markets, and civil society? (Clare Short & James Wolfensohn, Foreword to Narayan *et al.*, 2000: ix)

However, while the World Bank may concede that there is more to the world than its philosophy, the 'voices' it transmits are disembodied echoes, orchestrated within a theoretical and methodological framework designed from above. Local voices may well be cited, but the matrix discourses in which they are recontextualized and the higher-level practices that are based upon them remain the construction of the international development elite. And even within the radical participatory approaches described by Chambers, local voices are heard only in response to the impetus provided by outsiders. In effect, both approaches remain in some measure extractive and mediational: it is the international organizations on the one hand and professional development workers on the other who decide what information to elicit and who controls how this is utilized. This might be seen as a case of new wine into old skins, for in neither case have durable mechanisms been created for local communities to maintain sustainable and autonomous discourses that continuously redefine their own reality and determine the appropriate practices for solving their own problems and improving their living conditions (cf. Stiglitz, 2002: xvi, 50). Mindful of such limitations of participatory methods, Chambers (1997: 224) concludes his critique of standardized practice with a call for increased two-way discourse between the 'uppers' and the 'lowers' to 'promote procedures, norms and rewards which permit and encourage more open-ended participation at all levels'.

Others within development are more critical of this mediated conception of *voice*, with the poor themselves remaining structurally dependent on more powerful others and never in a position to forge alliances amongst themselves (Hobley, 2003: 19; Norton *et al.*, 2001: 42). Cornwall (2002: 5) emphasizes the problems of structural inequality in suggesting that even when spaces are created where the marginalized are able to participate, external social structures will continue to influence their ability to contribute their own perspectives within these spaces and 'issues of power and difference may not only undermine the very possibility of equitable, consensual decision making, they may also restrict the possibility of "thinking outside the box", reinforcing hegemonic perspectives and status-quo reinforcing solutions'. For these writers, an analysis of the socio-structural conditions and discourse relations within local communities is seen as a necessary first step in freeing up space for mobilization strategies that create 'an alternative social capital' and 'bring the poor into a direct relationship with the state through the principle of "voice" ... developing a collective identity and solidarity to counter the fragmentation and disunity engendered by their reliance on vertically organized and highly asymmetrical patron-client relationships' (Hobley, 2003: 30). Hobley (2003: 36) identifies three key variables in this process: *space*, as 'politically and socially constructed arenas in which individuals engage in decision-making and express their voice'; *voice* itself, as 'measures ranging from participation of people in decision-making and product delivery to lodging complaints, engaging in organized protest or lobbying [for] better service outcomes'; and *choice*, as 'both the right to exercise voice – (and therefore the obverse right not to) – and the provision of a diversity of channels through which voice can be articulated and responses delivered'.

The first of these variables, space, addresses the need to create a variety of discourse contexts in which different actors come together with their own expertise and authority. However, the effectiveness of such spaces depends on the means of participation that they make possible and the level of genuine choice they offer to local communities, on whether they indeed open up discussion to local voices rather than a minimal level of reactive input. But both these categories, voice and choice, remain under-analysed in the above definitions, which are to some extent little more than a list of desirables rather than a consideration of the workings of *voice* and the means of enabling these as *choice*. In particular, the definition of *voice* above could be criticized for being a vaguely labelled range of speech act universals rather than locally meaningful discourse acts. Such a perspective is likely to result in a reductionist view of participation as a *quantitative* commodity in which popular *voice* is unlikely to mean anything more than a diminished version of established discourse patterns. While increased participation within these parameters might represent 'amplification' (Cornwall, 2002: 8) of local participation within the existing discourse regime, it might well be asked what the limits are in amplifying already distorted voices. A more radical approach would be to enhance *voice* as the *quality* of participation in terms of increasing the range of speech acts open to local participants and broadening the means of performing these, including ways as yet unimagined. This begs the question of how 'choice' and 'rights' correlate in practice. Formally establishing *de jure* rights for local participants to express themselves is likely to be an empty gesture when governmental and international speakers automatically, and often unintentionally, exert *de facto* control over the proceedings through their familiarity with the language and discourse repertoires in which the two sides negotiate and through the inhibiting effect of their social and professional prestige. Establishing alternative negotiating strategies in which participants from local communities are in a position to contribute and to lead with the same amount of authority as national and local government officials and international development workers therefore goes beyond simply bringing relevant parties together and entails both analysing 'the power relations that need to be understood as part of any approach to support participatory governance' (Hobley, 2003: 4) and exploring how such relations are established through language, particularly if this language is not native to the local community.

In the next section I will provide a brief outline of an enhanced conception of *voice* in the work of two key figures in socially oriented linguistics, Dell Hymes and Basil Bernstein, and suggest that intercultural discourse within development can be furthered not through the scrapping of ancient community philosophies, institutions and bonds, as suggested by the UN Department of Social and Economic Affairs, referred to earlier, but rather through the enactment of these social features through the transnational languages of development. Such an approach extends the remit of ELF beyond ensuring mutual comprehension to identifying ways of incorporating the worldviews and social relations of local groups into their transnational discourse practice.

Voice from a Sociolinguistic Perspective

Dell Hymes, one of the principal architects in bringing ethnographic perspectives to bear in sociolinguistic studies, relates Bakhtin's (e.g. 1981: 262) concept of *voice* to language variety in the United States and the potential social exclusion of those who do not have a command of the socially esteemed varieties that are prevalent in educational and civil contexts. For Hymes the immediate tasks for socially concerned linguists at the time were to counter the simplistic view of language variety as merely an unsystematic grouping of deficient versions of the standard language and to replace this with an understanding of language variety as a systematic means of expressing individuality and difference:

> Even if the country remains, so far as the media detect, linguistically simply some sort of mush, those who believe in a society better than we now have should develop a well-grounded critique. What ideal or vision can we entertain in terms of language? Two ingredients of a vision are longstanding. One is a kind of negative freedom, freedom from denial of opportunity due to something linguistic, whether in speaking or reading or writing. One is a kind of positive freedom, freedom for satisfaction in the use of language, for language to be a source of imaginative life and

> satisfying form. In my own mind I would unite the two kinds of freedom in the notion of *voice*: freedom to have one's voice heard, freedom to develop a voice worth hearing. (Hymes, 1996: 64)

Hymes's concept of *voice* therefore goes beyond the emphasis in recent development literature on greater inclusion through the amplification of existing *voice* to stress that inclusion is as much a qualitative as a quantitative notion, that freedom to participate, or choice in Hobley's terms above, is as much a question of the means of participating as it is of the extent. A major basis of Hymes's work on *voice* is the notion of *ethnopoetics* (Hymes, 1996), the exploration of distinctive and consistent underlying structures in the narrative styles of particular subgroups. Much of Hymes's work is focused on storytelling and other forms of artistic production, but his approach has recently been applied to other genres such as asylum applications and education (Blommaert, 2008). The analytical framework I illustrate below shares the same concern in describing narrative as locally specific practice as Hymes's ethnopoetics and highlights many of the same features, but draws on a wider range of linguistic variables using the descriptive categories developed within Systemic Functional Linguistics (SFL) as a means of analysing language as a social phenomenon (Halliday, 1978; Halliday & Hasan, 1985).

SFL has a long history of work on *voice* drawing on the work of British sociologist Basil Bernstein. Roughly contemporaneous with Hymes's work on *voice* and subcultures in the United States, Bernstein's work focused on the linguistic bases of academic underachievement from working class children as a result of differences between their everyday means of communication and the generic conventions and expectations of the dominant sectors of society. Bernstein, like Hymes, uses the term *voice* to discuss the relationship between the right to be heard and the use of non-standard linguistic styles in realizing this right. Bernstein's framework and terminology are a little different from Hymes's, though the similarities are clear. Bernstein (2000: 206) describes *voice* as 'something like a cultural larynx which sets the limits on what can be legitimately put together'. By this he means that different cultures or social groups recognize discrete categories of knowledge, the contents of which are established and maintained by those at the top of the social hierarchy. This definition corresponds to Escobar's description, above, of dominant perspectives on development as hermetically sealed and self-contained discourses that are passed from 'uppers' to 'lowers'. The bounds of these categories are controlled in real time through the linguistic actions of individuals, either those in control, such as teachers, who regulate the flow of discourse, or those who automatically adhere to these regulations. Bernstein refers to these individual linguistic acts as *messages* (Bernstein,

2000: 12). However, there is a constant tension between the dominant *voice* and individual *messages* that allows alternative worldviews and power relationships to be smuggled into the dominant discourses a sentence at a time. And while each individual *message* does not represent a significant threat to the dominant *voice* and can be accommodated within it, Bernstein's framework suggests that the dominant *voice* can gradually be recalibrated through an increase in the number of non-standard *messages* introduced. In the following analysis I will draw on data from development discourse to show how such subversive *messages* can correspond to those same 'ancient philosophies' that, according to the 1951 pronouncement of the UN Department of Social and Economic Affairs, above, 'have to be scrapped', the 'old social institutions [which] have to disintegrate' and the 'bonds of cast, creed and race [which] have to burst'. I will then argue that, as a result of their successful recontextualization within the dominant development genre, these philosophies and bonds are 'legitimated' and provide the basis for an alternative, and effective, local *voice* to emerge through the medium of an *appropriated* English as a lingua franca.

Recalibrating Dominant *Voice* on the North Rupununi Savannahs of Guyana

The following texts come from development discourse between the local indigenous populations of the North Rupununi Savannahs of Guyana and an international development organization, the Iwokrama International Centre for Rainforest Conservation and Development (generally referred to as Iwokrama, though this is in fact the name of the rainforest in which they operate). As a means of facilitating broad-based community participation, progressively minded social scientists within Iwokrama worked with local community leaders to establish the North Rupununi District Development Board (NRDDB), which fostered outreach amongst the 13 dispersed villages of the North Rupununi and brought community members together every second month to meet with representatives from Iwokrama, other international organizations and the Government of Guyana. Although English is the second language of the majority of local participants, NRDDB meetings are conducted almost exclusively through English.

In this section I will analyse extracts from two contributions at an NRDDB meeting (4 November 2000). The first is from Sarah, a social scientist with Iwokrama, a position that affords her the prestige, or cultural capital (Bourdieu, 1991), associated with modern technical knowledge. The second is from Uncle Henry,[2] a local elder who worked extensively with Iwokrama and was one of the founders of the NRDDB and who thus had considerable prestige based on both local authority and outside knowledge. In this analysis I will demonstrate how Uncle Henry, a skilled orator, was able to draw on his hybrid prestige to *re-present* Sarah's account of Iwokrama plans to demarcate an area of the rainforest as a Sustainable Utilization Area (SUA). I will argue that the discursive means by which Uncle Henry achieved this not only represent a reframing of the dominant discourse through *messages* that encapsulate local *voice*, but that this real-time process goes some way in recalibrating the discourse of development locally.[3]

In presenting features of Uncle Henry's contribution I shall follow SFL practice in recognizing three distinct areas of meaning in discourse: the experiential, concerned with representations of real or imaginary worlds; the interpersonal, concerned with representing the speakers' stance towards the subject matter and their interlocutors; and the textual, concerned with the cohesive and rhetorical organization of texts (Halliday & Hasan, 1985). I shall contrast features of Sarah's and Uncle Henry's contributions within these three areas of meaning individually before discussing how they can be seen holistically as expressions of the contrasting *voices* of the two communities.

Starting with the representation of events and states of affairs, Sarah frames the SUA as a series of semiotic activities, such as meetings and discussions, and highlights the business potential of the scheme:

> So, the idea was, what they thought they could do was bring together communities, these government representatives, Iwokrama, to sit down and think about what would be the best way to plan the area, to plan the businesses that they would develop in the area, the management of the land in terms of SUA. The thinking behind it is that these people would meet quarterly, that's (xxxx)[4] the couple of months in between, and what they would do is sit down and talk about how the process is going and they could share what are their concerns and what they think should happen. So from the community perspective the idea was that the NRDDB representatives would be able to bring to the meeting what they think are important for their villages. Because, remember, the SUA is really Iwokrama developing businesses in the preserve. And those businesses are going to operating, it's – one possible business is logging; a second is ecotourism; a third is harvesting things like nibbi and cassava, for selling, they call it non-timber forest products.

Uncle Henry, in contrast, frames the concept of sustainable utilization in terms of the existing relationship between the indigenous communities and the forest, illustrating this connection through references to familiar objects and everyday events and contrasting the expertise of the local community as those who are closest to the forest to the abstract theoretical knowledge of outsiders:

> Now the meeting we attended with this group of all the representatives of various organizations: We sat down there to discuss relatively commonplace intuitions, but we discussed the Sustainable Utilization Area, in that the Wilderness Preserve is another area, that is where the zoning is important. Had they not that place zoned to identify the Sustainable Utilization Area, here is where you all knowledge – all of us knowledge comes into play. Because we are the people who are familiar with that forest, we are people closest to the forest, more than anybody else who live outside, because it's a way of life that's part of it, and we are the ones to give an advice. And we should state it in that vein. Because whenever you're down, whoever comes from there will return, we remain here. And whatever is built or constructed, whatever it is, we will remain. Of course some of it (has been lost). But then we're working to defend (xx) all of us, (xx) worry.
>
> Now, the Sustainable Utilization Area means the area which you can use natural resources (be) there. In the sustainable use you keep it … not going down. But if possible you keep it increasing so that those things, whatever it may be, whether it be (x), medicinal plants, frogs, centipedes, snakes, fishes, baboon, or what-you-call-it, there's nothing in there and you must not be (xxxxxx), so that our generation have just a few years to keep it. You take out, but then you must stop, to have that recycling going on, so that the interaction of the resources going on.

Analysing the two speakers' contributions for interpersonal features we see how Sarah switches between distancing herself from the decision makers in Iwokrama, referring to them in the third person in the above extract, and aligning herself with them as 'we' in the following example, where she expresses criticism of the local communities as 'you' (though this is softened by its possibly generic meaning here):

> … even though NRDDB would be meeting, it was big meetings, a lot of issues come up, and it's four days, and you never finish the discussions, so a lot of things leave hanging, and if we could have a meeting in between, just with the communities so we are clear about what it is you expect, and we are clear, there's a clear sense of what the communities want Iwokrama to do, and a clear sense from Iwokrama of what we are capable of doing.

Towards the end of her contribution Sarah uses negative politeness strategies (Brown & Levinson, 1987) such as 'we would like NRDDB to think about'; the expression of requests indirectly through conditional clauses; and the repeated use of distal 'could'. These features all serve to recall that Iwokrama workers are guests within the local community and that ultimately the local communities have a power of veto over any proposed Iwokrama activity. Through the interplay of these various features the interpersonal relationship constructed by Sarah in her contribution is appropriate to Iwokrama and the local communities as coworkers, but with each side possessing latent powers in the wings: the scientific knowledge and institutional structure of Iwokrama on the one hand and Uncle Henry's sanctioning of local community involvement on the other.

In Uncle Henry's contribution the emphasis on local expertise links into to his own authority as a community elder, and we see this enacted in several ways through the use of interpersonal features of language that would not be appropriate for professional experts. For example, Uncle Henry uses direct commands such as 'don't blame the snakes where you can't go (x) in the savannah', and, in the extract above, the strong personal modal 'must' to express obligation (twice) and the median personal modal 'should' for what he is entitled as a community elder to frame as appropriate behaviour. Uncle Henry also indexes his hybrid prestige as a local elder with outside expertise through his shifting personal stance, at times identifying with the community, addressing them as 'we', at times distancing himself from them, addressing them as 'you', as shown in the marked contrast between the two paragraphs of his contribution above. It is of particular interest with regards to Uncle Henry's dual status that he distances himself from the community when he refers to current bad practice, as in his later warning:

> Which means if you go and take all that natural resource you have there, you're going to be (depleting established connexion)

Uncle Henry markedly finishes his contribution with a declaration of his own unique status, a contradiction of the Iwokrama scientists' assessment of local wildlife patterns framed as a contrast between outside experts as 'they' and Uncle Henry's personal authority through 'to my mind' and the externalized thoughts of the first person 'I':

> Now they have a good idea, but I'm still a bit sceptical about certain areas I notice that are for sustainable – I look at the map, 'Oh oh of course it just ends there', and you have a wilderness reserve and you have a sustainable portion (xxxxxxx) – To my mind (xxxx after xx x)

> population, because this wildlife preserve (xx), as soon as applications start here, (we're started ... xx). And once they adapt, there are migration and migratory routes which they will take and they will find themselves right up in Pakaraimas for the next year. So these are things still to be discussed because there is not – I don't think that that is already confirmed where (x), those are just tentative demarcation.

Differences between the two speakers are also apparent in the textual organization of their contributions. Textual, or rhetorical, organization, by its very nature, can only be illustrated through an analysis of large stretches of text and, given constraints on space, I shall limit myself to a few comments on two key features here. Drawing on the descriptive techniques of Hasan and Cloran (described in Cloran, 2000) we can consider the extent to which discourse is either anchored in time and space to the immediate context of production, through the use of the present progressive and reference to copresent people and things, for example, or is 'decontextualized', through the use of such features as the 'timeless' present, hypothetical modality and reference to distant or generalized people and things. Stretches of discourse that are consistent in this regard are referred to as 'rhetorical units' and are provided with descriptive labels such as 'Commentaries', 'Reflections', 'Recounts' and 'Generalizations' (moving from most immediate to most decontextualized). In this regard, Uncle Henry develops his theme through Reflections on shared community life and the use of concrete examples of life close to the forest. Sarah, in contrast, tends more towards Recounts of meetings and Generalizations about life close to the forest, and her language can thus be seen to be more remote from the immediate context.

Another textual feature to consider is the development of texts through an analysis of how individual rhetorical units relate to each other. A particularly salient relationship here is that of *embedding*, in which one rhetorical unit is said to be contained within another both structurally and functionally. This is a strategy which is heavily drawn upon by Uncle Henry as he attempts to bring abstract ideas closer to local experience and understanding. The most elaborate example of this is where Uncle Henry begins his contribution, like Sarah, with a Recount of a past SUA meeting, but goes on to bring out its relevance to the local community through a Reflection on community life, a Commentary on the present context and a call for common Action – all highly contextualized rhetorical strategies. Sarah, in contrast, employs very few embeddings, and those she does use generally serve to theorize the SUA process through the use of largely decontextualized Plans, Recounts and Conjectures. Uncle Henry can thus be said to enhance local understanding of the issues involved in the SUA process by creating empathy as well as by aiding comprehension. Equally as importantly, Uncle Henry's use of embedding allows him to mirror Sarah's contribution at a superficial level through the use of similar 'matrix' rhetorical units, thus legitimating his contribution in the institutional context, while subverting the dominant genre through the introduction of alternative *voices* in the embedded recontextualizations.

Having looked at the different ways that the two speakers construct their contributions in terms of experiential, interpersonal and textual meaning, it is important to bear in mind that it is the combination of these three strands of meaning that ultimately expresses a speaker's *voice* as an encapsulation of community values. Thus, in my Guyanese data, Uncle Henry, a local elder with considerable experience and expertise in the field of development, is able to reframe contributions from development workers across a conjunct of these three variables as appropriate to his local position. Through Uncle Henry's skill, Sarah's accounts of development practice that are based on descriptions of organizational principles, that rely on the outside authority of science and the status of development workers, and that are couched rhetorically as relations between abstract categories, are transformed into accounts of local subsistence practice, underwritten by Uncle Henry's authority within the local community, and rhetorically presented in terms of everyday concrete realities, their causes and effects. However, as demonstrated by Uncle Henry's assertion that his personal understanding of local conditions is better than the outside experts', as described above, such reframing potentially goes beyond realizing the dominant discourses in locally relevant terms, for each act of reframing entails smuggling local realities, power relations and rhetorical styles into dominant discourses, re-creating and hence transforming them in the process, and so expanding the potential for future contributions that adhere to local social norms. Over time, the accumulation of such messages is capable of radically altering the terms of the dominant discourse and 'the limits on what can be legitimately put together'. As Bernstein (2000: 15, *emphasis in original*) puts it in relation to pedagogic practice, but in terms that can easily be translated to intercultural information exchange in general:

> The potential of change is built into the model. Although framing carries the message to be produced, there is always pressure to weaken that framing. There is very rarely a pedagogic practice where there is no pressure to weaken the framing because, in this formulation, pedagogic discourse and pedagogic practice construct always an arena, a struggle over the nature of symbolic control. And at some point, the weakening of the framing is going to violate the classification. *So change can come at the level of framing.*

Conclusion

I started this chapter by discussing the links between globalization and the spread of transnational languages to suggest that these phenomena presented both opportunities and dangers to developing communities. Although globalization opens up access to new markets and information, and the use of transnational languages such as English facilitates this process, there is a danger in that the virtual disappearance of political and linguistic borders will benefit the already advantaged at the expense of more marginalized groups. For, just as the existing economic and technical strength of the developed nations provides them with the opportunity to exploit new international markets to their advantage, so there is the danger that their native competence in transnational languages and their associated repertoires will enable them to control situations in which these languages are used. This has led to movements such as ELF, which aims to promote non-standardized English as a shared international language. The majority of research in ELF to date, however, has focused on ensuring mutual comprehension and is yet to explore more radical approaches, which would enable speakers from different cultural backgrounds to offer alternative worldviews, to create alternative interpersonal relations and to draw on alternative rhetorical traditions. This is clearly a goal that falls within the remit of ELF, as made clear in Mauranen's (2009: 3) outline of future directions in ELF-based research:

> English is the lingua franca of an enormous variety of social and cultural contexts, of which only a fraction has been investigated. Looking into new contexts calls for new ways of seeing context and situated language use. Contexts of ELF use typically involve different social formations from the speech communities of traditional analyses, and therefore norms, identities and practices get negotiated on new grounds as well. We need new conceptual and methodological tools for making sense of these often transient, frequently multilingual and always complex social and linguistic configurations that typify ELF-using situations.

In this chapter I have focused on the context of discourse within the field of international development itself as this is an area where local communities are using transnational languages, English in the case of my data, to discuss the effects of globalization on their communities and to offer alternatives to the 'globalist' approach as described by Fairclough. I outlined the history of participation within international development to show a trajectory from top-down prescriptivism to participatory methods and the focus on *voice* within current development thinking. I suggested, however, that the concept of *voice* was underdeveloped within development literature, amounting to a quantitative increase in participation in contexts controlled by the development organizations rather than a qualitative change in participation that enables local communities to take control of these contexts and to offer genuine alternatives to mainstream thinking on development. To enhance the development perspective, I drew on linguistic theories of voice, in particular Bernstein's framework, and supplemented these with SFL's conception of language as combining experiential, interpersonal and textual meaning to suggest a 'new conceptual and methodological tool' that linked these areas of meaning to the worldview and social organization of developing communities. In my analysis I showed how two speakers, one a community elder, the other a professional development worker, employed these linguistic resources differently, each in accordance with their social position, and suggested that through the gradual introduction of alternative *messages* there was a movement in the overall discourse towards a pattern of involvement that placed the community's worldview and social order on equal footing with those of professional development workers. As a result, rather than merely contributing from the sidelines to a discourse framed in the terms of the already advantaged, local participants were able, albeit in small measure, to alter the effects of globalization on their communities. From my analysis, therefore, I hope to have suggested ways in which developing communities can counter the 'globalist' tendencies of both the development process and transnational languages such as English through their appropriation of these languages themselves.

Notes

(1) Stiglitz, it should be noted, was on President Clinton's Council of Economic Advisers from 1993 to 1997, when he moved to the World Bank as Chief Economist and then Senior Vice President until he returned to academia in 2003. He is a forceful proponent of globalization and his critique of the policies of the International Monetary Fund (Stiglitz, 2002) discusses the failings of overly rapid and uniform globalization according to dominant 'western' model. In this respect his critique mirrors the distinctions between 'globalization' and 'globalism' discussed by Fairclough (2006).

(2) 'Uncle' is a general term of respect for elders and often outsiders in Guyana.

(3) Fuller descriptions of the context, analyses of Uncle Henry's and Sarah's contributions and discussion of hybrid discourse within the context of the NRDDB can be found in Bartlett (2012). General information about Iwokrama and the NRDDB can be found at www.iwokrma.org.

(4) In the transcriptions, (xx) represents unintelligible speech and e.g. (depleting) represents a best guess.

References

Bakhtin, M. (1981) *The Dialogic Imagination: Four Essays*. In M. Holquist (ed.) (C. Emerson and M. Holquist, trans.). Austin, TX: University of Texas Press.

Bartlett, T. (2012) *Hybrid Voices and Collaborative Change: Situating Positive Discourse Analysis.* London and New York: Routledge.

Bernstein, B. (2000) *Pedagogy, Symbolic Control and Identity: Theory, Research, Critique.* Oxford: Rowman and Littlefield.

Block, D. (2010) Globalization and language teaching. In N. Coupland (ed.) *The Handbook of Language and Globalisation* (pp. 287-304). Oxford: Wiley-Blackwell.

Blommaert, J. (2005) *Discourse: A Critical Introduction.* Cambridge: Cambridge University Press.

Blommaert, J. (2008) Bernstein and poetics revisited: Voice, globalisation and education. *Discourse and Society* 19 (4), 425-452. Bourdieu, P. (1991) *Language and Symbolic Power.* Cambridge: Polity.

Bourdieu, P and Wacquant, L. (1996) *An Invitation to Reflexive Sociology.* Cambridge: Polity.

Brown, P. and Levinson, S.C. (1987) *Politeness: Some Universals in Language Usage.* Cambridge: Cambridge University Press.

Chambers, R. (1997) *Whose Reality Counts? Putting the First Last.* Southampton: ITDG Publishing.

Cloran, C. (2000) Socio-semantic variation: Different wordings, different meanings. In L. Unsworth (ed.) *Researching Language in Schools and Communities: Functional Linguistic Perspectives* (pp. 152-183). London: Cassell.

Cornwall, A. (2002) *Making Spaces, Changing Places: Situating Participation in Development.* IDS Working Paper 170. Brighton: Institute of Development Studies.

Escobar, A. (1995) *Encountering Development: The Making and Unmaking of the Third World.* Princeton, NJ: Princeton University Press.

Fairclough, N. (2006) *Language and Globalization*. Abingdon: Routledge.

Halliday, M.A.K. (1978) *Language as Social Semiotic.* London: Arnold.

Halliday, M.A.K. and Hasan, R. (1985) *Language, Context and Text: A Social Semiotic Perspective.* Geelong, Victoria: Deakin University Press.

Held, D., McGrew, A., Glodblatt, D. and Perraton, J. (1999) *Global Transformation: Politics, Economics and Culture.* Cambridge: Polity Press.

Hobley, M. (2003) *Power, Voice and Creating Space: Analysis of Local-level Power Relations.* Paper prepared for DFID Bangladesh, Dhaka.

Hülmbauer, C., Böhringer, H. and Seidlhofer, B. (2008) Introducing English as a lingua franca: Precursor and partner in intercultural communication. *Synergies Europe* 3, 25-36.

Hymes, D. (1996) *Ethnography, Linguistics, Narrative Inequality: Towards an Understanding of Voice.* London: Taylor and Francis.

Mauranen, A. (2009) Introduction. In A. Mauranen and E. Ranta (eds) *English as a Lingua Franca: Studies and Findings.* Newcastle-upon-Tyne: Cambridge Scholars Publishing.

Narayan, D., Patel, R., Schafft, K., Rademacher, A. and Koch-Schulte, S. (2000) *Voices of the Poor: Can Anyone Hear Us?* New York: Oxford University Press.

Norton, A., Bird, B., Brock, K., Kakande, M. and Turk, C. (2001) *A Rough Guide to PPAs. Participatory Poverty Assessment: An Introduction to Theory and Practice.* London: Overseas Development Institute.

Robertson, R. (1995) Glocalization: Time-space and homogeneity-heterogeneity. In M. Featherstone, S. Lash and R. Robertson (eds) *Global Modernities* (pp. 25-44). London: Sage.

Seidlhofer, B. (2005) English as a lingua franca. *ELT Journal* 59 (4), 339-341.

Stiglitz, J. (2002) *Globalization and Its Discontents.* London: Penguin.

8 Digital Literacy, HIV/AIDS Information and English Language Learners in Uganda

Bonny Norton, Shelley Jones and Daniel Ahimbisibwe

> *After lunch we discussed what girls have learnt from each other's presentations. Girls responded positively that indeed it was very interesting and educating to each other, not only to get knowledge and understand about AIDS/HIV but also to learn a computer how it works, internet, how it works, getting information from internet and getting an opportunity to present their findings ... Unbelievable.*

> *Since now they have accessed the information they wanted to know, Henrietta said that now they have joined the group of knowledgeable people around the world.*

The excerpts above are drawn from the journal reflections of Daniel Ahimbisibwe, written in September 2006, during a digital literacy course he was teaching to a group of young women in rural Uganda. It captures the excitement the young women experienced at having the opportunity to learn how computers work, and, in particular, how to access valuable HIV/AIDS information on the internet. The course was part of an action research study undertaken by Bonny Norton, Shelley Jones and Ahimbisibwe, with the following two research questions: 'To what extent is digital literacy productive for accessing HIV/AIDS information in Ugandan communities?' and 'What facilitates the development of digital literacy?' In this chapter, we discuss the study and its findings, focusing on the impact of digital literacy on the identities of the participants, who were all English language learners.

Introduction

As many scholars now acknowledge, the 'digital divide' is no longer primarily concerned with the infrastructure of ICTs (information and communication technologies); it is centrally focused on the urgent need to build human capacity in poorly resourced global communities (Hawkins, 2002; Mitchell & Sokoya, 2007; Mwesige, 2004; Snyder & Prinsloo, 2007; Warschauer, 2003). The building of human capacity can best be achieved through providing access to ICTs, developing ICT skills and abilities, and improving proficiency in the languages of ICTs, the most dominant of which is English. The young women in our study faced challenges in each of these areas. The rural context in which they lived and their limited access to financial resources constrained their access to ICTs, which, in turn, inhibited their ability to develop ICT-based skills and knowledge. Further, although English was the medium of instruction in their upper primary and secondary schools, their access to English outside the school was very limited. In many ways, the challenges faced by these young women in terms of ICT access, skills and language proficiency are reflected in Mwesige's (2004: 95) statement below:

> Internet cafes are by and large a reserve of the haves of Ugandan society. Not only do these users have the disposable income required to have access, they also have the requisite requirement of language, for English remains the language of the Internet.

With regard to access to health information in particular, research is demonstrating how young women in Uganda, as in many parts of Africa, face numerous socio-economic, cultural and educational challenges that negatively impact their ability to access the information they require to make informed choices about sexual health and healthy sexual relationships (Jones, 2008; Jones & Norton, 2007; Norton & Mutonyi, 2007). With the acknowledged potential for ICTs to support capacity-building among girls and women in poorly resourced communities (Bakesha *et al.*, 2009; Hafkin & Taggart, 2001; Ochieng, 2000), the purpose of this study was to investigate how the development of digital literacy supports young, rural, Ugandan women's access to sexual health information.

Collections such as Thioune's (2003) argue that the internet can only become a tool for social development if it is applied in a way that addresses the quality of life of individuals and their hopes for the future. In addressing the daily realities and aspirations of the young women in our study, our particular focus was the way in which digital literacy and training in English dovetailed to provide the participants with access to sexual health information on the internet. Most health information available globally is in the English language, and English is an additional language for Ugandans. English is also an official language in the country, as it is in most countries in Sub-Saharan Africa, and command of the English language is important for educational and professional success. Therefore, teaching the digital literacy course in English was important for capacity-building. All of the participants had Luganda as a mother tongue, but Luganda is used primarily in oral contexts, and has few textual resources.

In this chapter, we demonstrate how the participants developed digital skills, enhanced their knowledge about HIV/AIDS and negotiated the English language in ways that resonated powerfully with their lives. As Huyer and Sikoska's (2003: 33) note, 'ICT projects should tackle capacity-building issues and themes with application to women's daily lives'. We make the argument that digital literacy can provide girls and women in poorly resourced communities with much-needed opportunities to develop greater human agency with respect to health, in general, and HIV/AIDS, in particular.

Background to the Study

The study, which took place in 2006, involved a group of Ugandan secondary school girls of approximately 17 years of age who attended Kyato Secondary School (KSS),[1] located in a village in southwestern Uganda. The study was supported by a grant from the British Columbia association of Teachers of English as an Additional Language (BCTEAL), in Canada. While the primary purpose of the BCTEAL grant was to develop materials to 'integrate knowledge about AIDS with English literacy instruction', we also drew on funds from a federal grant (Social Sciences and Humanities Research Council of Canada) to investigate whether digital access to HIV/AIDS information for English language learners in Kyato might be a particularly powerful means to access HIV/AIDS information. The action research study included development of materials for a digital literacy course taught in English by Ahimbisibwe; the development and analysis of two participant questionnaires, administered, respectively, before and after the course; and analysis of observations written by both Ahimbisibwe as course instructor, and participants as learners.

Literature Review

A review of the literature relevant to our study places the research in a wider educational context, and is drawn from work in two distinct areas: (1) research on 'the new literacies'; and (2) research on applied linguistics and HIV/AIDS.

New literacies

Research on new literacies that is relevant to our project is associated with the work of Barton and Hamilton (1998), Hornberger (2003),

Martin-Jones and Jones (2000), Prinsloo and Baynham (2008), and Street (2001). These researchers take the position that literacy practices cannot be isolated from other social practices, and that literacy must be understood with reference to larger historical, social and economic processes. Thus, while earlier psychological perspectives conceived of reading and writing as the acquisition of particular behaviours and cognitive strategies, more recent insights from ethnography, cultural studies and critical theory have led to the recognition that literacy is not only a skill to be learned but also a practice that is socially constructed and locally negotiated.

Associated with new literacies is the increasing research on digital literacy, multiliteracy and multimodality (see Coiro *et al.*, 2008). The central tenet of this research is that developments in ICT profoundly affect literacy practices across different sites of learning, and that a 'text' is not only printed material, but includes visual, oral and multimodal products. The complex ways in which schools, families and communities engage in digital literacy practices have become an important site for literacy research and theory, and provide significant insights into the ways in which people learn, teach, negotiate and access literacy both inside and outside school settings. However, as many scholars note (Andema *et al.*, 2010; Mutonyi & Norton, 2007; Snyder & Prinsloo, 2007; Warschauer, 2003), much of the research in this area has focused on wealthier regions of the world, and there is a great need for research in poorly resourced communities to impact global debates on digital literacy.

Applied linguistics and HIV/AIDS

In the literature on applied linguistics and HIV/AIDS, Higgins and Norton (2010) note that while HIV/AIDS has been an object of study for sociolinguists and discourse analysts for approximately two decades, most of this research has examined contexts relevant to gay men in resource-rich nations. The bulk of this research has focused on stigma, risk and sexual identification in face-to-face interactions (cf. Jones & Candlin, 2003). The use of conversation analysis, for example, has provided insight into the ways in which HIV/AIDS counselling is interactionally constructed (Maynard, 2003; Silverman, 1997), while Jones (2002) has examined how speakers frame their activities when handing out informative pamphlets to men they identify as gay in Hong Kong's city parks.

Applied linguistics research on HIV/AIDS in resource-poor contexts is a much more recent development. In a review of sociolinguistic research in public health domains in Sub-Saharan Africa, Djité (2008: 94) concluded that there is a 'relative dearth of sociolinguistic studies in the area of health' despite the millions of people who are infected across this continent. While studies are still relatively few in number, applied linguists have begun to turn their attention to HIV/AIDS in these contexts, focusing specifically on the creation of knowledge as it is constructed in language and multimodal semiotic systems (e.g. Kendrick *et al.*, 2006; Mitchell, 2006; Norton & Mutonyi, 2010). These studies reveal the presence of differing worldviews and perspectives at the levels of institutional structures and in the form of cultural practices. Such research is seen to be important for funding agencies in diverse development contexts, which have increasingly acknowledged the importance of understanding local contexts and cultures in order to make progress in culturally appropriate ways (Craddock, 2004; Farmer, 1994).

In the collection of articles in Higgins and Norton (2010), it is made clear that research on HIV/AIDS in any geographic setting must take into account the role of context in the production of knowledge. This is particularly important in resource-poor areas, where educational efforts are often compromised by the limited availability of resources, unequal gender relations and cultural belief systems that differ from Western, biomedical perspectives. In this spirit, we turn next to the research context in which our study took place.

The Research Context

Uganda, where our research study took place, is one of the poorest countries in the world, ranked 145 out of 177 countries on the Human Development Index. It is also one of the countries that had been hit the hardest by the HIV/AIDS epidemic. In Africa, HIV/AIDS transmission occurs predominantly through heterosexual contact (Malinga, 2001), and almost 50% of the HIV/AIDS-infected population is youth. Although the male:female ratio of HIV infection among adults is 1:1, it is 1:4 among adolescents, and some research indicates that girls in the 15-19 year age range are up to six times more likely to contract HIV than boys in their age cohort (Malinga, 2001; Mirembe & Davies, 2001). In addition to physiological factors, the reasons for the acute differential in HIV/AIDS infection rates between young men and women are related to significant sociocultural and economic factors. Young women from poor, rural backgrounds, such as the participants in this study, are particularly at risk as transactional sex is often the only way they are able to forge a better future for themselves by, for example, using money earned through sexual relationships to pay school-related expenses (Jones & Norton, 2007).

In Kyato village, which borders a trading centre that is approximately seven miles from the nearest town centre, Ganda, poverty is endemic and acute. There is no running water, and the limited electricity available comes from solar power available publicly only at Kyato Community Library. Most of the participants' families survive by subsistence-level farming, with small incomes derived primarily from men's employment as labourers, tailors or taxi drivers. Women can sometimes earn a very small income through the sale of crafts such as mats and baskets, or the sale of extra food grown in family gardens. The official per capita income is less than $1 US per day. Malnutrition, disease and poor living conditions are widespread. Every participant in this study had been affected in some way by HIV/AIDS: each had lost friends, siblings, relatives and even parents to the disease. HIV/AIDS was never far from their thoughts, and it constituted a perpetual source of anxiety and fear.

Despite the widely acknowledged sex-related dangers young women in Uganda face, they receive minimal sexual health education in school. It is included in subjects like biology, Christian religious education and health education, but there is no comprehensive sex education component of the curriculum (Jones & Norton, 2007), nor are there many other possibilities for youth to access the sexual health services, information and resources they need. Studies have shown health clinics to be generally lacking in outreach, and unfriendly towards youth. Based on the emerging and promising potential of technology to connect learners to global databases (Warschauer, 2003; Wasserman, 2002), we sought to link HIV/AIDS education and digital literacy in our action research. We were also aware that our learners have a mother tongue other than English, and so promoting access to the digital world would not only provide extensive access to HIV/AIDS information, but, given the predominance of English on global health websites, enhanced opportunities for English language learning.

The Study

In order for the participants to access health websites at the closest internet café in Ganda, they needed a comprehensive introduction to computers and digital technology, as well as hands-on practice. Jones, who had worked closely with the participants on a daily basis for one year (2004-2005) for her PhD research, developed the digital literacy course, which took into account the fact that the participants had had very little experience with computers or the internet. The course was comprised of an intensive six-session, 46-hour curriculum that took place from August to September 2006. The instruction took place in both the Kyato community library, where a computer and solar power were available, as well as the internet café in Ganda, which was about a 45-minute walk from Kyato village. In order to address our two research questions, we developed two questionnaires, which we refer to as Q1 and Q2, respectively. These questionnaires were written in English, because English is the language of instruction in schools, and the print most familiar to the participants. English is also used for ICT-related terminology. In Q1, administered before the course, we asked the participants their expectations of the course, their interest in computer literacy, what they knew of the internet and the extent of their interest in health information and HIV/AIDS in particular. Q2, administered at the end of the course, included the following areas: What participants had learnt from the course; what benefits technology and the internet might have for the future; what health information they had acquired; and what information about HIV/AIDS they might still like to get. Ahimbisibwe, the course instructor, also kept a detailed journal during the course, and adapted the course to suit the needs of the learners.

Findings

Questionnaire 1

In Q1, we learnt that 10 of the 12 participants had never used a computer before. Of the two who had, one had used it 6-10 times in the past year, in the Kampala district; the other had used it about once a month in the Kyato community library. The computers had been used for such activities as writing letters and essays. All participants indicated that they would like to use a computer more often. With regard to the internet, although 11 had heard of it, four had little knowledge of exactly what it was. As Sofia noted, 'I have heard about the word internet but I don't know its meaning'. There were five, however, who understood that the internet was associated with access to information, as exemplified by Sofia's comment, 'I know that internet is a world wide web where you can get information from different countries'. The remaining two participants focused on the communication possibilities of the internet, as Henrietta noted, 'The word internet means the world wide web. This means people can communicate through computers'. Not one participant had used the internet over the past year, but all of them indicated that they would like to use the internet more often. Most indicated that instruction and practice was necessary to enable them to use the internet. As Doreen noted, 'I will need training because I don't know how to use it', while Shakila wrote, '1st teach me about the internet and provide as many as possible so that we use them frequently'.

When asked, 'What health information, if any, would you like to get from the Internet?' 11 of the 12 participants indicated that they would like to get information about HIV/AIDS. Participants were interested in a range of issues, including the causes of AIDS; how to reduce AIDS; how to help people live longer; how to treat people with AIDS; and how to prevent AIDS. Henrietta, in particular, focused on the impact of AIDS on youth: 'I want to know more about HIV/AIDS because it is the killer of the youth and we don't know more about it'. The one participant who did not mention AIDS, Sofia, expressed an interest in the brain and heart, 'The health information I like is to know about the brain of human beings because some are thinking more and others less and also on heart diseases'.

When asked what other information (apart from health) the participants would like to get from the internet, there was a wide range of responses. Shakila noted, for example, that she wanted 'Information concerning with problems of girls and jobs of women in all the world'; Caroline noted that she wanted 'information about different kinds of people from different countries'; Tracy wanted knowledge about 'female bodies, how do they look like'; and Henrietta wanted 'to know more about English'. In response to the question about their 'main interest' in learning more about the internet, Sofia added the following new information, 'I want to know everything which can help my life now and in the future'. The desire to connect with Canadian people was also mentioned as a desirable outcome of internet access. As Henrietta noted, 'I will learn more about myself from sharing view with Canadian people'; and Jenenie noted as follows, 'My main interest in learning more about the internet is that I want to make friends outside my country like in Canada'.

With reference to course expectations, six participants hoped that the course would increase their employability. Gelly wanted more job opportunities; Penina wanted to be an entrepreneur; Tracy, a doctor; Gloria, a dressmaker; Sofia, a business person; and Jenenie, the head teacher of a secondary school. The remaining participants wished to learn more about computers, and how to use them for communication, entertainment and access to information. In response to the question, 'How do you think you could benefit from learning to use the computer?' Henrietta and Jenenie added the following additional information. Henrietta noted that 'I will understand more about English language', while Jenenie noted that she would become 'mentally modernized'.

The digital literacy course

The data from the digital literacy course was also very revealing. The first session of the course, which took place on Sunday, 20 August 2006, in the Kyato community library, introduced the participants to the objectives of the course, and the research study more broadly. The 12 participants also signed consent forms and completed Questionnaire 1. In his journal, Ahimbisibwe notes, 'I could tell from the faces of the girls that they were interested', and he comments that questions from the participants were 'endless'. Such pressing questions included: 'What is a computer? How does it work?' The second session provided an introduction to computers and other technological equipment such as printers, digital cameras and digital recorders. The participants were also introduced to internet vocabulary such as search engine, website, keywords, toolbar and home page. 'They were all enthusiastic to start', writes Ahimbisibwe. After lunch, each participant had 15 minutes on the library computer, and learnt to open a Microsoft program, type a few words, and save a file. 'Each girl was fidgeting to be the first one to sit on computer as it was their first time to use the computer', Ahimbisibwe says. Indeed, he notes, 'it was not enough to some of them. Up to evening they wanted to go on and on'.

In preparation for the third session, which focused on the internet, Ahimbisibwe visited the internet café in Ganda and did a Google search on people and places that would be familiar to the participants, including their home village and the names of the researchers. He then photocopied the documents and made copies for each of the participants. During the third session, 'all the girls were so attentive and eager to see what I have for them', notes Ahimbisibwe. The day was a very productive one, in which the participants learnt much about the internet and its potential, and reviewed the materials that Ahimbisibwe had brought.

Session four was the first visit to the Ganda internet café, reached by local taxi, and took place on Sunday, August 27. As noted above, not one of the participants had ever used the internet before. The participants worked in pairs to search for information on HIV/AIDS, and, as Ahimbisibwe notes, 'the girls were very excited by the whole thing. You could hear them exclaiming at whatever they saw on the monitor'. In the discussion that followed, the participants noted that the following were the issues they would like to learn more about: How AIDS spreads and ways of avoiding it; the number who have died of AIDS throughout the world; signs and symptoms of AIDS; the origin of AIDS; the treatment of AIDS; antiretroviral drugs; prevention of mother to child transmission; testing centres. 'The questions were so many', Ahimbisibwe notes.

In the fifth session, which started in the library and continued in the internet café, the participants worked in pairs to search for the information that they had identified as relevant to HIV/AIDS. Ahimbisibwe notes that after the participants had found the particular information they wanted on HIV/AIDS, they 'wanted to look at other interesting things on the internet as it was the chance and they don't know when they will get another one to look at other things'. In the discussion after the visit to the internet café, the participants shared the information they had found, and Ahimbisibwe made the following significant observation, as quoted above: 'Since they have accessed the information they wanted to know, Henrietta said they have joined the group of knowledgeable people around the world'.

It was in the sixth session, held on September 3, that Ahimbisibwe commented on the 'unbelievable' events in the classroom, as quoted at the beginning of this chapter, and the course ended with a final visit to the internet café, on Wednesday, September 6. Ahimbisibwe notes in his journal how enthusiastic the participants were, because they knew how to use the computer and the internet. The participants had planned ahead, and knew what topics to research. 'Although they still had problems with how to handle the mouse and move the cursor properly, but they knew what they were doing'. Ahimbisibwe adds, however, that issues of broadband became a challenge for the participants. 'Another difficulty they face is some computers are very slow when it comes to the internet so they were complaining that all their time went without actually getting to the website'. After lunch, Ahimbisibwe led a discussion and writing session about what the participants had learnt, and the participants completed the second questionnaire.

Questionnaire 2

While space does not permit a comprehensive review of what each participant had learnt in the digital literacy course, which was the focus of Questionnaire 2, we will provide key data with respect to access to information in general, and access to information about HIV/AIDS in particular. First, it was clear that participants needed to learn how to use a computer before they could access health information on the internet. The comment from Henrietta captures many of the responses to the question, 'What did you learn from this course?'

> I learnt how to use a computer/introduction to the computer. I learnt to access information on the internet. I learnt how people can communicate through internet. I learnt how people get information from the internet. I learnt the methods of preventing HIV/AIDS and all about AIDS.

The participants noted that 'computers make the work easier', that they 'save time', that they are essential for 'accessing information', and that they promote 'communication with other people'. The role of English in internet information was noted by Henrietta, who wrote that she 'had learnt the English language' on the internet, because it is 'arranged properly'. A number also noted that knowing about computers and the internet is important for future employment. As Gelly noted:

> I have learn how to use a computer, how to write the information on the computer and how to search the information on it. It can help me to get job opportunities in my future because now days every job needs to be with an experience to computer such as being an office manager, secretary accountancy and others.

Participants noted that there was still much they would like to learn about computers, such as developing their own websites, uploading photographs and using Skype (or, as Tracy noted, 'learn to talk to somebody while his or her image appears on a screen'). With reference to cultural practices, Doreen noted that 'I would like to learn more about the behaviours of other girls outside Uganda because me as I am I behave the way I behave like a Ugandan girls so what about others?'

With reference to access to health information, and HIV/AIDS more specifically, there was overwhelming consensus that access to the internet had provided crucial and comprehensive information about HIV/AIDS. By way of example, Yudaya noted,

> I have got health information from the internet which concern to the HIV/AIDS. Now I know how to prevent AIDS/HIV and other information about it. AIDS stands for acquired immune deficiency syndrome and what of HIV is human immune deficiency virus.

Gelly noted that she had been surprised to find that the 'highest percentage of people who die AIDS are youth/teenage this is very dangerous because me also I am a teenager'. Shakila, from a slightly different perspective, discussed not only how to protect herself, but how to advise others:

> From the internet I searched different information on some of the health information is about AIDS/HIV from the internet. Now I know how to protect myself from HIV/AIDS, how to know that someone is HIV positive, what to do if I become affected that I rest, I don't work hard, I have to look for treatment that I can get ARVS that stop the cells to multiply. I knew the symptoms of AIDS but I got all these from the internet. Through the use of internet just know I can advise different things to my friends about HIV/AIDS.

In a similar spirit, Sofia noted not only that 'I can be prevented using condom' but that 'I can counsel somebody with AIDS by telling him that being HIV positive it doesn't mean the end of your life'. Gelly noted, in addition, that, 'someone with AIDS may experience the wide range of different diseases and opportunistic infection'.

A number of participants were particularly concerned about the way in which AIDS had affected their own country of Uganda, and noted that they had learnt more about the relationship between AIDS and development. Fortunately, much new and important local information was also learnt on the internet, such as the role of TASO, Uganda's leading AIDS Support Organization, which has 'tried to look after the affected people through rendering services'.

Other health information, particularly relevant to Uganda, was also searched on the internet, including information on malaria and early pregnancies. For example, Sofia noted as follows:

> From the internet I have got some other information like the information about malaria and so I want also to know more about it like how it spread, its symptoms and how it can be prevented because malaria is a very big problem in our area so more information is needed from that.

With regard to early pregnancies, Doreen noted as follows:

> On the internet I searched many health information including AIDS/HIV/STD and other diseases like malaria. Apart from these I searched about girls who become pregnant when they are still at school. I found it and they are very many who become pregnant and some are ending up affected with AIDS so what should we do?

As if in response, Tracy noted as follows:

> It was very important and interest for me to know how to prevent pregnancy when I am still studying like using contraceptives and abstinence from sex. I became happy because some of us don't know how to prevent pregnancies and we do lack some information.

When asked what other information they would like to share with the researchers, many participants expressed their appreciation for the course, as exemplified by Shakila: 'For me I just thank you for your organization because it has been good and beg you to help and organize other courses like that one because we learned many things. So thanks'.

Discussion

In our research project, we sought to determine, with respect to the participants in our study, if digital literacy was productive for accessing information about HIV/AIDS, and the conditions that facilitate the development of digital literacy. At a quantitative level, it is interesting to note that although Q2 was modelled on Q1, and participants were given the same number of pages (4) in which to write their responses, the responses in Q2 were considerably longer and more developed than those in Q1. A computer word count provided an approximation as to the difference between the total length of responses in Q2 as opposed to Q1: There were 6294 words in Q2 and 3260 words in Q1. This suggests that the participants had much to say about the course and their internet searches, and their learning was reflected in the comprehensiveness of their written responses.

Our central finding, then, is that the internet provided multiple opportunities for participants to gain access to information about HIV/AIDS and to use English in meaningful ways. Perhaps more interesting, however, are our findings with respect to our second research question, 'What facilitates the development of digital literacy?' To address this question, we have found research on identity and language learning very helpful, particularly with reference to work on investment, imagined communities and imagined identities. Although these areas are highly related, we will address each in turn, as they represent somewhat different perspectives on the development of digital literacy.

Investment and digital literacy

With regard to investment and digital literacy, Norton (2000, 2012) has argued that if learners 'invest' in learning a language, they do so with the understanding that they will acquire a wider range of symbolic and material resources, which will in turn increase the value of their cultural capital and social power. The construct of investment conceives of the language learner as having a complex identity, changing across time and space, and reproduced in social interaction, both oral and written. It provides for a particular set of questions associated with a learner's commitment to learning the target language. In addition to asking, for example, 'To what extent is the learner motivated to learn this language?' the researcher asks, 'What is the learner's investment in the language practices of this classroom?'

There is abundant evidence to suggest that the participants in this study were highly invested in the language practices of the digital literacy course. In Q2, all the participants noted how much they had learnt in the course, and how interested they were in the diverse aspects of the course. Their appreciation was effusive, with participants like Shakila noting that the course 'has been good and beg you to help and organize other courses like this one because we learned many things'. Ahimbisibwe also noted frequently how excited the participants were. 'I could tell by their faces that the girls were interested', he notes on the 20th August; 'they were all enthusiastic to start' he continues on the 23rd; and on September 3rd, noted that it was 'unbelievable' what progress the participants had made.

Part of the girls' investment in the language practices of the digital literacy course was the opportunity to access the English language in multiple new ways. Some of the participants saw engagement with ICTs as not only a tool through which to communicate, but also as a tool that would help them communicate in English. For example, in response to the question, 'How do you think you could benefit from learning to use the computer?', Henrietta noted that she would 'understand more about English language'.

The three particular areas of interest noted by Ahimbisibwe also provide important clues as to why the participants were highly invested in the language practices of the course: the participants had access to information about HIV/AIDS; they had learnt how computers and the internet work; and they had been given the opportunity to share their learning with their peers in presentation format. Prior to the course, Ahimbisibwe notes, these were all 'very new things which they didn't have hope to access in the near future'.

The research context provided at the beginning of this chapter gives some explanation as to why these language practices were hitherto unavailable to the participants. Information about HIV/AIDS is difficult to access in remote Ugandan communities, and HIV/AIDS is a topic that both parents and teachers tend to avoid. As Norton and Mutonyi (2007) note, HIV/AIDS clubs are one of the few sites in which young people can access information on the disease, and 'Talk what others think you can't talk'. Further, access to computers and other technology is very difficult in rural Uganda, primarily because of the expense involved, and the great inequities between urban and rural areas (Mutonyi & Norton, 2007). In addition, as Jones and Norton (2007) note, young women in particular struggle to fund even the most basic necessities of life, and paying for computers and internet access would be a luxury way beyond the budgets of young rural women. It was interesting to note Ahimbisibwe's observation that after the participants had found the information they wanted on HIV/AIDS, they turned their attention to 'other interesting things on the internet' as they didn't know when they would be given this opportunity again.

The student-centred pedagogy of the course, which included pair and group work, class presentations and regular student–teacher interaction, was also novel for these young women, who were accustomed to large, teacher-fronted classrooms. In Jones's doctoral research, participants had shared with her their experiences of many unsatisfactory classrooms, as evidenced in the following extract (Kendrick *et al.*, 2006: 110):

Shelley: How is learning English through doing a project like this different from learning English in the classroom?
Rose: In class teachers write on the blackboard – and we just listen …
Shelley: In the research project how do you use English?
Rose: Communication.
Shelley: Do you learn more by studying English or by communicating in English?
Rose: Communicating …
Shelley: Why?
Rose: Because when you communicate, you think your own English.

It is clear from the data that the participants in the study were 'thinking [their] own English', and it is this ownership of meaning-making that was central to their investment in digital literacy.

However, the participants' investment in digital literacy extended beyond issue of health, to include ecological, educational and gender issues of particular relevance to development. In response to the Q2 question, 'Is there any other information you would like to share with the researchers?', Penina, for example, commented: 'Thank you for your information but I suggest an idea that next turn let's be on the environment and the animals'. Tracy said: 'Yes! I would like to share information about how the liberation of women has helped in development'. Henrietta stated: 'I want to share the information with researchers about education. Who introduced education, how did he understand that people should get education'. Doreen remarked: 'Of course! There other information which I would like to share with the research. It is about education in both girls and boys, and how we can develop our talents like reading storybooks, singing, etc'. And Caroline responded: 'Yes. The information about rape and defilement, the factors leads to its increase in Uganda and how to overcome it'.

The participants were also invested in digital material on global issues of importance to them. At the time this research was conducted, the Iraq War was into its third year and the participants were very interested to learn more about the war and international figures, such as Saddam Hussein and George W. Bush. Doreen wrote 'On the internet also I got information about many people for example Saddam Hussein whereby I searched his image and I see him with some of his information. I didn't searched Saddam only but also I searched our president Museveni and I managed to see him on the Internet so this was so great for me'. Tracy explained how the internet provided her with information she had not been able to get otherwise, and thus enabled her to extend her representations of the war: 'I searched for Bush George's picture on the internet via Google search, I saw how Bush looks like. More also, I looked for Saddam's picture. It was very interesting because I was just hearing of their names without seeing them'.

Imagined communities and digital literacy

Related to the construct of investment is that of imagined communities and imagined identities (Anderson, 1991; Kanno & Norton, 2003; Norton, 2001; Pavlenko & Norton, 2007). Benedict Anderson (1991: 6), who first coined the term 'imagined communities', argues that what we think of as nations are imagined communities, 'because the members of even the smallest nation will never know most of their fellow-members, meet them, or even hear of them, yet in the minds of each lives the image of their communion'. Thus, in imagining ourselves connected with our fellow human beings across space and time, we can feel a sense of community with people we have not yet met, but perhaps might hope to meet one day. Developing this notion with reference to language education, Norton and colleagues argue that in many language classrooms, learners may be given the opportunity to invest not only in the classroom community, but also in communities of the imagination – a desired community that offers possibilities for an enhanced range of identity options in the future. They argue that such imagined identities can be highly varied, from the imagined community of the more public professional, such as doctors, lawyers and teachers, to that of the more local homemaker or farm worker.

Language learners have different investments in a range of identities, and of particular interest in this study was the extent to which such investments were productive for the development of digital literacy. In spite of the digital divide, and the fact that none of the participants had had any sustained contact with the internet before this study, they quickly embraced the digital as a means through which they could appropriate new identities and engage with a wider range of communities. Tracy, for example, specified her interest in becoming part of a global academic community, as she wanted: 'To talk with people from different countries like to acquire some information from outside universities'. Likewise, Joanne commented: 'I would also like to get discussion with other students in other country. And also I would like to get skills how I can also start my own project in future'. Of great significance, however, is that the participants did not wish to simply become consumers of information; they also wanted to be producers of information. Penina imagined herself contributing knowledge and ideas to others through publication: 'According to me I want to learn it to become one of the most people who can use it and to become publicable'. Sofia expressed a similar idea: 'I would like to share with the researcher in writing academic book or research'. Such global knowledge production is strongly advocated by scholars who wish to ensure that African ideas, knowledge and experience are well represented in the international literature (Andema *et al.*, 2010).

While some the participants expressed their desire to take an active part in global knowledge production, others were primarily interested in expanding their friendship networks outside Uganda. As Jenenie noted, 'My main interest in learning more about the internet is that I want to make friends outside my country like in Canada' while Gelly stated: 'I heard that computers are usually used on the internet so I would like to know how to use it, and how to send messages from outside countries'.

In the process of engaging in digital literacy with respect to imagined communities, gender issues were also central concerns for these young women (cf. Mitchell & Sokoya, 2007). Doreen expressed her interest in learning more about the lives of other girls in the world to expand her understanding of what it means to be a girl beyond the only context she knew – that of rural Uganda. Shakila, similarly, sought to learn about the experiences of girls in different parts of the world by accessing information on the internet, and in particular, what she called 'information concerning with problems of girls'. With a related focus, Tracy wanted to know about 'female bodies, how do they look like', suggesting that she was interested in expanding her understanding of herself as a young woman, as well as her general understanding of the physical body, '.... because I am soon becoming a doctor'.

Imagined identities and digital literacy

Norton (2010: 356) argues that 'an imagined community assumes an imagined identity, and investment in the target language must be understood within this context'. There is much evidence to suggest that the development of digital literacy provided an enhanced range of identity options for the future of these young women, identities that could be considered imagined identities. Particularly profound is the comment by Henrietta, that 'they have joined the group of knowledgeable people around the world'.

In a related comment, Sofia noted that her 'main interest' in learning more about the internet was that it enabled her to 'know everything which can help my life now and in the future'. In similar comments, several participants expressed the desire to engage in activities that would enable them to develop, change, or deepen their understanding about themselves as young women in the larger global context. These comments speak to the need for educational opportunities that cultivate girls' capabilities and empower them to engage more fully in the world (Jones, 2011).

Future employment was a central concern for these young women, most of whom struggled economically. Penina wanted to be an entrepreneur; Tracy wanted to be a doctor; Gloria, a dressmaker; Sofia, a business person; and Jenenie, the head teacher of a secondary school. To realize such imagined identities would be rare for many rural Ugandan women, but the participants hoped that digital literacy would help them achieve their ambitions. Caroline expressed her belief that, given time and experience with ICTs, she would become more confident and better able to interact effectively and meaningfully with people around the world. Similarly, Jenenie imagined herself as 'popular' in a global context: 'My main interest in learning more about the internet is that I want to make friends outside my country like in Canada so that I become popular worldwide through writing letters'.

Using the internet to access information about people and places with whom they had personal connections was of great interest to the participants, as it seemed to bridge the gap between the virtual and the real world, linking their identities (as, for example, students, community members and research participants) with the larger world on the internet. For example, Shakila stated:

> I got information about the location, history of [Kyato] Community Library, I searched information about Shelley her background, what she did in Uganda and Canada particularly. I searched information about Mr [Masinde] the founder of [Kyato Secondary School] and why he established the school the aim, location and the beginning and history of it. I searched the main players of [Kyato] Community Library ... and their history. And where the library started from.

Conclusion

In responding to diversity in language and literacy education, McKinney and Norton (2008) have noted that teachers need to consider not only what is educationally possible, but what is also educationally desirable. In many poorly resourced communities, in Africa and other parts of the world, what is 'possible' may appear bleak and discouraging. Indeed, without resources provided by sponsors, our study would not have been possible. Sustainability therefore remains a major challenge not only in our project, but also in other national projects in Uganda and beyond. However, what is clear from our study is that the hopes and desires of young people in the most rural parts of Africa are no less ambitious than those of young people in Singapore, Seattle or Sydney. The young women in our study wanted access to current and reliable information on health, job opportunities, diverse international communities and the English language. Further, they not only want to be receivers of global information; they want to produce information, make their own websites, Skype with friends and engage actively in global knowledge production.

Our study not only provides convincing evidence that digital literacy is highly productive for accessing information about HIV/AIDS in Ugandan communities but also demonstrates that learners are interested in a wide range of topics, including gender and development. The study also confirms that digital literacy takes place, most effectively, when learners are invested in the language practices of their classrooms and communities, and when they can draw on digital information to develop an enhanced range of identity options for the future. This has important implications for English language learning and teaching. The English language learners in our study were able to imagine and appropriate identities as autonomous learners, informed global citizens and HIV/AIDS counsellors. The challenge for the global community is to collaborate with African partners to ensure that the imagined identities of English language learners are not only pedagogically desirable but also educationally possible.

Acknowledgements

This chapter is a revised version of an article published by the *Canadian Modern Language Review* (see Norton, Jones and Ahimbisibwe, 2011). Copyright permission from the University of Toronto Press is gratefully acknowledged.

We would like to extend our warmest thanks to the young women who took part in our study. We also greatly appreciate funding from BC TEAL (British Columbia Teachers of English as an Additional Language) and the Social Sciences and Humanities Research Council of Canada.

Note

(1) Pseudonyms are used for the names of the school, village and research participants to protect the identities of those who were associated with this study.

References

Andema, S., Kendrick, M. and Norton, B. (2010) ICT, cultural knowledge, and teacher education in Africa. In F. Sudweeks, H. Hrachovec and C. Ess (eds) *Proceedings of the 7th International Conference on Cultural Attitudes Towards Technology and Communication 2010* (pp. 450-457). Murdoch, Australia: Murdoch University.

Anderson, B. (1991) *Imagined Communities: Reflections on the Origin and Spread of Nationalism* (Rev. edn). New York: Verso.

Bakesha, S., Nakafeero, A. and Okello, D. (2009) ICTs as agents of change: A case of grass-roots women entrepreneurs in Uganda. In I. Buskens and A. Webb (eds) *African Women and ICTs: Investigating Technology, Gender, and Empowerment* (pp. 143-153). London: Zed Books.

Barton, D. and Hamilton, M. (1998) *Local Literacies*. New York: Routledge.

Coiro, J., Knobel, M., Lankshear, C. and Leu, D. (2008) *The Handbook of Research on New Literacies*. Mahwah, NJ: Elbaum.

Craddock, S. (2004) Beyond epidemology: Locating AIDS in Africa. In E. Kalipeni, S. Craddock and J. Ghosh (eds) *HIV & AIDS in Africa: Beyond Epidemiology* (pp. 1-10). Malden, MA: Blackwell.

Djité, P.G. (2008) *The Sociolinguistics of Development in Africa*. Clevedon: Multilingual Matters.

Farmer, P. (1994) Aids-talk and the constitution of cultural models. *Social Science and Medicine* 38, 801-809.

Hafkin, N. and Taggart, N. (2001) *Gender, Information Technology, and Developing Countries: An Analytic Study*. Washington, DC: Academy for Educational Development (AED)/ USAID.

Hawkins, R.J. (2002) Ten lessons for ICT and education in the developing world. In G. Kirkman, P.K. Cornelius, J.D. Sachs and K. Schwab (eds) *The Global Information Technology Report 2001-2002: Readiness for the Networked World* (pp. 38-43). Oxford: Oxford University Press.

Higgins, C. and Norton, B. (eds) (2010) *Language and HIV/AIDS*. Bristol: Multilingual Matters.

Hornberger, N. (ed.) (2003) *Continua of Biliteracy*. Clevedon: Multilingual Matters.

Huyer, S. and Sikoska, T. (2003) *Overcoming the Gender Digital Divide: Understanding ICTs and Their Potential for the Empowerment of Women*. INSTRAW Research Paper Series No. 1, April 2003. Washington, DC: United Nations International Research and Training Institute for the Advancement of Women.

Jones, R. (2002) A walk in the park: Frames and positions in AIDS prevention outreach among gay men in China. *Journal of Sociolinguistics* 6, 575-588.

Jones, R. and Candlin, C. (2003) Constructing risk across timescales and trajectories: Gay men's stories of sexual encounters. *Health, Risk & Society* 5, 199-213.

Jones, S. (2008) Secondary school for girls in rural Uganda: Challenges, opportunities and emerging identities. PhD thesis, University of British Columbia.

Jones, S. (2011) Girls' secondary education in Uganda: Assessing policy within the Women's Empowerment Framework. *Gender and Education* 23 (1), 1-29.

Jones, S. and Norton, B. (2007) On the limits of sexual health literacy: Insights from Ugandan schoolgirls. *Journal of Diaspora, Indigenous, and Minority Education* 1 (4), 285-305.

Kanno, Y. and Norton, B. (2003) Imagined communities and educational possibilities. *Journal of Language, Identity, and Education* 2 (4), 241-249.

Kendrick, M., Jones, S., Mutonyi, H. and Norton, B. (2006) Multimodality and English education in Ugandan schools. *English Studies in Africa* 49, 95-114.

Malinga, F. (2001) Uganda: Designing communication and education programs to combat HIV/AIDS. *Association for the Development of Education in Africa Newsletter* 12 (4).

Martin-Jones, M. and Jones, K. (eds) (2000) *Multilingual Literacies*. Amsterdam: John Benjamins.

Maynard, D. (2003) *Bad News, Good News: Conversational Order in Everyday Talk and Clinical Settings*. Chicago, IL: University of Chicago Press.

McKinney, C. and Norton, B. (2008) Identity in language and literacy education. In B. Spolsky and F. Hult (eds) *The Handbook of Educational Linguistics* (pp. 192-205). Malden, MA: Blackwell.

Mirembe, R. and Davies, L. (2001) Is schooling a risk? Gender, power relations, and school culture in Uganda. *Gender and Education* 13, 4, 401-416.

Mitchell, C. (2006) In my life: Youth stories and poems on HIV/AIDS: Towards a new literacy in the age of AIDS. *Changing English* 13, 355-368.

Mitchell, C. and Sokoya, G. (2007) New girl (and new boy) at the internet café: Digital divides/digital futures. In S. Weber and S. Dixon (eds) *Growing Up Online: Young People and Digital Technologies* (pp. 211-225). New York: Palgrave Macmillan.

Mutonyi, H. and Norton, B. (2007) ICT on the margins: Lessons for Ugandan education. *Language and Education* 21 (3), 264-270.

Mwesige, P.G. (2004) Cyber elites: A survey of internet café users in Uganda. *Telematics and Informatics* 21, 83-101.

Norton, B. (2000) *Identity and Language Learning: Gender, Ethnicity and Educational Change*. Harlow: Longman/Pearson Education.

Norton, B. (2001) Non-participation, imagined communities, and the language classroom. In M. Breen (ed.) *Learner Contributions to Language Learning: New Directions in Research* (pp. 159-171). Harlow: Pearson Education.

Norton, B. (2010) Language and identity. In N. Hornberger and S. McKay (eds) *Sociolinguistics and Language Education* (pp. 349-369). Bristol: Multilingual Matters.

Norton, B. (2012) Investment. In P. Robinson (ed.) *Routledge Encyclopedia of Second Language Acquisition* (pp. 22-24). New York: Routledge.

Norton, B. and Mutonyi, H. (2007) Talk what others think you can't talk: HIV/AIDS clubs as peer education in Ugandan schools. *Compare: A Journal of Comparative Education* 37 (4), 479-492.

Norton, B. and Mutonyi, H. (2010) Languaging for life: African students talk back to HIV/AIDS research. *Language Policy* 9 (1), 45-63.

Norton, B., Jones, S. and Ahimbisibwe, D. (2011) Learning about HIV/AIDS in Uganda: Digital resources and language learner identities. *Canadian Modern Language Review* 67 (4), 569-590.

Ochieng, R.O. (2000) *The Empowerment of Women through the Internet: The Africa Women Experience*. Paper presented at the International Telecommunication Union, Geneva.

Pavlenko, A. and Norton, B. (2007) Imagined communities, identity, and English language. In J. Cummins and C. Davison (eds) *International Handbook of English Language Teaching* (pp. 669-680). New York: Springer.

Prinsloo, M. and Baynham, M. (eds) (2008) *Literacies, Global and Local*. Philadelphia, PA: John Benjamins.

Silverman, D. (1997) *Discourses of Counselling*. London: Sage.

Snyder, I. and Prinsloo, M. (eds) (2007) The digital literacy practices of young people in marginal contexts. *Language and Education* 21 (3).

Street, B. (ed.) (2001) *Literacy and Development: Ethnographic Perspectives*. New York: Routledge.

Thioune, R.M. (ed.) (2003) *Information and Communication Technologies for development in Africa: Opportunities and Challenges for Community Development*. Ottawa, Canada: International Development Research Centre.

Warschauer, M. (2003) *Technology and Social Inclusion: Rethinking the Digital Divide*. Cambridge, MA: MIT Press.

Wasserman, H. (2002) Between the local and the global: South African languages and the internet. *African and Asian Studies* 1 (4), 303-321.

9 Language Policy in Singapore: Singlish, National Development and Globalization

Lionel Wee

Introduction

Unlike the other cases of 'developing' nations discussed in this volume, Singapore has long since developed into a First World nation. In fact, Singapore is now aggressively attempting to reinvent itself as a global/cosmopolitan city. Nevertheless, the successful economic development of Singapore provides an interesting case for policy makers in other contexts, not least because of Singapore's successes and missteps in its language policy, particularly in its treatment of the English language. For example, a sociolinguistically natural consequence of the widespread confident adoption of English is the development of a nativized variety, in Singapore's case, Singlish. But the Singapore government has been directing much effort towards trying to discourage, if not eliminate, the use of Singlish. Developing countries are often keen to encourage the use of English as a part of their strategy for socioeconomic development. Like Singapore, many countries, particularly those in Asia and Africa, adopt a pragmatic perspective on English, seeing it as an important tool for accessing valuable scientific and technological knowledge, as well as for developing a viable local workforce that is attractive to foreign investment, especially in the service industries. One important thing to learn from Singapore's experience, then, is to be prepared for sociolinguistically natural outcomes of any policy aimed at encouraging the widespread adoption of English. At the very least, unnecessary official angst over a localized variety should be avoided.

In this chapter I discuss some of the implications for Singapore's language policy given its global/cosmopolitan city aspirations. I focus on the government's positioning of English and, in particular, its negative stance towards Singlish, a colloquial variety of English. I touch on the other languages used in the country only insofar as they have a bearing on the points being discussed in this chapter. This focus on English and Singlish is motivated by the fact that among the four official languages recognized by the language policy, it is these two which are most directly implicated in the context of the development of a global city narrative.

Language Policy in Singapore

Singapore is a linguistically and ethnically diverse country with a population of about 3.2 million (2000 Census of Population). Officially, its racial composition is roughly 76.8% Chinese, 13.9% Malay, 7.9% Indian, while the remaining 1.4%, classified as 'Others', comprise mainly Eurasians and Europeans. Because Singapore has no natural resources of its own, in the 1960s its leaders were convinced that economic survival was possible only if Singapore joined the Federation of Malaysia, and they worked hard to bring that about in 1963. However, just over two years later, Singapore reluctantly gained its independence when it left the Federation in 1965. This departure was due in part to political differences over the issue of whether ethnic Malays ought to be granted special rights. Malaysia preferred a *bumiputra* policy, one that recognized Malay as the sole official language and endowed ethnic Malays with special rights. In contrast, Singapore was uncomfortable with the idea of privileging one particular ethnic group over others.

Singapore's departure from the Federation meant that its leaders were faced, quite suddenly, with the task of building a nation out of an ethnically and linguistically diverse population, and with developing the nation's economy without access to any natural resources. According to Lee Kuan Yew, Singapore's first prime minister:

> (1)
> … the future looked very bleak, but we had to make a living for our people… we succeeded in doing by two basic strategies. First, we made direct links with the industrial countries – Europe, America, Japan – and got their companies, their MNCs [multi-national companies] to invest in Singapore, manufacture and then re-export to the world, primarily to the developed countries. Next, we made Singapore into a First World oasis in a Third World region. In other words, in a Third World region, we created an oasis with First World standards of security, health, efficiency, communications, transportation, education, convenience for all those from the First World to come here and set up their camp, their base, their headquarters… (*NHK Interview*, 18 December 1999, Singapore)

Singapore's language policy is a reflection of these imperatives: the need to ensure parity across the various ethnic groups as a way of maintaining interethnic harmony, and the need to attract foreign direct investment. The former motivated the recognition of three mother tongues. Each of the major ethnic communities was assigned an official mother tongue: Mandarin for the Chinese, Malay for the Malays and Tamil for the Indians.[1] The latter motivated the recognition of English as an official language – though not as a mother tongue because it was, and still is, seen as a language that marks a Western identity. English is deemed necessary, however, both as an interethnic lingua franca and for global economic competitiveness. This makes it particularly vital that English be seen as ethnically neutral, so that any socioeconomic advantages that come with proficiency in the language will not be associated with a specific ethnic community, which might otherwise raise the danger of interethnic tension. The mother tongues, on the other hand, are supposed to ensure that Singaporeans remain rooted to their Asian heritage even as they compete globally. In this way, the policy encourages bilingual proficiency in English and the officially assigned mother tongue.

This language policy has worked well so far, allowing Singapore to move fairly rapidly from being an economically impoverished country to one that is prosperous and modern, and to do so while maintaining smooth relations across the different ethnic groups. However, development is an ongoing process, and in recent years, given the intensity of global competition, Singapore has sought to reinvent itself as a global or cosmopolitan[2] city. Thus, according to Goh Chok Tong, the second prime minister:

> (2)
> Our... strategy to meet future competition is to gather talent and make Singapore a cosmopolitan city... This is how cities like London, New York, Hong Kong and Shanghai (before the War) became successful... Attracting global talent is essential for creating the best for Singaporeans... Singapore must become a cosmopolitan, global city, an open society where people from many lands can feel at home. (1997 National Day Rally speech)

Because cities are mainly associated with the functions of residence, business and entertainment, they do not carry the same connotations of commitment to a national identity. They are thus better able to conceptually accommodate a culturally plural and diverse population. The idea of a global city inherits these properties of a city, but adds to them other properties such as 'importance, modernity and being at the center of world affairs' (Perrons, 2004: 231).

This shift into a global city narrative does not mean that Singapore is abandoning its identity as a nation-state, though it does present interesting challenges, since the global city narrative sits rather uneasily with the country's language policy, which, as we have just seen, was constructed in a different developmental context. From a development perspective, the attempt to reinvent Singapore as a global city represents an economic 'next step', given that the political leaders feel that economic growth and competition is now increasingly taking place at the level of the city rather than the state, and that the strategic focus needs to be on high-end provision of and innovation in the service, technological and financial sectors (Sassen, 2001: xix-xxi, 8-9).

'Good' English and the Anti-Singlish Stance

Singapore's language policy treats English as a purely 'practical' language, one that 'should be taught... without cultural nuance or reference' since it supposedly represents the idea of 'modernity' and its association with progress, science, technology and capitalism (Wee, 2007: 253-254). This pragmatic positioning of English means that the policy has no place for Singlish, a colloquial variety of English that is characterized by, among other features, a lack of inflectional morphology, reduplication, lexical items borrowed from Malay and Chinese and discourse particles, as in the following example.

(3)
He always eat hot-hot curries, then kena stomach ache, hor?

'He always eats very hot curries and then gets a stomach ache, right?'

Its exclusion from policy is because the Singapore government sees Singlish as a threat to the ability of Singaporeans to acquire competence in 'good', that is, standard, English. The latter is prized as a linguistic resource in a world of global economic competition, and the government is concerned that the presence of Singlish will interfere with the learning of the standard variety. That is, the government fears that learners will be unable to distinguish between the two and end up mixing features of Singlish with those of the standard, thus contaminating the grammar of the latter.[3] It is for this reason that Lee Kuan Yew, minister mentor since 2004, has labeled Singlish a 'handicap' (*The Sunday Times*, 15 August 1999).

Expressing a similar position, Goh Chok Tong (then the second prime minister and currently senior minister) made the following argument against Singlish:

> (4)
> We cannot be a first-world economy or go global with Singlish... The fact that we use English gives us a big advantage over our competitors.
>
> If we carry on using Singlish, the logical final outcome is that we, too, will develop our own type of pidgin English, spoken only by 3 [million] Singaporeans, which the rest of the world will find quaint but incomprehensible. We are already half way there. Do we want to go all the way? (Goh, 1999)

Goh had even expressed the hope that in time to come, Singaporeans will no longer speak Singlish:

> (5)
> Singlish is broken, ungrammatical English sprinkled with words and phrases from local dialects and Malay which English speakers outside Singapore have difficulties in understanding... Let me emphasise that my message that we must speak Standard English is targeted primarily at the younger generation... we should ensure that the next generation does not speak Singlish. (*The Straits Times*, 29 August 1999)

However, the government's anti-Singlish stance is problematic because of the following:

(1) Singlish can help create a bond of solidarity amidst a Singaporean disapora. This is an issue that the government itself has been concerned with, as the shift to a global city narrative is intended to make Singapore as attractive as possible to people from all over the world, including Singaporeans who have migrated overseas.
(2) As part of an attempt to counter the outward migration of Singaporeans, the government has attempted to specifically target 'foreign talent'. The hope is that such 'foreign talent' will come to work, live and ultimately even take up citizenship in Singapore. In this regard, Singlish may also be relevant in helping newly arrived citizens integrate into Singapore society.
(3) The government has also come to realize that it is difficult to lay claim to a 'global city' status in the absence of an energetic and creative cultural scene. But where the culture industries are concerned, Singaporean films, for example, cannot be successful overseas if the actors only speak 'proper/good' English. The use of Singlish contributes to a sense of what is authentic about the Singaporean identity and contrary to Goh's assertion (4), it may indeed be possible to 'go global with Singlish'.

Singlish and the Singaporean Diaspora

The government has for some time now had to accept the fact that many Singaporeans are traveling, working abroad and even emigrating.[4] Goh (1997), therefore, speaks of 'Singapore communities in other cities' and appeals to a sense of national loyalty and familial ties that they will (hopefully) feel regardless of where they may be:

> (5)
> In a very mobile world, more Singaporeans will go abroad to work… There are… sizeable Singapore communities in other cities – Sydney, Perth, London, Paris, Tokyo, Beijing, Bangkok, Manila … It is a facet of globalization and regionalization that we need to reflect on and address…
>
> Abiding bonds to family and friends and deep loyalties to Singapore are crucial in this new situation. We must never forget that Singaporeans owe one another an obligation, and the more able ones, in whom Singapore has invested the most, have a special obligation to society. We must all join hands to keep Singapore together.

This is a government discourse that tries to combine the notion of a Singaporean diaspora with continued fidelity to the nation-state. Cultivating a diasporic identity is a useful political strategy for positioning the nation-state to meet the challenges of globalization (Yeoh & Willis, 1997), especially since 'discourses of diaspora' typically presume the existence of a commonality across 'diverse flows of people in different parts of the world' (Ong, 2006: 59). But the government seems reluctant to recognize that Singlish might prove helpful to this strategy, even though it is clear that for at least some Singaporeans working abroad, the opportunity to use Singlish constitutes one important way in which they can feel Singaporean. For example, in her observation of Singaporeans working in Beijing, Kong (1999: 579) points out that among their 'ways of recreating Singapore in everyday life' is 'the opportunity to lapse into the use of Singlish, thus reducing the social distance and re-establishing connectivities'. This use of Singlish to neutralize social gaps is in fact one of the reasons put forward by Singlish supporters for claiming that it warrants a legitimate cultural space in Singapore's linguistic landscape (Goh & Woo, 2009: xiii).

And ironically, as Wee (2010) observes, the government itself has used Singlish in a diaspora context such as Singapore Day. Singapore Day is a largely annual event (there was no Singapore Day in 2010) organized by the government and held in different parts of the world. It is aimed at getting Singaporeans who are living or working overseas to come together, and the goal is to help them maintain a sense of connection with their home country. In April 2009, a Singapore Day was held in London and according to a news article,[5] the event made occasional use of Singlish, such as the lexical item *chope,* which is used to indicate the reservation of a seat. The same article also begins with a tongue-in-cheek observation that the Singlish discourse particles *lah* and *lor* were being bandied about as Singaporeans prepared to gather for the event:

> (6)
> Britain's busiest train station reverberated with lots of *lahs* and *lors* yesterday morning.

An event like Singapore Day thus helps prove the point of Singlish supporters, since Singlish is being used in a context of building national cohesion. That is, it is precisely in such a global context that occasional switches into Singlishcan help establish a sense of shared 'Singaporean-ness'.

Attracting Foreign Talent

In addition to trying to cultivate a sense of connectedness among Singaporeans located in other parts of the world, Singapore also hopes to attract talented foreigners as potential new citizens, to replace those Singaporeans who may decide to emigrate permanently. The hope is that this image of Singapore as a global/cosmopolitan city will prove attractive to affluent, highly educated and mobile individuals. According to Goh Chok Tong:

> (7)
> Therefore we must incorporate into our society talent from all over the world, not just Chinese, Malay or Indians, but talented people whatever their race or country of origin – East Asians, Southeast Asians, South Asians, Arabs from the Gulf and Middle East, North Americans, Europeans, Australasians, even Latin Americans and Southern Africans... Some will integrate into our society and settle here. For them we hope this spirit will eventually evolve into one of loyalty and rootedness to Singapore. (1997 National Day Rally Speech)

Because the foreign talent policy aims to persuade such talent to take up Singaporean citizenship, the success of this policy could well change the country's demographics and will eventually impact upon the language policy. Japanese, Korean, French or American foreign talent who become citizens obviously cannot be expected to embrace Mandarin, Malay or Tamil as their official mother tongues. Rather, the concept of mother tongue will have to be broadened to include many more languages than the current three, including – crucially – English. This means that the state will need to abandon its stance where the English–mother tongues dichotomy supposedly corresponds to a Western–Asian distinction. This insistence on opposing English (the 'Western' language) to the 'Asian' mother tongues will no longer be tenable. As Wee and Bokhorst-Heng (2005: 176-177) observe:

> This might mean that, in so far as the state is still intent on encouraging Singaporeans to keep in touch with their mother tongues, this will have to be done 'softly', via persuasion but accepting that the final choice lies with the individual. Furthermore, once the mother tongue issue is ceded more toward the personal domain, then it becomes clear that what language a particular Singaporean may consider his or her mother tongue is also something that can no longer be mandated by the state; this, too, will be a matter of personal choice.

Recall that the government's understanding of a mother tongue is that it represents the cultural heritage and identity of an ethnic community. This is regardless of the actual linguistic experiences of individuals. As a consequence, a Chinese Singaporean is expected to accept Mandarin as his or her mother tongue regardless of whether he or she has grown up with the language or not. But as Singapore society becomes culturally and linguistically more complex, it becomes less feasible to treat the notion of a mother tongue as the property of an ethnic community, in the sense that only the mother tongue is an appropriate carrier of the community's ancestral values and no other language can be considered to be an adequate medium.

In particular, the mother tongue should not be pre-assigned by the state as a significant, if not essential, aspect of the speakers' cultural identity, such that loss of the language is (allegedly) tantamount to the destruction of that culture and where, as a demonstration of their fidelity to the community and its associated values, speakers are obligated to preserve their knowledge and use of the language. Rather, the mother tongue has to be understood as one that is more reflective of an individual's particular set of lived experiences. Only then would the language policy be better able to accommodate the growing diversity of the population.

This, however, would also require the state to stop insisting on positioning English as a purely pragmatic language that should have no place in Singaporean identity. This also leads us back to the issue of Singlish. The state has been encouraging newly arrived immigrants to learn English in order to better integrate into Singapore society. But while the use of 'standard'

English is certainly useful, it lacks the necessary cultural associations that would allow it to serve as a resource for identity work at the national level.

In fact, it seems clear that both locals as well as new citizens tend to treat the acquisition and use of Singlish as an indicator of successful integration. Thus, a recent news article ('New Singaporeans', Cai Haoxiang & Elgin Toh, *The Straits Times*, 29 August 2010) profiles immigrants from China, Myanmar and India who 'lapse into Singlish easily' and 'who have become thoroughly Singaporeanised'. The same article describes Meng Qingyi, a 'newly minted citizen' from China, as having been taught Singlish by her Singaporean school friends. It also describes Eddy Goh, originally from Myanmar, whose 'strong Singaporean-accented English and lapses into Singlish make him indistinguishable from any teenager here'.

Singlish in the Culture Industries: Films and Tourism

Though the Singapore film industry is still at a relatively young stage of development, a number of films have been produced that have done relatively well at the local box office. Some earlier successes include *Army Daze* (1996) and *Money No Enough* (1998). The former is a comedy about the military experiences of a group of enlistees from a variety of socioeconomic and ethnic backgrounds, and the latter a comedy-drama about the financial problems faced by a group of Chinese-educated friends. Both films dealt with issues that resonated with local audiences, and this resonance was in no small part due to the fact that the films also made strong use of language that was officially frowned upon by the Singapore government. *Army Daze* used a lot of Singlish, and *Money No Enough* a lot of Hokkien,[6] in order to authentically reflect the speech patterns of their respective characters. Other films have enjoyed both local and international success, such as Eric Khoo's *Mee Pok Man* (1995) and *12 Storeys* (1997). Both deal with themes of social alienation among working-class Singaporeans, and also make use of Singlish, again, in order to provide a realistic portrayal of the characters. *Mee Pok Man* was invited to be screened at more than 30 film festivals, and *12 Storeys* was selected to be featured at the Cannes International Film Festival.

More recently, *Singapore Dreaming* (2006), by Colin Goh and Woo Yen Yen, became the first Singaporean film to win the Montblanc New Screenwriters Award at the 54th San Sebastian International Film Festival. It also won the Best Asian/Middle-Eastern Film Award at the 20th Tokyo International Film Festival. This film focuses on a Singaporean working-class family as they aspire towards a better life. *Singapore Dreaming* is particularly interesting because the promotional trailer for the film was banned from local free-to-air television by the government, due to what was deemed as excessive use of Singlish and the Chinese dialects. But as Colin Goh points out in an interview (emphasis in original)[7]:

> (8)
> This is something Singapore's censorship authorities and language police completely don't understand. It's a LOT easier to write in a single language. But the fact is, Singaporeans DON'T speak like that. We mix languages, even several times in a single sentence, and code switch constantly. If you want to write Singaporean dialogue that reflects the way Singaporeans actually speak, and want to have a film that Singaporeans respond to, you have no choice.

Colin Goh's remarks about mixing and switching as reflections of 'the way Singaporeans actually speak' are true to an extent. However, they have to be qualified by the fact that in films there is sometimes a tendency to exaggerate the degree of 'Singlish-ness' for humorous effect, especially in comedies. But the twist in this observation is that even in 'real life', Singaporeans, especially educated Singaporeans who are fairly competent in the standard variety, will tend to engage in playful and highly creative manipulations of the language, such practices being intended also to be humorous (Wee, 2011). So, filmic exaggerations of Singlish are, in fact, not too far from some of its real life uses.

Ironically, the Singapore government itself is on occasion willing to treat Singlish as a manifestation of Singaporean-ness, such as when it commodifies Singlish as a part of the tourist experience (Wee, 2011). Thus, in (9) below, the Singapore Tourism Board (STB)[8] actually describes Singlish as Singaporeans' 'own brand of English', one that they 'fondly refer to'. As with the government's use of Singlish on Singapore Day, this, too, undermines its own claims that Singlish has no value. The STB even adds that the mixed nature of Singlish is 'not surprising' given Singapore's multi-racial background – which is the very same argument that supporters of Singlish have been making.

> (9)
> Over the years, Singaporeans have developed their own brand of English fondly referred to as 'Singlish'. With our multi-racial background, it's not surprising that 'Singlish' borrows from the many different languages spoken in Singapore. Here's a collection of 'Singlish' terms which you might find handy on your visit to Singapore.

As the last sentence in (9) indicates, the STB has also included on its website explanations of some Singlish terms, some of which are shown in (10) below. These are aimed at tourists, on the grounds that they may otherwise find it difficult to understand what (some) Singaporeans might be saying. More significantly, the explanations in (10) encourage these foreign visitors to learn bits of Singlish so as to better understand the locals. This is a move that undermines the government's claim that foreigners are unwilling or unable to learn Singlish in order to communicate with locals, and that because of this, Singaporeans should stop using the language altogether. In this example, foreigners are in effect encouraged to indulge in learning bits of Singlish as part of their experience of being in Singapore.

(10)

(i) Action (verb)
Derived from the English language meaning to show off.
Example: 'That fellow always like to action, walking around with his Rolex over his shirt sleeves'.

(ii) Boh-Chup (adj)
Derived from the Hokkien dialect meaning couldn't care less.
Example: 'Ah, boh-chup, I'm not going to hand in my assignment'.

The discussions in this and the preceding sections show that Singlish could indeed be useful in maintaining a sense of connectedness among Singaporeans located in various parts of the globe, in helping new citizens better integrate in Singapore society, and in contributing to the marketing of Singaporean cultural commodities.

In the next section, we explore the possibility that these uses of Singlish are not necessarily independent, but can, in fact, feed off each other.

The Identity Economy

Dávila (2001: 2, cited in Comaroff & Comaroff, 2009: 16) suggests that the 'marketing and making' of an identity may be closely connected to each other, such that 'commercial representations may shape people's cultural identities as well as affect notions of belonging and cultural citizenship in public life'. To see how this might be the case, we need to appreciate that in a consumer-oriented society, goods are prized as much for their symbolic as their material properties (Bauman, 1998). And while the identity of the consumer often depends on the choice of goods being consumed (Warde, 1982), so too are producers validated by having their particular goods recognized and valued in the marketplace. In the case of cultural goods, such as those associated with the film and tourism industries, recognition and appreciation of the products – by locals as well as foreigners – are usually predicated on some perception that they are 'authentic' reflections of the culture that they represent. Thus, in their own extension of Dávila's insight from the commodification of ethnic identities to that of national identities, Comaroff and Comaroff (2009: 130-131, italics added) point out that

> Both situate themselves in what, these days, is taken to be the true nature of people and things... [though] nationhood has both to encompass internal heterodoxy and to subsume it within a superordinate one-ness, as a result of which it may submerge its *own* sense of ethno-cultural particularity in a civic conception of citizenship; which is how, for example, 'Britishness' and liberal democracy, the particular and the universal, come to suffuse each other in the ideological scaffolding of the United Kingdom. But both ethnicity and nationality, in their contemporary guise, depend on the interplay of blood, culture, substance, sovereignty. *And both may claim a natural copyright over their heritage-as-property: property that appears to be highly replicable without losing its aura; property whose commodification often adds value to, rather than cheapens, identity; property that, however widely it circulates at the behest of the market, typically resists the abstraction of its essence into pure exchange value or the reduction of its exuberant, messy particularity to bland ordinariness.*

What this means is that the Singapore government needs to acknowledge that consumer interest, especially interest from the international market, is not limited to officially approved or established forms of culture, such as the Asian Civilizations Museum, the Malay Village or Chinatown. It can also involve forms of culture (including varieties of language) that the government may deem undesirable. There appears to be a relatively widespread interest in the consumption of cultural products that provide the consumer with some 'insight experience' into the culture of others, especially among well-educated and affluent individuals. Brown-Saracino (2009: 192) refers to such individuals as 'cultural omnivores'. One possible reason for such interest, according to Comaroff and Comaroff (2009: 140), is that

> the identity economy feeds, and feeds off, a deep ambivalence in modern life: a sense of exile from 'authentic' being that seeks to requite itself in encounters with 'authentic' otherness – albeit in consumable form.

Of course, the recognition of cultural goods may not necessarily be focused on Singlish per se. But there is little doubt that the use of Singlish – despite its officially stigmatized status – does contribute to the perception of authenticity and, as a consequence, does raise the likelihood of recognition. And positive reaction to cultural goods, in turn, can feedback into Singaporeans' own sense of pride in what it means to be distinctively Singaporean and in this way contribute to cultivating the kind of connectedness that the government is keen to encourage in the face of a Singaporean diaspora, as well as the kind of integration that the government is hoping to encourage between locals and new citizens.

If the Singapore government is at all intent on taking advantage of and participating in this identity economy – and there is every reason to believe that it is, as seen in the Tourism Board's references to Singlish (see (9) above) – then it has to be prepared to be less bound to its own anti-Singlish ideologies and adopt a more pragmatic attitude.

Implications for Singapore's Language Policy

A central issue in the study of globalization has been the claim that globalization processes are weakening the nation-state, if not actually making it obsolete (Ohmae, 1996). Such a claim, however, fails to seriously consider the potentially creative responses the nation-state might mount in the face of globalization. In the case of Singapore, we have seen that the reinvention of itself as a global city is indeed one such response. Not surprisingly, while the government has been quite prepared to confront the economic and political challenges associated with this reinvention, it has been less ready to grapple with the linguistic and cultural implications. But if this next step in Singapore's development is to be managed smoothly, these implications have to be confronted. In this closing section, I want to spell some of the implications of the shift into a global city narrative for Singapore's language policy.

I have argued elsewhere (Stroud & Wee, 2010; Wee & Bokhorst-Heng, 2005) that Singapore's language policy needs to be opened up, so as to provide for greater individual autonomy. That is, allow individuals to make their own decisions about which language they would consider their mother tongue, on the basis of their particular lived experiences. This move towards greater individual autonomy is necessary because the government has aggressively embarked on a foreign talent policy in order to attract educated, successful and affluent individuals from all over the world, encouraging them to take up Singaporean citizenship. The motivation for this foreign talent policy stems from the combined effect of the outward migration of Singaporeans and Singapore's own low fertility rate. These two factors have led the government to worry that not only are Singaporeans not replacing themselves, but they are also migrating, leading to the loss of educated and mobile citizens, which could ultimately have deleterious consequences for the nation's economic growth. But because the foreign talent policy encourages individuals of different ethnic and linguistic backgrounds to take up citizenship, it is likely that this could result in the demographic profile of the country becoming even more heterogeneous than it already is. Consequently, a language policy that insists on allowing only Asian languages to be mother tongues while denying this status to English is not going to be feasible, especially if some of the foreign talent comes from, say, the United States or Australia. This argument for individual autonomy still holds, but now we have an additional reason, given that Singlish can be useful in a diasporic context and it is potentially valuable in the identity economy.

Moreover, whether the government likes it or not, it is simply not practical to ban or attempt to eliminate Singlish, especially if the targets of this move are Singaporeans who are located overseas, since being located overseas makes them even less susceptible to the dictates of a language policy. Furthermore, as we have seen, the government itself occasionally even finds it useful to acknowledge the value of Singlish in establishing a sense of connectedness and solidarity. Inaddition, the decisions of international audiences and film festival organizers to recognize Singaporean films (and possibly other cultural goods) are also beyond the government's regulation, and a persistently anti-Singlish stance would only look foolish in retrospect should more such recognition be forthcoming. Therefore, rather than continue asserting that Singlish is a lingua non-grata, the government would actually find it more useful to adopt a laissez faire approach. In essence, this would mean the following: allow individuals who are actively engaged in the production of cultural products to use language as they see fit, and let the market of consumers (locally and internationally) be the judge of value of these products. And allow individuals who are working and living overseas engage in the use of Singlish if they so wish – especially if this helps to reinforce and sustain a sense of connectedness.

Notes

(1) In addition to being the official mother tongue of the Malay community, Malay is also the national language. But this national language status is mainly symbolic. Malay is used in the national anthem and in military commands, but there is no official obligation to learn the language. The emphasis, instead, is for each individual to learn the mother tongue assigned by the government as emblematic of the culture and identity of his or her ethnic community. There is consequently no language that strongly embodies a national identity, and cultural identification is instead supposed to be directed towards specific ethnic communities.

(2) The terms are used interchangeably by Singapore's political leaders.

(3) This is an all-too-common argument stemming from a prejudice against stigmatized varieties. It is often used to justify the conclusion that the stigmatized variety ought to be eliminated from the classroom, for example, because of the confusion and contamination it supposedly causes, even though the available evidence suggests that stigmatized varieties either have no effect on the learning of the standard or can actually have a positive effect (Siegel, 1999). In the context of Singapore, this line of thinking feeds the government's concern that Singlish truly is an economic threat that has to be eliminated. It was this anti-Singlish stance that led the government, in 2000, to initiate the Speak Good English Movement (SGEM). For details, see Chng (2003) and Rubdy (2001).

(4) A survey by Tan (2005: 89) suggests that 27% of Singaporeans have considered emigrating.

(5) 'Singapore Day in London draws the crowds', *The Sunday Times*, 26 April 2009.

(6) The Singapore government recognizes only Mandarin as the official mother tongue of the Chinese community, and discourages the use of the other Chinese dialects (Bokhorst-Heng, 1999).

(7) www.singaporedreaming.com/q&a_writers.htm.

(8) www.visitsingapore.com/publish/stbportal/en/home/about_singapore/fun_stuff/singlish_dictionary.html.

(9) 'Proposal to Develop Integrated Resorts' (Singapore Government Press Release, dated 18 April 2005).

References

Bauman, Z. (1998) *Work, Consumerism and the New Poor*. Buckingham: Open University Press.

Bokhorst-Heng, W. (1999) Singapore's speak Mandarin campaign: Language ideological debates and the imagining of the nation. In J. Blommaert (ed.) *Language Ideological Debates* (pp. 235-265). Berlin: Mouton de Gruyter.

Brown-Saracino, J. (2009) *A Neighborhood That Never Changes*. Chicago, IL: University of Chicago Press.

Chng, H.H. (2003) 'You see me no up': Is Singlish a problem? *Language Problems & Language Planning* 27, 45-62.

Comaroff, J.L. and Comaroff, J. (2009) *Ethnicity, Inc*. Chicago, IL: University of Chicago Press.

Dávila, A. (2001) *Latinos Inc.: The Marketing and Making of a People*. Berkeley, CA: University of California Press.

Goh, C.T. (1997) *National Day Rally Speech*. Singapore: Ministry of Information and the Arts.

Goh, C.T. (1999) *National Day Rally Speech*. Singapore: Ministry of Information and the Arts.

Goh, C. and Woo, Y.Y. (2009) *The Coxford Singlish Dictionary* (2nd edn). Singapore: Angsana Books.

Kong, L. (1999) Globalization and Singaporean transmigration: Re-imagining and negotiating national identity. *Political Geography* 18 (5), 563-589.

Ohmae, K. (1996) *The End of the Nation-State: The Rise of the Regional Economies*. New York: Touchstone Press.

Ong, A. (2006) *Neoliberalism as Exception: Mutations in Citizenship and Sovereignty*. Durham: Duke University Press.

Perrons, D. (2004) *Globalization and Social Change: People and Places in a Divided World.* London: Routledge.

Rubdy, R. (2001) Creative destruction: Singapore's speak good English movement. *World Englishes* 20, 341-355.

Sassen, S. (2001) *The Global City*(2nd edn). Princeton, NJ: Princeton University Press.

Siegel, J. (1999) Stigmatized and standardized varieties in the classroom: Interference or separation. *TESOL Quarterly* 33 (4), 701-728.

Stroud, C. and Wee, L. (2010) Language policy and planning in Singaporean late modernity. In L. Lim, A. Pakir and L. Wee (eds) *English in Singapore: Modernity and Management* (pp. 181-204). Hong Kong: Hong Kong University Press.

Tan, E.S. (2005) Globalization, nation-building and emigration: The Singapore case. In B.P. Lorente, N. Piper, H-H. Shen and B. Yeoh (eds) *Asian Migrations* (pp. 87-98). Singapore: Asia Research Institute, Singapore University Press.

Warde, A. (1982) Consumption, identity-formation and uncertainty. *Sociology* 28 (4), 877-898.

Wee, C.J.W-L. (2007) Afterword: Language, capitalist development, cultural change. In V. Vaish, S. Gopinathan and Y-B. Liu (eds) *Language, Capital, Culture: Critical Studies of Language and Education in Singapore* (pp. 249-257). Rotterdam: Sense Publishers.

Wee, L. (2010) 'Burdens' and 'handicaps' in Singapore's language policy: On the limits of language management. *Language Policy* 9 (2), 97-114.

Wee, L. (2011) Metadiscursive convergence in the Singlish debate. *Language & Communication* 31 (1), 75-85.

Wee, L. and Bokhorst-Heng, W. (2005) Language policy and nationalist ideology: Statal narratives in Singapore. *Multilingua* 24, 159-183.

Yeoh, B. and Willis, K. (1997) *Singapore Unlimited: Configuring Social Identity in the Regionalization Process.* Paper presented at University of Nottingham Department of Geography Seminar Series.

10 English, Scientific Publishing and Participation in the Global Knowledge Economy

Theresa Lillis and Mary Jane Curry

Introduction

The notion that economic growth nationally and globally is dependent on knowledge, rather than labour, land or industrial production, has been discussed since the 1950s and has become central to global economic policy and practice since the 1990s, and is captured in the phrase 'knowledge economy', along with other terms such as 'knowledge society' and 'information society'. This emphasis on knowledge as the base of a successful economy has meant that scientific knowledge – used in this chapter, unless otherwise indicated, to refer to both natural and human sciences[1] – constitutes a specific value or commodity to be generated and harnessed for economic growth and explicitly called for in developing as well as developed countries. The ways in which such knowledge is produced, circulated and governed is, therefore, of crucial importance at national, regional and transnational levels. Scientific publications – in particular the scientific journal article – are a key vehicle for knowledge production and constitute a key source of knowledge capital, essential for accruing other important resources necessary to building a knowledge base, and, securing scientific influence, for example, for attracting research funding, being invited to contribute to international conferences and other types of scholarly activity. Thus, success in scientific article publication needs to be seen as key not only to activity at the levels of individual scholars, departments and institutions, but, in both direct and indirect ways, to a nation or region's participation in knowledge-generating capacity more generally.[2]

English is nested within this imperative to grow knowledge in highly consequential ways. As we discuss below, English is often construed by academic institutions and key evaluating institutions, such as the Institute for Scientific Information (ISI), as an academic *lingua franca* which can facilitate the transnational exchange of ideas, new knowledges and understandings, which in turn can help sustain economic growth and development. As such, in policy documents and research reports, its status is often taken as given with little explicit debate about how the dominant position of English may be impacting on opportunities for knowledge generation and economic growth. However, the dominance of English as the medium of scholarly exchange is far from unproblematic, not least because this dominance is partly sustained through its nested position within policies and practices of high-income countries and Anglophone centre-based evaluation systems, which powerfully shape opportunities for the kinds of knowledges that are produced, circulated and valued.

This chapter discusses the current importance attached to developing a 'knowledge (based) economy' for national and international development, focusing in particular on one key strand of knowledge-making capacity – scientific publishing – and emphasising the powerful position of English within this strand. The chapter brings together quantitative and qualitative data: the former collated from a range of available statistics on global scientific article publishing and the latter from the small, but increasing, number of ethnographic studies exploring scholars working and writing on the 'periphery'. Throughout, we use the terms 'centre'/'Anglophone centre' and 'periphery' in order to highlight the power and resource differentials between contexts of, and for, knowledge production, drawing on both economic and linguistic categorisations: the centre/periphery perspective outlined by World Systems theorists such as Wallerstein (1991) and SousaSantos (1994), and the inner/outer/expanding circles of English speakers used by Kachru (1992). While aware of some limitations in such framing, empirically and theoretically, we consider that they provide a meaningful way of articulating some of the politics surrounding language and knowledge production.[3]

A key argument we make is that there needs to be greater recognition of the nested position of English within practices surrounding scientific activity which extends well beyond 'language' per se but is rather built into policy and practices governing who gets to participate in knowledge production globally.

The Knowledge Economy and Development

The notion of the 'knowledge economy' became significant in policy discussions globally with the publication of the Organization for Economic Cooperation and Development's (OECD, 1996: 4, 7) *The Knowledge-Based*

Economy, where knowledge is stated as being 'a driver of productivity and economic growth' and knowledge economies are 'based on the production, distribution and use of knowledge and information'. A similar position was taken up in the equally influential World Bank's *The World Development Report: Knowledge for Development* (1998), which states that 'economies are built not merely through the accumulation of physical and human skill, but on the foundation of information, learning and adaptation'. Foundational thinking in this area is found in the work of Daniel Bell (e.g. 1973), who claimed that information rather than energy was now the transforming resource (see Robertson, 2005 for overview). Key empirical indicators in this move towards knowledge as the base of economic growth include the move away from industrialised production towards service industries – for example, in 1956, white-collar workers in the United States outnumbered blue-collar workers for the first time in US history; a rise in the number of highly skilled or professional workers in service industries; and increased use of technology across all occupations (Kenway *et al*., 2006; Schement & Curtis, 1997; Wyatt & Heckler, 2006).

It is important to recognise that the notion of the knowledge economy, from its first uses, has been (and is) at the same time a description of changing production practices (predominantly in the centre/North), a powerful discourse for making sense of shifts in economic development and an economic mission statement or prescription for global economic development, whereby knowledge/information is construed as a solution to post-industrial/late capitalist societies. Academic commentators have pointed to the vague and slippery way in which 'knowledge economy' has been, and is, used, including the shift from description to prescription and vice versa, and the slippage in policy documents between core (and different) terms which are often used interchangeably: these include *knowledge, technology, information*. 'Knowledge economy' is used alongside or instead of 'information society', 'learning economy', 'learning society' and related terms such as 'knowledge workers' and 'knowledge work' (for overview, see Kenway *et al*., 2006). However, while the notion and discourses surrounding the 'knowledge economy' are highly problematic – 'steeped in hyperbole and laced with prediction' (Peters, 2001: 12) – scholars also emphasise that whatever its discursive or material base, the 'knowledge economy' is a profoundly influential phenomenon, such that 'knowledge economy' and its commonplace glosses are viewed as powerful 'determinants of social and economic change' (Bimber, 1995).

This emphasis on knowledge for economic growth has involved a significant shift in key funders' emphasis, away from projects centring on capital and labour, towards growing knowledge capacity (see Stiglitz, 1999, economist of the World Bank). With regard to 'international development', such a shift involves a radical reconfiguration:

> Development ... becomes a matter of narrowing knowledge gaps through national policies and strategies for *acquiring, absorbing* and *communicating* knowledge, and addressing information problems through national policies designed to process the economy's financial information... (Olssen & Peters, 2005: 335, their emphasis)

It is salutary here to note that the narrowing of knowledge gaps in World Bank policy is construed in terms of consumption – policies that will enable poorer countries to 'acquire, absorb and communicate' knowledge. This vision of developing countries and regions as consumers of knowledge from the centre, rather than producers of their own knowledge, contrasts with the more explicit human rights approach and discourse, reflected in OECD and United Nations Educational, Scientific and Cultural Organization (UNESCO) policy documents (see, for example, UNESCO Forum, 2009b: 2). In the foreword to the 2010 *World Social Science Report*, it states

> Article 27.1 of the Universal Declaration of Human Rights stipulates that everyone has the right to share in scientific advancement and its benefits. This is not the best known of the fundamental human rights, but it is not the least important. (UNESCO, 2010a: v)

Advocating a more agentive role for developing countries in setting their own research agendas is strongly evident in areas which have an obvious applied potential, as in the area of health research. The criticism here is that the gap in scientific publications between low-income countries and the rest of the world continues to grow (Paraje *et al.*, 2005), and the concern is that research problems are being framed – and solutions derived – without the central involvement of local researchers (see, for example, Freeman & Robbin, 2006).

Of course, advocating for 'local', or non-centre, control over research and research agendas[4] is at odds with the market-led principles governing the knowledge economy where competition is key: within nation-states over research resources; between nation-states (as within the EU) and between regions of the world (for example, the United States, the European Union, Asia). This competition over knowledge, and thus science as a resource essential to a nation's economic success, is evident in statements routinely made by governments (for examples, see http://www.scotland.gov.uk/Topics/Business-Industry/science; http://advancingknowledge.com) and echoed in transnational science reports, such as the National Science Foundation *Key Science and Engineering Indicators* (2010: 3).

Emphasis on competition often sits alongside a more critical agenda within the same reports. Thus, in the 2010 *World Social Science Report*, concern about the disparities between regions of the world in scientific activity is clearly signalled in its subtitle, 'knowledge divides', yet at the same time the competitive nature (and goal) of such scientific capacity building is presented uncritically (for example, see UNESCO, 2010b: 274). Thus, although 'the knowledge economy' is often talked of in the singular, it is, in fact, highly differentiated and might more accurately be described as a plurality of competing economies, at state and regional levels (Kenway *et al*., 2006), and its use includes diverse positions on the extent to which a neo-liberal agenda should also pay some attention to challenging social inequalities, through policies aimed at 'social inclusion' (see Jessop, 2002, as discussed in Fairclough, 2006).

In brief, the emphasis on knowledge as the driver of economic success means that scientific activity, including publication, is a key and competitive business. High-income countries see the building of science as central to sustaining their own economic position globally; lower-income countries within the framing of 'international development' are construed as needing knowledge to grow their economies, yet the challenges such countries face are clearly immense. Whilst knowledge growing is presented in some policy circles as a human right, at the same time the competitive nature of science and knowledge building positions lower-income countries as potential consumers rather than producers of knowledge, raising fundamental questions about agency and control.

The position of English is often not mentioned in such debates.[5] Yet, as we discuss in the following sections, English has a dominant status within scientific activity, particularly in relation to the most valued products of science, publications in 'high status' journals, which constitute a significant form of symbolic capital so essential to building competitive knowledge-based economies.

Scientific Knowledge Production and the Status of English

Economic input and scientific output

Scientific production remains within the control of a few countries and, to a large extent, reflects the more powerful economic position of those countries globally. The amount of money devoted to General Expenditure on Research and Development (GERD) is much less in low- and lower-middle-income countries than in upper-middle- and high-income countries, with production – here measured in terms of scientific article output – closely mapping against GERD.

Quantifying the exact number of journals and articles being produced globally and mapping these against countries and regions is not straightforward, as categories used vary from source to source (and also reflect geopolitical ideologies as, for example, in the classification of Mexico in many sources as part of 'Latin America' rather than North America). We have therefore compiled Table 10.1 from a number of sources, in order to offer a snapshot of publication patterns around the world: it compares regions of the world – including selected countries from those regions – in terms of GERD with their share of world journal article output (in the natural sciences and technology), a key measure of knowledge production (countries whose article output totals less than one-tenth of 1% of world share are not included). Countries whose names are in italics are members of the OECD.

Table 10.1 demonstrates that Europe and the United States have a large share of article production around the world. Overall, research publications are highly concentrated in a few countries and regions, with more than 80% of the world's scientific articles coming from the OECD area. Table 10.2 provides data on share of social science article output for certain regions of the world, based on journals indexed in the Thomson Reuters Social Science Citation Index (country-specific data not available). While percentages vary across the natural and social sciences, the overall domination of the same regions remains constant.

The country/regional level view emphasises the paltry share of world knowledge production in all disciplines held by countries/regions outside the historical 'triad' of the United States, Europe and some parts of Asia. Variation in numbers of researchers, the final column in Table 10.1, likewise indicates the current knowledge-building capacity in different nations, as reflected in numbers of researchers as a percentage of the population, and stark contrasts can be noted between countries, such as, on the one hand, the United States, Sweden and the UK and, on the other hand, Mexico, Turkey, India and South Africa.

The number of researchers per million inhabitants also signals the importance of universities for building knowledge-growing capacity. In a summary of 'The Case for African Higher Education, Research and Innovation', Kearney (2009) illustrates the link made between this capacity, science

Table 10.1 General expenditure on research and development (GERD), share of world science journal article output, and researchers per million by region and income level (regions and selected countries)[†]

Region/country/income classification	*GERD as % of GDP**	*Researchers per million (2007)**	*Share of science articles (%) (2007)***
North America 31.20			
High income			
United States	2.82 (2008)	4663	27.6
Canada	1.84 (2008)	4260	3.60
Europe/Central Asia 29.88[a]			
High income			
Sweden	3.75 (2008)	5239	1.30
Switzerland	2.90 (2004)	3634 (2002)	1.20
Denmark	2.72 (2008)	5670	0.06
Austria	2.66 (2008)	4123	0.06
Germany	2.54 (2007)	3532	5.80
France	2.02 (2008)	3496	4.00
Belgium	1.92 (2008)	3435	0.09
United Kingdom	1.88 (2008)	4269	6.20
Slovenia	1.66 (2008)	3490	0.10
Netherlands	1.63 (2008)	3089	1.80
Norway	1.62 (2008)	5468	0.05
Portugal	1.51 (2008)	3799	0.40
Czech Republic	1.47 (2008)	2886	0.40
Ireland	1.42 (2008)	3090	0.30
Spain	1.34 (2008)	2944	2.70
Italy	1.18 (2008)	1616	3.50
Hungary	0.96 (2007)	1733	0.03
Greece	0.57 (2007)	1873	0.06
Slovak Republic	0.47 (2008)	2331	0.10
Upper-middle income			
Russian Federation	1.03 (2008)	3191	1.80
Poland	0.61 (2008)	1623	0.90
Romania	0.59 (2008)	908	0.10
Lower-middle income			
Turkey	0.72 (2007)	680	1.10

East Asia/South Asia 20.1			
High income			
Japan	3.44 (2007)	5573	6.90
South Korea	3.21 (2007)	4627	2.40
Taiwan	2.63 (2007)***	Not available	1.60
Singapore	2.52 (2007)	6088	0.50
Upper-middle income			
Malaysia	0.64 (2006)	717****	0.10
Lower-middle income			
China	1.44 (2007)	1071	7.40
India	0.80 (2007)	137	2.30
Africa 1.16			
Upper-middle income			
South Africa	0.93 (2007)	361	0.30
Lower-middle income			
Egypt	0.23 (2007)	617	0.20
Middle East 0.80			
High income			
Israel	4.86 (2008)	Not available	0.80
Latin America 2.60			
Upper-middle income			
Brazil	1.10 (2007)	694	1.50
Argentina	0.51 (2007)	980	0.40
Chile	0.68 (2004)	548****	0.20
Mexico	0.37 (2007)	353	0.50
Oceania 2.70			
Australia	2.06 (2006)	4224	2.30
New Zealand	1.21 (2007)	4365	0.40

†Income groupings use World Bank (2010) classifications per capita. World Bank income ranges are as follows: High income = US$11,906+; Upper-middle income = US$3856-11,905; Lower-middle income = US$976-3855; low income = US$975 or less.

Note on sources: Asterisks are used to indicate data source. Where asterisks appear in column heading, this indicates that most of the data in that column are from that one source.

[a]Not all countries are represented in each region; regional totals thus may be larger than the sum of country totals included.

*UNESCO Science Report (2010b).

**National Science Foundation *Key Science & Engineering Indicators* (2010).

***OECD (2009) *Factbook*.

****UNESCO *Mapping research systems in developing countries* (2009c).

Table 10.2 Social sciences article output by world region

Region	*% Thomson SSCI articles 1998-2007 (N = 226, 940)*
North America	52.2
Europe	38.0
Asia	8.9
Oceania	4.7
Latin America	1.7
Africa	1.6
CIS [former Soviet states]	1.2

Source: Adapted from UNESCO World Social Science Report (2010a), Table 4.2.

and progress, emphasising the particular challenges faced in African higher education contexts:

> Present problems date from the policies adopted in the last decades of the twentieth century, when this sector suffered severe reductions in donor investment in favour of the more rapid returns perceived from basic and primary education... Two decades of reduced allocations to higher education resulted in the dramatic decline of African universities, and though demand for higher education grew in the region, the chances of a young person born in sub-Saharan Africa acceding to higher education were roughly eighteen to twenty times lower than those of their peers born in industrialized countries. (Kearney, 2009: 17)

Of course, Table 10.1 also shows that clear variation exists within regions of the world, even within upper-income European states in terms of GERD and research productivity: notably, France, Germany, Italy and the United Kingdom far outpace other countries in the region. In other regions, certain countries stand out in terms of high research productivity (e.g. Japan and China within Asia; South Africa within Africa).

Table 10.1 also signals, but does not capture, changes over time in world share of article output. The share held by the United States and Europe has declined in recent years and is predicted to continue to decrease, in contrast to increased GERD and publications output from regions such as Asia and Latin America (UNESCO World Social Science Report, 2010a). In particular, China is making noticeable gains in share of world productivity (OECD, 2008), a trend partly attributable to massive increases of GERD. Although wary of making specific predictions, researchers (e.g. Shelton, 2008) and government organisations (e.g. the United States' National Science Foundation) appear to agree that the share of knowledge production by the United States and the EU will be challenged by the continued investment in GERD in places such as China, Brazil and India. Fears that the declining share of knowledge production signals the saturation of research capacity in previously dominant economies, such as the United States, match concerns in such economies about losing the 'competitive edge' globally.

Of course, current levels of financial investment in research and development are only one, albeit important, contributor to high research productivity. In addition, a range of geohistorical factors continue to exert a powerful influence on opportunities for scientific production and engagement, not least the pivotal role of Anglophone-centre states in research activity and policy, including journal publication, and journal evaluation practices. Nested within all of these is the status of English.

The status of English in academic knowledge production globally

In almost every academic field, the dominance of English as the language of academic publishing is well documented (Lillis & Curry, 2010). More than 95% of indexed natural science journals and 90% of social science journals use all or some English (Thomson Reuters, 2009a). Further, English is the language of the majority of the 4654 journals listed in UNESCO's DARE database of social science periodicals (UNESCO, 2009a). While scientific writings continue to be published in a range of languages, English dominates in journals listed in high-status indexes, notably those generated by the Institute for Scientific Information (ISI) such as the Science Citation Index (SCI) and the Social Science Citation Index (SSCI). Table 10.3

Table 10.3 The 10 most prevalent languages in social science journals

Language	*% Ulrich's refereed journals in 2004 (N = 3046)*	*% Thomson SSCI articles 1998-2007 (N = 226, 984)*
English	85.3	94.45
French	5.9	1.25
German	5.4	2.14
Spanish	4.0	0.40
Portuguese	1.7	0.08
Chinese	1.5	0.00
Dutch	1.5	0.01
Japanese	1.0	0.06
Polish	0.9	0.00
Italian	0.6	0.01

Source: UNESCO World Social Science Report (2010a), Table 4.3.

shows rankings of languages of publication for social science journals from all geographic regions that are included in these indexes: note the dramatic reduction in percentage of languages following English, with non-Western languages virtually invisible.

The majority of journals included in the SCI and SSCI indexes are not only published in English but also edited in Anglophone-centre contexts. Table 10.4 illustrates this disparity in the global distribution of journals across broad academic fields.

With some variation across academic fields, the United States, the United Kingdom and a small number of other European countries host the majority of journals included in prestigious indexes such as those published by ISI/ Web of Science; this distribution parallels the statistics on GERD and share of article output presented in Table 10.1. What is not captured in these statistics is the increasing number of English-medium journals published outside of Anglophone contexts in response to the growing dominance of English in scholarly publication and, more specifically, in response to systems of academic evaluation that privilege English-medium publications. The practice of English-medium journals being published outside of Anglophone contexts is well established in the natural sciences and is a growing phenomenon in the social sciences (Lillis & Curry, 2010). This phenomenon of the growing number of English-medium journals in non-English-dominant contexts illustrates not only the increasing use of English for knowledge production but also its embedding in local and transnational systems of rewards, whereby publishing 'in English' is often a proxy for 'high status' or 'international' (for fuller discussion, see Lillis & Curry, 2010, chap. 2).

In short, a range of geohistorical factors continue to exert a powerful influence on scientific production, most of which are predominantly Anglophone-centre based or derived, and thus contribute to the dominant position of English: the establishment and control of transnational scientific journals; the development of publication evaluation systems, including the 'impact factor' devised by Garfield (1972) to measure the value or 'impact' of a journal, and increasingly used to evaluate scholars; particular systems and practices of gatekeeping in publication; the linguistic medium used and ideologies around its use. Whilst, to some extent, these are each discrete phenomena, they are also highly intermeshed. Thus the medium that is assumed to be the language of science, English, is not just the 'language' of science, but is rather the language of the richer countries at the heart of scientific production, the language of the most prestigious journals and the language of evaluation and reward systems. When we talk of the position of 'English' in scientific knowledge production, therefore, we need to be aware of the much longer trail of practices and systems that this positioning brings in its wake.

Table 10.4 Geographic distribution of journals indexed in ISI and Ulrich's global serials directory

Country/region	*Number of ISI journals (Science Citations Index, 2009)* *	*Number of ISI journals (Social Science Citations Index, 2009)**	*Ulrich's Global Serials Directory: (refereed academic periodicals)***
North America	*2698*	*1119*	*9591*
United States	2612	1092	8902
Canada	86	27	689
Europe	*3083*	*874*	*10,525*
United Kingdom	1494	555	5358
Netherlands	643	140	2025
Germany	512	90	1617
France	177	25	512
Switzerland	158	25	441
Spain	60	31	359
Hungary	21	3	95
Slovakia	16	3	85
Portugal	2	2	33
Asia	*382*	*20*	*2062*
China	114	8	674
Japan	200	8	633
India	68	4	755
Africa	*37*	*18*	*428*
South Africa	29	16	245
Nigeria	8	2	183
Latin America	*113*	*33*	*623*
Brazil	65	10	363
Mexico	22	11	107
Chile	16	8	63
Argentina	10	4	90
Oceania	*123*	*70*	*1094*
Australia	97	61	898
New Zealand	26	9	196
Rest of world	*968*	*123*	*3673*
Total	7404	2257	27,996

Sources: *Thomson Reuters (2009b) ISI Web of Knowledge Journal Citation Reports.
**Ulrich's Global Periodicals Directory.www.ulrichsweb.com. Accessed December 2010.

Scholars as Knowledge Producers: Challenges, Interests, Inequalities

That there is a disparity between contexts of research and scientific outputs is evident in the statistical data presented in previous sections. What case study and ethnographic research adds to the picture is an understanding of how macro-economic factors (notably GERD), coupled with the dominant position of the Anglophone centre in science production and evaluation systems, impact on individual scholarly life and work. In this section, we turn our attention to the growing number of studies (including some reflective commentaries found in published works and academic blogs) which have sought to describe, understand and explore how scholars outside of the Anglophone centre are engaging in this academic marketplace. This is a relatively small field within the fields of academic literacy/writing/TESOL, whose growth in part parallels the increasing pressure on scholars to produce texts in English. We summarise key themes emerging from this work, including our own longitudinal study with 50 scholars from central and southern Europe (http://creet.open.ac.uk/projects/paw/) and discuss what this work adds to our understanding about opportunities and constraints for participating in knowledge generation.

Material conditions of scholarly work

A key issue foregrounded in case studies of scholarly writing for publication in peripheral contexts is that of the negative impact of the specific material conditions in which scholars work. 'Poverty, political instability, living conditions and lack of scholarly support systems – along with other such matters of unequal distribution or access to resources – shape the different practices and outcomes' (Canagarajah, 2002: 108). In his work with Sri Lankan scholars (including his own reflections), Canagarajah (1996, 2002) foregrounds the importance of such 'non-discursive' requirements for success in academic publishing, thus making an obvious point, but one often lost in the vast enterprise of English for Academic Purposes (EAP) with its predominantly 'language'-based discussions of the problems faced by 'peripheral' scholars in academic writing and writing for publication. He points to some of the larger challenges faced by scholars, such as sustaining scholarly activity in war or conflict areas, as well as some of the smaller (but vital) resource problems such as limited access to current journals and to necessary materials for production – paper, computers, multiple photocopies, return postage, style manuals. Similar material constraints have been noted by other researchers, and additionally include a lack of funding opportunities for research and limited opportunities to attend conferences (e.g. Flowerdew, 2001; Lillis & Curry, 2010). The following recent blog entry by a scholar from Malawi illustrates some of the challenges and frustrations of being a periphery scholar:

> One of the duties of an academic is to conduct research in their area of interest and specialization. Well, finding equipment for doing research is in itself a big huddle in most African universities. Apart from this, there is the daunting task of trying to disseminate your research findings in international conferences.
>
> By this I mean, getting your research paper accepted for some international conference may bring joy to the researcher. BUT, wait a minute, the researcher would have to fund from his own pocket for expenses like conference registration fees, transport, accommodation and other associated costs.
>
> This in itself is a stab in the back of an African researcher, because normally host institutions do not have funds for these expenses. This is because most universities in Africa are funded by their governments and definitely the funding is never enough. Of course it's understandable since the governments have 'priorities within priorities' in their national budgets. The governments have to fight for national food security, clean water, infrastructure development etc for the masses and funding academic research would never make it into the priority list.
>
> However, this situation might lead others to conclude that there is no academic research being done in Africa which is not necessarily true. Unfortunately, world university rankings take research publications into account. So you better not be surprised to see many African universities not faring well in the rankings! (http://bkankuzi.blogspot.com/2008/02/challenges-of-doing-academic-research.html. Accessed 15 November 2010)

Poor conditions of scholarly employment are a basic factor influencing opportunities for scientific activity. Whilst (shortage of) time is often viewed as a constraint by scholars around the world, limited time is clearly a problem when scholars are forced to take up several jobs because of low academic salaries. Mweru (2010), investigating the low rates of publishing by sub-Saharan African scholars, held focus group discussions with 25 Kenyan scholars of various ranks working at a public university in Nairobi.

Participants, who taught in five different departments, were 'faculty members who had not yet published a journal article or who had only published one article in the past three years' (Mweru, 2010: 110). She also conducted interviews with the chairs of the five departments. Mweru identified key themes in the data related to limited publications: 'lack of time and low salaries' (Mweru, 2010: 110). Given scholars' low salaries, 'if they did find some extra time, it was spent on teaching extra classes in private universities or colleges to supplement their incomes' (Mweru, 2010: 110). Likewise, the impact of working conditions on scholars in Central and Eastern Europe has also been noted, where scholars often hold two or three jobs (including non-teaching or academic jobs) because academic salaries are so low (Lillis & Curry, 2010).

Of course, in the context of the global position of English, limited amount of time for scholarly activity is further exacerbated by the need to write and disseminate research in the medium of English (in addition to researching and working in local, national and regional languages) and to compete for publication in Anglophone-centre journals. It is well documented that a considerable additional amount of time is required by peripheral scholars to write in English (see, for example, Curry & Lillis, 2004; Swales, 1990).

Access to English as a networked resource

Given the widespread practice in institutions around the world of treating English as the 'default' language of science, scholars are indeed under pressure to publish in English in order to have their work recognised and to build research capital for continued scientific work. It may seem obvious, therefore, that a key goal to ensure access and participation in scientific endeavour should be to increase individual competence in 'academic English'; indeed considerable research time and energy has gone into establishing the key features of 'academic' English, either as a generic resource or in disciplinary-specific fields and genres (see *Journal of English for Academic Purposes* as an example) and there is evidence that periphery scholars using English for scientific work are keen to have access to such knowledge (for examples of programmes, see Salager-Meyer, 2008; Shashok, 2010). However, case study research shows that individual competence in managing such features may be less significant than the capacity to access English along with or via 'literacy brokers' (Lillis & Curry, 2006), such as language professionals, authors' editors, translators and academics (see Shashok & Kerans, 2000). Gaining access to such human resources, in particular valuable brokers such as centre academics who have insider knowledge of journals' ideologies and practices, is often the result of spending a period of time in centre contexts which in itself constitutes a form of academic capital and serves to differentiate between privileged and non-privileged 'non-native English speaking' scholars (see Salager-Meyer, 2008). Several researchers have emphasised the constraints faced by scholars who are 'off-network' (Casanave, 1998; Flowerdew, 2000; Swales, 1987: 43).

Therefore, it is the capacity to access English as a resource attached to other key resources – such as centre academics, centre-based networks – rather than necessarily gaining individual control over English construed as an autonomous medium that is important. In our research, what emerged as particularly significant for ensuring publication in Anglophone-centre journals is the interrelationship between local and transnational network activity, in which English is used as a resource by different people at different points in time (Curry & Lillis, 2010; Lillis & Curry, 2006).

Ideologies of English in production and evaluation

Whilst in some academic circles there is an emphasis on English as a plural phenomenon – whether in terms of varieties (e.g. World Englishes) or practices (i.e. *languaging*, as in Phipps & Gonzalez, 2004), an ideology of a standard, appropriate English pervades reviewing and evaluation practices. Categorical statements about the inappropriateness of language used in articles submitted for publication are evident in reviewer comments, an example of which is included below:

> As regards the language the text also needs some revision. There are formulations that, in my view, are a little bit over the top and too pretentious... Maybe it is not the language but it is just too Latin for a North-West European. (Lillis & Curry, 2010: 150)

While the reviewer here seems to have trouble pinning down exactly what is troubling him or her, he or she appears to be quite disturbed by the text, and the comments clearly index that such concern relates to linguistic, rhetorical and intellectual traditions different from his or her own. There are many issues raised by such comments (for further discussion, see Lillis & Curry, 2010: 149-154), but the key point we wish to make here about this particular comment is that it is highly consequential: the author decided not to revise and resubmit the paper to this journal, even though the editor's letter explicitly invited her to do so. She could not make sense of, or did not know how to engage with, this particular comment. Similar consequences for periphery scholars have been noted by other researchers: Flowerdew (2000) points to the profoundly negative experience of a Hong Kong scholar from having his use of English criticised as being 'non native', and Englander (2009), in case studies with Mexican scholars, illustrates how such experiences feed into authors' identities as scholars with rights (or not) to participate in specific academic communities in specific ways.

Less obviously negative, yet potentially more oblique, discourse practices also impact on peripheral scholars' uptake of reviewer comments, and therefore their potential participation and success in scientific publishing. Canagarajah (2002: 171) notes problems caused by rhetorical practices in journal editors' correspondence to periphery scholars: 'The euphemistic modes of expression and politeness strategies create considerable problems of interpretation. This difficulty... perhaps accounts for the fact that very few periphery scholars resubmit their papers for consideration'.

A standard response by editors and reviewers when they 'recognise' a text as being written by a 'non-native user of English' is to call for it to be 'polished' or edited by a 'native speaker'. However, this reaction says more about the pervading ideology of a 'standard' English, than any simple (empirically identifiable) dichotomy between the 'English' used by so-called 'native' or 'non-native' users of English. This is borne out by the fact that reviewers can 'misrecognise' the linguistic identity of writers, as illustrated by Belcher (2007), where a comment about the need for 'NES' (native English speaking) editing was made about an 'NES' text. Furthermore, such an ideology ignores diversity in English practices globally and the possibility that writers may prefer to use rhetorical traditions associated with local (or translocal) English(es) or languages/language practices other than English (see, for example, Mauranen, 1993) and may indeed have serious concerns about the use of Anglophone-centre rhetorical practices for knowledge making. An example of the latter is reported by Duszak (2006) drawing on investigations by Gajda (1999) into Polish scholars' concerns about writing in English: these included what they referred to as the 'feuilletonisation' of academic genres involving a shift towards greater use of rhetorical features such as metaphor and hedging. A more general comment is made by Canagarajah (2001: 33), who, reflecting on his own writing, says writing in English has made him 'intellectually and rhetorically lazy'.

Contributing knowledge from the periphery

Even if/where 'non-discursive requirements' can be mitigated by improved material circumstances, or English can be crafted so as to appear 'NES like', periphery scholars may face further obstacles with regard to the value attributed to their research, notably related to the location of their research. Canagarajah (2002: 121) notes that where scholars' research topics focus on issues important to the local context 'the subjects treated don't fall within any existing (center) disciplinary discourse'. They are, thus, difficult to place in particular journals and to win the approval of journal gatekeepers. Likewise, Flowerdew (2001: 134) noted that one of the criticisms made by centre journal editors of peripheral scholars was that they are too 'parochial'. Mweru (2010: 111), in her work with Kenyan academics, reports scholars' sense of 'a negative attitude towards sub-Saharan-based scholars and their research, and a disregard for the issues that were addressed in [their] articles'.

There is strong evidence from our research with central and southern European scholars that research outside of Anglophone-centre contexts tends to be clearly 'marked' (as 'non-centre', non-Anglophone, peripheral). This can, in some instances, be to the scholar's benefit if, at that specific moment, a journal is seeking a 'non-centre' contribution. However, the downside is that work which, through its non-Anglophone-centre location, serves an 'exotic' function (Lillis & Curry, 2006) can only hold on to its value as 'exotic' as long as it remains a rarity. As one Spanish scholar stated:

> If journals published research about Spain every year, readers would develop understanding about the Spanish context. But of course this would mean readers wanting to know about Spain for Spain's sake, not as counterpoint, contrast to UK or US. (Lillis & Curry, 2010: 147)

Recent work by Flowerdew and Li (2009: 11) on Chinese scholars' activity has echoes of this 'exoticisation' process in journal article evaluation. One Chinese scholar states:

> I think on the whole they [the journals in the Anglophone centre] have – to put it unpleasantly – an 'orientalist discourse'... To follow internationalization, you need to cater to their interest, through self-colonialism.

Sustaining local/non-centre research tradition

Whilst we have emphasised throughout the significance of English-medium-centre journals, it is also the case that research continues to be published in many languages and that the status attributed (through national and transnational evaluation systems) to specific indexes, such as those generated by ISI, can obscure this fact. For example, Brazil's (natural) science publications overwhelmingly continue to be in Portuguese (UNESCO, Science Report, 2010b). Many scholars continue to publish in local, national or regional languages, in addition to publishing in English (see Curry & Lillis, 2010, for Slovak, Hungarian, Spanish and Portuguese scholars; Flowerdew & Li, 2009 for Chinese scholars; Buckingham, 2008 for Turkish scholars).

Scholars seek to sustain local publishing in local communities for a range of reasons, notably the very research-building capacity that is seen to be so crucial for economic success: for supporting younger scholars, sharing expertise and sustaining local (national/regional) traditions of research interests and paradigms.

Conclusion

If knowledge is the key to international development – whether defined in terms of competition in the global marketplace or in terms of universal human rights to participate in knowledge generation – having opportunities to engage in high-status scientific knowledge generation and publication activity is crucial. English currently holds a pivotal position within this activity, particularly, as we have foregrounded here, in terms of scientific article production and evaluation. Quantitative data show the paltry share of scientific article production in all disciplines held by countries/regions outside the historical 'triad' of the United States, Europe and some parts of Asia. Case study research indicates that peripheral scholars are under pressure to publish in English yet face considerable obstacles in doing so, including not least the material conditions of their scholarly work and the ideologies of English embedded in evaluation practices. Furthermore, it seems clear that it is the capacity to access English as a resource attached to other key resources – such as centre academics, centre-based networks, rather than necessarily gaining individual control over English construed as autonomous medium, that leads to publication opportunities and success.

We are aware, of course, that we have focused on only one type of knowledge production – scientific research articles which appear in high-status indexes. We consider this focus important because of the academic capital that such publications accrue. However, we recognise that more work is needed in this area: firstly to track the precise ways in which the development agenda in local sites is mediated by such capital; and secondly to explore the extent to which local research and publishing communities, using English as well as local languages, are succeeding in intervening in this agenda.

Acknowledgements

We would like to thank Anna Robinson-Pant for comments on an earlier draft. We would also like to thank UNESCO Division of Public Information for permission for the adaptation of Table 4.2 and the reprinting of Table 4.3 from the *World Social Sciences Report: Knowledge Divides*, 2010.

Notes

(1) 'Science' is used in its Latin-based meaning *scientia*, as knowledge making in general, rather than the natural sciences only, and as currently used in many parts of the non-Anglophone world.

(2) Journal articles are clearly not the only type of knowledge production valued in development debates or by key funders such as the World Bank and UNESCO. The UNESCO *Global Monitoring Report on Education for All* commissions 'background papers' rather than articles to feed into their global surveys and reports (www.unesco.org/new/en/education/themes/leading-the-international-agenda/efareport/background-papers/2010) and involves contributors to their reports from non-academic sectors, such as NGOs. We suggest, however, that scientific (academic) publication profiles play an important 'indirect' role here notably in commissioning practices: academics are invited to contribute to such reports on the basis, in part at least, of their publication profiles.

(3) A key limitation is that both models seem to work with quite rigid notions of space and, particularly Kachru's three circles, imply static processes and practices around language, rather than dynamic across time and space. Nevertheless, we continue to find the notions of centre and periphery valuable in exploring the politics of scientific text production.

(4) For examples of 'indigenous knowledges' as part of participatory research design, see Chambers, 1997. We are grateful to Anna Robinson-Pant for making this connection explicit.

(5) It is interesting to note that in the *World Social Science Report 2010*, explicit mention is made of the hegemonic (and problematic) position of English, whereas in the *World Science Report 2010*, no such comment is made.

References

Belcher, D. (2007) Seeking acceptance in an English-only research world. *Journal of Second Language Writing* 16, 1-22.

Bell, D. (1973) *The Coming of Post-Industrial Society: A Venture in Social Forecasting.* New York: Basic Books.

Bimber, B. (1995) The three faces of technological determinism. In M.R. Smith and L. Marx (eds) *Does Technology Drive History? The Dilemma of Technological Determinism* (pp. 79-100). Cambridge: MIT Press.

Buckingham, L. (2008) Development of English academic writing competence by Turkish scholars. *International Journal of Doctoral Studies* 3, 1-18.

Canagarajah, A.S. (1996) Nondiscursive requirements in academic publishing, material resources of periphery scholars, and the politics of knowledge production. *Written Communication* 13(4), 435-472.

Canagarajah, A.S. (2001) The fortunate traveler: Shuttling between communities and literacies by economy class. In D. Belcher and U. Connor (eds) *Reflections on Multiliterate Lives* (pp. 23-37). Clevedon: Multilingual Matters.

Canagarajah, A.S. (2002) *A Geopolitics of Academic Writing.* Pittsburgh, PA: University of Pittsburgh Press.

Casanave, C.P. (1998) Transitions: The balancing act of bilingual academics. *Journal of Second Language Writing* 1 (1), 175-203.

Chambers, R. (1997) *Whose Reality Counts?* London: Intermediate Technology Publications.

Curry, M.J. and Lillis, T. (2004) Multilingual scholars and the imperative to publish in English: Negotiating interests, demands, and rewards. *TESOL Quarterly* 38 (4), 663-688.

Curry, M.J. and Lillis, T. (2010) Academic research networks: Accessing resources for English-medium publishing. *English for Specific Purposes,* special issue on *EAP in Europe* 29, 281-295.

Duszak. A. (2006) Looking globally, seeing locally: Exploring some myths of globalization in academia. *Revista Canaria de Estudios Ingleses* 53, 35-45.

Englander, K. (2009) Transformation of the identities of nonnative English-speaking scientists as a consequence of the social construction of revision. *Journal of Language, Identity and Education* 8, 35-53.

Fairclough, N. (2006) *Language and Globalization.* London: Routledge.

Flowerdew, J. (2000) Discourse community, legitimate peripheral participation, and the nonnative-English-speaking scholar. *TESOL Quarterly* 34 (1), 127-150.

Flowerdew, J. (2001) Attitudes of journal editors to nonnative speaker contributions. *TESOL Quarterly* 35 (1), 121-150.

Flowerdew, J. and Li, Y. (2009) English or Chinese? The trade-off between local and international publication among Chinese academics in the humanities and social sciences. *Journal of Second Language Writing* 18, 1-16.

Freeman, P. and Robbin, A. (2006) Editorial: The publishing gap between rich and poor: The focus of AuthorAID. *Journal of Public Health Policy* 27, 196-203.

Gajda, S. (1999) Jezyk nauk humanistycznych. In W. Pisarek (ed.) *Polszczyzna* (pp. 14-32). Krakow: Osrodek Badan Prasoznawczych.

Garfield, E. (1972) Citation analysis as a tool in journal evaluation. *Science* 178, 471-479.

Jessop, B. (2002) *The Future of the Capitalist State.* Cambridge: Polity Press.

Kachru, B. (ed.) (1992) *The Other Tongue: English Across Cultures.* Urbana, IL: University of Illinois Press.

Kearney, M.L. (2009) Higher education, research and innovation: Charting the course of the changing dynamics of the knowledge society. In V.L. Meek, U. Teichler and M.L. Kearney (eds) *Higher Education, Research and Innovation: Changing Dynamics. Report on the UNESCO Forum on Higher Education, Research and Knowledge 2001-2009* (pp. 8-23). Kassel, Germany: International Centre for Higher Education Research.

Kenway, J., Bullen, E., Fahey, J. and Robb, S. (2006) *Haunting the Knowledge Economy.* New York: Routledge.

Lillis, T. and Curry, M.J. (2006) Professional academic writing by multilingual scholars: Interactions with literacy brokers in the production of English medium texts. *Written Communication* 23 (1), 3-35.

Lillis, T. and Curry, M.J. (2010) *Academic Writing in a Global Context: The Politics and Practices of Publishing in English.* London: Routledge.

Mauranen, A. (1993) *Cultural Differences in Academic Rhetoric.* Frankfurt: Peter Lang.

Mweru, M. (2010) Why Kenyan academics do not publish in international refereed journals. *World Social Science Report: Knowledge Divides* (pp. 110-111). Paris: UNESCO.

National Science Foundation (NSF) (2010) *Key Science and Engineering Indicators Digest.* Washington, DC: National Science Foundation.

Olssen, M. and Peters, M.A. (2005) Neoliberalism, higher education and the knowledge economy: From the free market to knowledge capitalism. *Journal of Education Policy* 20(3), 313-345.

Organization for Economic Cooperation and Development (OECD) (1996) *The Knowledge-Based Economy*. Paris: OECD.

Organization for Economic Cooperation and Development (OECD) (2008) *Science, technology and industry outlook highlights*, accessed 20 July 2009.www.oecd.org

Organization for Economic Cooperation and Development (OECD) (2009) *Factbook 2009: Economic, Environmental and Social Statistics*. Paris: OECD Publishing.

Paraje, G., Sadana, R. and Karam, G. (2005) Increasing international gaps in health-related publications. *Science* 308, 959-960.

Peters, M. (2001) National education policy constructions of the 'knowledge economy': Towards a critique. *Journal of Educational Enquiry* 2 (1), 1-22.

Phipps, A. and Gonzalez, M. (2004) *Modern Languages: Learning and Teaching in an Intercultural Field.* London: Sage.

Robertson, S. (2005) Re-imagining and rescripting the future of education: Global knowledge economy discourses and the challenge to education systems. *Comparative Education* 41 (2), 151-170.

Salager-Meyer, F. (2008) Scientific publishing in developing countries: Challenges for the future. *Journal of English for Academic Purposes* 7, 121-132.

Schement, J. and Curtis, T. (1997) *Tendencies and Tensions of the Information Age: The Production and Distribution of Information in the United States*. New Brunswick, NJ: Transaction.

Shashok, K. (2010) How AuthorAID in the Eastern Mediterranean helps researchers become authors. *The Write Stuff* 19 (1), 39-42.

Shashok, K. and Kerans, M. (2000) Translating the unedited science manuscript: Who fixes what shortcomings? In *I Congrés Internacional de Traducció Especialitzada: Actes* (pp. 101-104). Barcelona: Universitat Pompeu Fabra.

Shelton, R. (2008) Relations between national research investment and publications. *Scientometics* 74 (2), 191-205.

Sousa Santos, B. (1994) *Pela mão de Alice: o social eo político na pós-modernidade*. Porto: Edições Afrontamento.

Stiglitz, J. (1999) *Public policy for a knowledge economy, remarks at the Department for Trade and Industry and Center for Economic Policy Research, London*, 27 January, accessed 15 January 2011. www.cherry.gatech.edu/REFS/ED/KEPS/policy%20for%20know%20econ%20World%20Bank.pdf

Swales, J. (1987) Utilizing the literature in teaching the research paper. *TESOL Quarterly* 21, 41-68.

Swales, J. (1990) *Genre Analysis: English in Academic and Research Settings.* Cambridge: Cambridge University Press.

Thomson Reuters (2009a) *Current Contents*, accessed 22 June 2009. www.thomsonreuters.com

Thomson Reuters (2009b) *ISI Web of Knowledge Journal Citation Reports*, accessed December 2010. www.thomsonreuters.com

Ulrich's Global Periodicals Directory (UGPD) (2010) Ulrich's Global Periodicals Directory accessed December 2010, www.ulrichsweb.com

United Nations Educational, Scientific and Cultural Organization (UNESCO) (2009a) *DARE database*, accessed 22 July 2009. http://databases.unesco.org

United Nations Educational, Scientific and Cultural Organization (UNESCO) (2009b) *Forum on Higher education, Research and Knowledge 2001-2009*, accessed 30 November 2010. www.unesco.org

United Nations Educational, Scientific and Cultural Organization (UNESCO) (2009c) *Mapping Research Systems in Developing Countries: Synthesis Report*, accessed November-December 2010. www.unesco.org

United Nations Educational, Scientific and Cultural Organization (UNESCO) (2010a) *World Social Science Report: Knowledge Divides,* accessed November-December 2010. www.unesco.org

United Nations Educational, Scientific and Cultural Organization (UNESCO) (2010b) *Science Report. The Current Status of science around the world*, accessed November-22 December 2010. www.unesco.org

Wallerstein, I. (1991) *Geopolitics and Geoculture.* Cambridge: Cambridge University Press.

World Bank (1998) *World Development Report: Knowledge for Development*, accessed 22 December 2010. www.worldbank.org

World Bank (2010) *Development Report Statistical Annex.* Washington, DC: World Bank, accessed 22 December 2010. www.worldbank.org

Wyatt, I.D. and Heckler, D. (2006) Occupational changes during the 20th century. *Monthly Labor Review* March, 35-57.

11 Language in Economic Development: Is English Special and is Linguistic Fragmentation Bad?

Jean-Louis Arcand and François Grin

Introduction

The part that language might play in economic development has long intrigued scholars from various disciplines. However, no clear story has emerged from the investigations published to date, and the empirical evidence remains inconclusive (Nettle, 2000); even the choice of terms used in the literature ('fragmentation' to suggest a negative connotation, 'multilingualism' to suggest a positive one) reflects this ambiguity. The issues at hand are exceedingly broad, and the nature of the links that one wishes to identify, and then measure, is difficult to pinpoint precisely: what do we mean exactly by 'development'? And since 'language' pervades just about every facet of individual and social life, including economic processes, what manifestations of language should we assume to play a specific role in determining development-related outcomes?

The very existence of such a link is not self-evident, and most economic analyses, including those in the field known as development economics, tend to assume language away on the grounds that the economic processes at hand (encapsulated in terms like 'exchange', 'value', 'market', etc.), which they view as universal, transcend linguistic variables. It is only in recent years that 'culture', which, as an explanatory variable, had largely been relegated to the fringes of development economics as merely contextual, has been allowed to drift back near the centre of the field. Typical recent examples include work by Nobel laureate George Akerlof (Akerlof & Kranton, 2000) on the relationship between economics and identity or the study of the role played by religiosity in economic development (Barro & McCleary, 2003).

The distinct question of whether languages differ from one another in the ways in which they affect development, and then if one particular language, such as English, influences development in specific ways, can only be addressed in a second stage, after the previous set of questions has been dealt with. Note that we are not primarily interested in what would be the reverse causation, namely, providing an economics-based explanation of the relative fortunes of different languages, and the rise of English to its current position of prominence, though, as we shall see below, we will need to provide a partial answer to this question in order to investigate the impact of a given language on economic development in a statistically rigorous manner.

In this chapter, we develop an approach connecting 'language' as an independent and 'development' as a dependent variable, with a special emphasis on languages associated with the former colonial powers, particularly English. We shall return in a moment to the meaning (and hence also the limitations) of any connection of this kind that may be established. We define 'development' in a mainstream sense, focusing on relatively macro-level indicators, even if the methodology is, in the main, rooted in applied microeconomics. Our chief indicator of development is GDP per capita. This choice and its implications are discussed in the following section. Any attempt to establish this type of a relationship at a general level, rather than in reference to one specific developmental story, necessarily leaves aside a number of questions, some of which are studied elsewhere, while others remain, to our knowledge, unexplored, and it is useful to begin by listing some of the issues not addressed here.

We, therefore, deliberately put aside a wide range of perfectly legitimate questions regarding the interplay between language and economic activity, including some that are likely to be connected with development. For example, we do not address the internal communication practices of businesses that may 'develop' more or less successfully depending on the languages in which this internal communication takes place. This is not to deny that internal communication practices within firms may be one conduit through which language impacts on their economic performance and, by way of consequence, on aggregate measures of development. However, our main concern is on establishing the plausibility and magnitude of a link between language, on the one hand, and development, on the other hand, rather than focusing on the specific operations of such a link.[1] To this end, we draw on another subfield of economics, namely, language economics, which has only rarely been confronted with development questions. In the third section of this chapter, we discuss classical perspectives on economic development, which ignore language, before presenting causal connections between language and development, first proposed by Arcand (1996).

In our empirical work, which constitutes the crux of the original contribution of this chapter, we shall depart from a well-known strand of economic and political research that blames linguistic and cultural 'fragmentation' for the economic problems confronting many developing countries (in particular, those in Sub-Saharan Africa). Indeed, as we shall show below, there is relatively convincing empirical evidence that much of this literature is misguided because it has failed to adequately deal with the endogenous nature of ethnolinguistic fragmentation. The adjective 'endogenous' applies to a variable that is a function of other variables in the model, as opposed to 'exogenous', which can be assumed not to be determined by them. For example, if we study food production by subsistence farmers in Sub-Saharan Africa, it is likely to be positively connected to ownership of certain agricultural tools; at the same time, the fact that a farmer owns such tools is likely to be connected to the fact that he produces more food (and hence generates a surplus which in turn can be used to buy these tools). So when studying food production, it would be imprudent to assume that ownership of tools can be treated as an exogenous variable. An exogenous variable is something like recorded rainfall, a factor which influences a farmer's production, but is unaffected by it.

In our case, we do not view linguistic diversity (whether it is given a positive-sounding label such as 'multilingualism', or a negative-sounding one such as 'fragmentation') as independent of the other variables that play a part in the relationships we are studying; contrary to existing empirical work, which treats ethnolinguistic fragmentation as an exogenously given datum, we use a more complex approach, which allows for ethnolinguistic fragmentation to be determined by deep historical forces associated with colonialism.

Our empirical work throws up a number of thorny methodological challenges, including how to measure the stock of competence in a *lingua franca* such as English. In the main, however, these challenges are linked to the fact that even if we agree on a plausible 'story' connecting relevant linguistic variables with economic development, a host of other variables may be correlated with both the former and the latter. Thus, establishing the specific role of language as a (co-)determinant of development requires careful econometric procedures.

The following sections go into a fair amount of detail, explaining how we go about disentangling complex relationships in which economic development and language – or ethnicity-related traits – intervene. However, our main results, which fundamentally question received wisdom on these matters, can be accessed in our concluding section, without having to go through each of the technical steps involved. The findings are striking: namely, that 'fragmentation' (or 'multilingualism') may actually be associated with *higher* levels of GDP per capita.

What Do We Mean by 'Development'?

There are many ways to define economic development. In the empirical work that follows, we adopt the simplest (and highly reductionist) convention of confining our attention to GDP per capita. As has been argued by several generations of development economists since the 1950s, when the sub-discipline development economics emerged, and even when one eschews intertemporal concerns first raised by Nobel Prize laureate Samuelson in a famous paper from 1951, income is clearly an imperfect metric by which to measure development.

As should be obvious from the proliferation of alternative indicators such as the United Nations Development Programme's (UNDP) Human Development Index, or the focus of a number of world-renowned research institutions on very particular indicators (the International Food Policy Research Institute's use of child anthropometrics being a typical example), development is a multidimensional process that can be measured along a plethora of dimensions. Maternal and infant mortality rates, access to clean drinking water, the prevalence of infectious diseases, the empowerment of women, literacy or school enrolment rates, measures of the incidence of poverty or access to sufficient calorie and protein intake, life expectancy at birth – these and other indicators are all 'sold' by various constituencies as the 'best' indicator of economic development.

But it remains that GDP per capita is the only indicator that, because of its universal money-metric (and, once it is converted into purchasing power parity, one that is comparable across countries with vastly different consumption patterns and non-traded goods sectors), is applicable across all countries and during all time periods. In future research, we will seek to extend our results to other measures of development. For the time being, in order to circumscribe our search for a link between language and economic development using quantitative evidence, we will, therefore, confine ourselves to using GDP per capita as our dependent variable.

Combining Language and Development

Language plays a modest role in economic analysis, reflecting the twin notions that economic processes, being fundamental, transcend language and culture and that the latter, consequently, does not significantly affect economic variables. Since the mid-1960s, however, a small field of specialization has emerged, under the label of 'economics of language', precisely to explore these neglected questions. Much of this literature studies the effect of language skills on labour income or proposes economic approaches to the selection, design and evaluation of language policies (see Vaillancourt, 1985; Lamberton, 2002; or Grin, 1996, 2003, 2010 for surveys). However, the subfield of development economics has traditionally paid little attention to language, although linguists have often suggested that language must play some part in development (for a recent discussion, see Seargeant & Erling, 2011), sometimes in its capacity as a tool for communication, but more frequently as a key element of culture (Abou & Haddad, 1997; Chaudenson & de Robillard, 1990).

Let us begin by briefly considering the strand of literature that examines the effects of ethnic, linguistic or cultural 'fragmentation' on economic performance, such as Easterly and Levine (1997), Lian and Oneal (1997) and Alesina and LaFerrara (2005). Typically, these authors use an aggregate measure of ethnic, linguistic or cultural diversity, such as the Greenberg index of diversity,[2] and examine its statistical relationship with GDP per capita. Upon finding a negative relationship, they conclude that societal multilingualism is detrimental to economic performance. This literature, however, appears to rely on a rather essentialist brand of anthropology which assumes that diversity automatically makes societies prone to internal conflict, or at least hampers the development of trust that forms the bedrock of stable political and economic institutions. Actual communication processes are left out of the explanation (which begs the question of how intergroup trade develops in the first place), and the role of individual bilingualism is largely ignored (Nettle, 2000). Thus, finer-grained explanations need to be considered. While acknowledging that language barriers may restrict international trade, Noguer and Siscart (2003) conclude that this effect is considerably weaker than asserted by other authors in earlier work; Ku and Zussman (2010) use data on second-language skills showing that acquiring a foreign language (in their case English) 'can mitigate the impact of historically determined language barriers'. However, given the empirical evidence that we present below, we believe that we have uncovered a central fallacy in the arguments of those who hold that diversity is necessarily a fetter on economic growth and development.

One of the few contributions focusing on the effects of language on development processes as such is the work of Arcand (1996), which examines different conduits through which the former may influence the latter. Four such main conduits are identified:

(1) Transaction costs are lower among people who share a common language, thus facilitating, both in number and magnitude, transactions that might not occur otherwise; this negative effect of linguistic difference, however, can largely be obviated through other communication

strategies, whether through second-language learning generating widespread bilingualism, or using receptive competence in the form of 'intercomprehension' (particularly between relatively closely related languages), or resorting to language mediators possessing the necessary second-language skills.

(2) Contractual relationships, for example between a landlord and a peasant working on the former's land, may be complicated by the fact that if they speak different languages, this might hamper the landlord's capacity to precisely monitor the tenant's working effort. This, in essence, is an imperfect information issue. To circumvent this problem, the landlord must offer contractual terms for the lease of the land, which depart from optimality and thus result in lower economic performance. In other words, we would expect, *ceteris paribus*, an economy where most of the contracting takes place between people who share the same language to be more productive, all other things being equal, than one where such contracts are less common, and more effort needs to be expended to monitor or supervise a tenant's work (because in and of itself, expending such effort carries a cost). There again, this problem can be mitigated by widespread individual bilingualism or non-linguistic forms of social control that impel the tenant to deliver high productivity. And it is important to note that the effect just mentioned arises in situations where the respective roles of 'principal' and 'agent' (such as landowner and tenant) are unevenly distributed among language groups, suggesting that the source of the economic effect, if any, is linked to patterns of wealth distribution as much as to language: if both roles were equally represented across language groups, the aggregate negative effect on the economy might disappear altogether through expanded possibilities of intralinguistic contracting.[3]

(3) Uncertainty weighs heavily on credit transactions, which are crucial to economic activity by providing insurance. The implication, closely related to the preceding case, is that credit across language groups may, rightly or wrongly, be perceived as riskier than within a given language group. Conversely, if social norms prevent lending to members of the same group above a certain interest rate, intralinguistic credit will be constrained. Either way, restrictions on access to credit are likely to hamper development. Let us note, however, that such barriers may be linked to cultural traits (such as religious affiliation) that have little to do with language.

(4) Network externalities are another classical problem. 'Externalities' refer to the fact that one actor's action may generate unintended positive or negative side-effects. 'Network externalities' concern processes of this kind specifically connected to 'networks', usually in terms of

> information or communication. For example, when a person chooses to use a particular word-processing software, he or she does so for personal reasons (cost, convenience, etc.). However, this generates a positive externality, because people who *already* use this software will have one more person with whom they can directly exchange text files. Another typical example would be that of a telephone network: when an additional user joins the network, it expands, thereby increasing the value of the network to all existing users. To use a language example, if a person decides to learn Swahili (for whatever reasons), the value of Swahili *to those who already speak it* will increase, because they have gained one more potential interlocutor, without having had to incur any cost. In our case, network externalities may appear if there is convergence towards the use of one language, usually the 'larger' language boasting the larger number of speakers. Such externalities may arise through easier trade or faster adoption of new technologies. This effect, however, is predicated on the assumption that there is no alternative, in terms of developing 'networks', to sharing the same L1, or mother tongue.

Arcand then moves on to contributions from the closely related field of growth theory, which offer stepping-stones for introducing language into a narrative of development. Though the econometric tools we deploy at the macro level are, of course, far too coarse to allow us to explore these various causal pathways, they should be kept in mind, as the correlations we uncover in what follows are meaningless if they are not interpreted with the conceptual lenses offered by the various mechanisms sketched above.

Constructing an 'English Language' Variable for a Cross-section of Countries

We would ideally like to measure the effect of linguistic variables that are likely to play an important role in development processes. If we were to assume that the determining variable is the language(s) of schooling, the analysis would require having, for example, data on the percentage of school programmes, for each year in the syllabus, respectively taught through the medium of one or another language, along with information on which subjects are taught through what language, and whether all educational streams share the same linguistic regime, and, if not, what percentage of the school-going population is enrolled in what type of stream and so on. If we content ourselves, as an independent variable, with the distribution of language skills in a given country at a given time (hence leaving aside the question of how such skills are acquired, and what policies are conducive to such acquisition), we would then need detailed information on the population's linguistic repertoires, that is, what languages are known, by whom, at what level, orally and in writing, productively and receptively.

This, however, raises a number of difficulties. The first is that for the most part, data of this type simply are not available. Existing data are incomplete, imprecise, of questionable reliability and of restricted comparability. The second problem is that even if complete, detailed, reliable and comparable data were available, a fundamental problem would remain, namely, how to deal with unobserved variables. This problem deserves closer examination and will be the focal point of our empirical strategy which is detailed below.

Taking account of the paucity of data, the most reasonable choice of a language variable for quantitative treatment is one that describes the extent of skills in a given language in a given society at a given time. This is why we have chosen to measure 'English' as the level of the stock of knowledge of the language. More precisely, we approximate it by multiplying the average TOEFL score recorded in each country multiplied by the number of people in that country who have actually sat the TOEFL test.[4] This stock of linguistic knowledge may impact on economic development through different channels, such as 'access to knowledge and development of human capital' or 'integration in international trade flows'.

Empirical Methodology

If we agree that the existence of a link between some language-related variable (cast here in the role of an independent variable) and economic development (the dependent variable) is plausible, the measurement of this link requires taking account of a host of control variables. The latter may be correlated with both language *and* economic development. If such a 'third' factor is, for example, correlated positively both with GDP per capita and the stock of English competence as measured by our TOEFL variable, and if we fail to include it in our empirical specification, this could lead to a positive correlation between English competence and GDP per capita that would be entirely spurious: more seriously, in terms of the question we are seeking to answer, the ensuing correlation would in no way be tantamount to a causal effect of language on economic development. Quite apart from the difficulty of properly and completely identifying these control variables, it is highly likely that the corresponding data will not be available anyway.

One strategy for circumventing this problem, popularized in the literature on the empirics of economic growth in a celebrated paper by Acemoglu *et al.* (2001), is to use an instrumental variable (IV) approach. Intuitively, as applied to the problem at hand, the idea is to generate exogenous variation in the language variable using another variable (known as the 'instrument') which does not have any direct effect on our measure of economic development, but which does affect language. Therefore, if the instrument only affects economic growth because it affects our language variable, correlation between the instrument and economic growth provides proof that economic growth *is* affected by the language variable. In practice, the procedure works as follows: (1) we establish, through OLS (ordinary least squares) regression, that the instrument *does* affect our language variable (e.g. the stock of English-language competence); (2) we come up with a (hopefully) convincing story to the effect that the instrument has no reason to affect our development variable (such as GDP per capita); (3) we construct a new language variable that replaces the original language variable; more precisely, we estimate the level of English language competence that is *predicted* by the instrument, and this estimation will replace the original language variable, because, by definition, this estimation *cannot* be the product of something that would also influence GDP per capita; (4) we regress GDP per capita on this new language variable; (5) we interpret the resulting estimated coefficient as representing the causal impact of English language competence on GDP per capita.[5] At the risk of belabouring this point, correlation is not the same thing as causality. If one finds a strong (positive or negative) correlation between ethnolinguistic diversity and GDP per capita, this does not necessarily mean that there is a causal link flowing from one variable towards the other. The statistical procedure that we have outlined above attempts to disentangle correlation from causality and estimate the magnitude of the unidirectional causal link flowing from ethnolinguistic diversity towards GDP per capita.

Finding instrumental variables for right-hand-side (RHS) variables in growth regressions has become something of a cottage industry, and is more a question of art than of science. It is also a question of constructing variables that are not found in most economic datasets, such as the World Bank's World Development Indicators, or the International Monetary Fund's (IMF) International Financial Statistics. Most importantly, since the lack of a direct effect of the instrumental variable on the left-hand-side (LHS) variable in the growth or GDP per capita regression cannot be statistically put to a definitive test, it is essential that a plausible story be told as to why the exogeneity assumption (that is, the assumption that GDP per capita does *not* depend on the instrument) might reasonably be assumed to hold.

In the context of the impact of the English language on economic growth, the aforementioned work of Acemoglu *et al.* (2001), henceforth AJR, provides a useful benchmark for comparisons, as well as several candidate instrumental variables. In their work, AJR are interested in estimating the causal impact of economic institutions (which they quantify using a measure of protection against expropriation risk) on the logarithm of GDP per capita in 1995. Their key instruments are provided by the mortality of white settlers at the time of colonization (their sample of countries, which we shall conform to, is made up of ex-colonies), the proportion of European settlers in the country in 1900, the democracy score of the country in 1900, as well as a measure of the constraints on executive power, also in 1900. The interested reader is referred to AJR for details concerning the construction of all of these variables, which have become standard workhorses in the empirical growth literature.

The AJR argument is that each of these variables affects institutions, but has no direct effect on GDP per capita *in 1995*. For example, the proportion of European settlers in 1900 will have a profound influence on whether the country adopted neo-European forms of economic governance at the turn of the 19th century, which in turn will affect economic institutions today as measured by the protection against expropriation risk. Similarly, settler mortality, when extremely high at the time of colonization, will lead to 'extractive' institutions being initially put in place, in which the colonizing power would merely exploit the colony without investing in institutional construction[6]: the argument is that this will then lead to poor institutions today, while settler mortality, which does not reflect the epidemiological resistance of the country's current population, should have no *direct* impact on today's GDP per capita.[7] Summary statistics on the various variables used in this chapter are provided in Table 11.1 and will be referred to as needed in what follows.

Table 11.1 Descriptive statistics, 54 country sample

	Mean	*Standard deviation*	*Minimum*	*Maximum*
Log GDP per capita	7.971	1.001	6.110	10.220
Africa dummy	0.472	0.503	0	1
Asia dummy	0.145	0.355	0	1
Distance to the equator	0.175	0.132	0	0.670
Ethnolinguistic fragmentation	0.444	0.314	0	0.890
Log stock of TOEFL competence	9.413	1.653	5.910	12.854
Protection against expropriation risk	6.421	1.469	3.500	10.000
Settler mortality	4.775	1.226	2.150	7.990
Constraint on the executive in 1900	2.218	2.087	1	7
Democracy score in 1900	1.582	2.871	0	10
Proportion white settlers in 1900	15.43	24.740	0.000	99.000

Empirical Results: A First Pass

In Column 1 of Table 11.2, we present the 'first-stage reduced form', in which our English language variable is regressed on two standard control variables (the distance to the Equator, which proxies for geography, as well as ethnolinguistic fragmentation[8]) and the AJR settler mortality instrument.

Table 11.2 Econometric results (standard errors in parentheses)

	1	*2*	*3*	*4*
Dependent variable	*Log stock of TOEFL competence*	*AJR baseline result*	*Log GDP per capita in 1995*	*Log GDP per capita in 1995*
Estimation method	*OLS*	*IV*	*IV*	*OLS*
Intercept	12.127 (1.121)	3.767 (0.822)	−1.088 (2.203)	7.635 (0.854)
Africa dummy				−1.041 (0.325)
Asia dummy				−0.738 (0.386)
Distance to the equator	−2.423 (1.867)	−0.694 (0.767)	2.910 (0.892)	1.749 (0.886)
Ethnolinguistic fragmentation	−0.325 (0.810)	−1.069 (0.273)	−0.405 (0.410)	−0.181 (0.486)
Stock of TOEFL competence			0.927 (0.217)	0.075 (0.083)
Protection against expropriation risk		0.747 (0.132)		
Settler mortality	−0.449 (0.207)			
Constraint on the executive in 1900				
Democracy score in 1900				
Test of exogeneity of protection against expropriation risk: *p*-value		0.014		
Test of exogeneity of stock of TOEFL competence: *p*-value			0.000	
R^2	0.109			0.439
N	54	54	54	54

Our data are the same as those of AJR, though our sample size is slightly smaller because of the lack of data concerning TOEFL examinees for some ex-colonies included in the AJR dataset. As one would expect, higher settler mortality leads to a lower stock of English competence as measured by our TOEFL variable, and this result is highly significant at conventional levels of statistical confidence[9]: presumably the causal pathway through which this result is obtained is similar to that through which high settler mortality leads to poor levels of economic institutions. Extractive colonies may be associated with the lack of a well-functioning schooling system for the local population, and few opportunities for advancement within the colonial civil service, all of which would render the economic returns to mastering English extremely low. (A useful thought experiment in the francophone world would be to compare Guinea-Conakry, where settler mortality was extremely high and schooling for the local population was essentially non-existent, with nearby Senegal where, despite widespread discrimination, Africans eventually found opportunities for advancement within the colonial civil service or that of the colonizing power – Leopold Sedar Senghor being the most notable example).

The corresponding structural equation, in which we then explain GDP per capita in 1995 (as in AJR) using the exogenous portion of TOEFL competence (i.e. that part of TOEFL competence which is explained by the instruments), is presented in Column 3 of Table 11.2. The reason we need to do this goes under the technical term of 'endogeneity' in econometrics: is GDP per capita high because TOEFL competences are high, or are TOEFL competences high because GDP is high? All of the procedures in this chapter attempt, to the extent that it is possible, to cut this Gordian knot and to distinguish between correlation and causality. The underlying steps are those explained earlier.[10]

As shown by the estimated coefficient (Column 3 of Table 11.2), a 1% increase in the stock of TOEFL competence leads to a 0.927% increase in GDP per capita, which would *prima facie* suggest that English language skills do indeed have a positive influence on income. These estimates can be treated as percentages because both the stock of TOEFL competence and the dependent variable are measured in logarithmic terms: the ensuing coefficients can therefore be interpreted as a ratio of relative changes, known in economic analysis as 'elasticities'.[11,12]

By dint of comparison, Column 2 of Table 11.2 reports the result of estimating the standard AJR result for their measure of institutions. Given that, unlike income, there is no obvious metric with which one can compare differences in 'protection against expropriation risk' and differences in TOEFL scores, we need to find a manner of quantifying the magnitudes of their respective effects on income per capita. The most obvious solution is to reason in relative terms. For a variable distributed according to the normal distribution, 95% of the observations will fall within two standard deviations of the mean. In order to quantify the impact of institutions or linguistic competence on income, we consider a change of one standard deviation in each of these variables and look at the resulting changes in income. A one standard deviation change in the 'protection against expropriation risk' variable (1.469, as reported in the descriptive statistics in Table 11.1) leads to a 109% change in GDP per capita (not reported in the tables). In comparison, a one standard deviation change in the stock of TOEFL competence (1.653) leads to a 153% change in GDP per capita. A preliminary conclusion that might be drawn from these results is that English language competence is just as important as economic institutions, indeed is quantitatively more important, in determining who is rich and who is poor in today's world.

Before proclaiming that competence in English as measured by our TOEFL variable is as important as economic institutions in explaining economic growth and development, it is wise to subject the previous result to a number of elementary robustness checks.

For the sake of brevity, we shall not discuss them in detail, but merely present a gist of the corresponding tests. First, we add geographic control variables. This inclusion substantially changes the results; in particular, the stock of TOEFL competence no longer has any significant effect on GDP per capita. What is more, this lack of statistical significance can be established using a standard OLS regression, without resorting to an IV approach.

The OLS results in question are, therefore, presented in Column 4 of Table 11.2. Additional experimentation, not reported here, involving estimating the equations on the African and non-African sub-samples separately, confirms the lack of effect of TOEFL competence on GDP per capita.

Let us, however, carry the investigation a few steps further and question the assumption that variables denoting linguistic or ethnic features of society can, in general, be treated as exogenous.

Can One Safely Assume Ethnolinguistic Fragmentation to Be Exogenous?

If one agrees, at least initially, that it is unwise to presume that our measure of English language competence can be assumed to be exogenous in an AJR-type regression analysis of income per capita, a second question then, almost of necessity, rears its ugly head. Is it reasonable to assume that ethnolinguistic fragmentation, as it is usually measured in the economic growth literature, is exogenous with respect to income per capita, despite the fact that, in our empirical specification, ethnolinguistic fragmentation is measured in 1960 and income per capita is measured in 1995? Could there not be unobservables that, over time, have contributed simultaneously to lower GDP per capita and higher ethnolinguistic fragmentation and which we have not adequately controlled for in our structural equations? If one maintains the same level of statistical agnosticism concerning the exogeneity of ethnolinguistic fragmentation as one does concerning the exogeneity of institutions (curiously, the literature has chosen *not* to), the answer should be a resounding 'yes'.

In Table 11.3, we, therefore, reconsider our earlier results, as well as those of AJR and their followers, and relax a number of assumptions. First, we shall include institutions (the AJR protection against expropriation risk variable), the stock of TOEFL competence, and ethnolinguistic fragmentation all at once and, given the wealth of instruments provided by AJR, we shall allow all three of them to be jointly endogenous RHS variables (which means that instead of using the observed values of these variables, we replace them by their predicted value using the instruments). We will then let the data speak for themselves and guide us in terms of which variables can, on statistical grounds (and, of course, under the hypothesis that the AJR instruments are valid), be safely assumed to be exogenous with respect to GDP per capita in 1995.

The results of the three first-stage reduced forms for the stock of TOEFL knowledge, protection against expropriation risk and ethnolinguistic fragmentation are presented in Columns 5, 6 and 7 of Table 11.3. Concentrating on the ethnolinguistic fragmentation equation (Column 7), we find that the proportion of European settlers in 1900 is associated with a higher degree of ethnolinguistic fragmentation in 1960. Though the precise causal pathways through which this correlation obtains could be numerous, displacement of local populations by European colonizers and 'divide and rule' strategies put in place to maintain colonial 'peace' are plausible candidates, or that when there was little fragmentation to begin with, settlement was more difficult, because Europeans were up against a less malleable colony.

The ensuing structural equation (in which ethnolinguistic fragmentation, protection against expropriation risk and the stock of TOEFL competence are all allowed to be endogenous) is presented in Column 9 of Table 11.3. Several results are extremely striking. First, the coefficient associated with ethnolinguistic fragmentation is positive (though not significant). Second, as in our previous results which also included

Table 11.3 Econometric results (standard errors in parentheses)

	5	6	7	8	9	10	11	12	13
Dependent variable	*Log stock of TOEFL competence*	*Protection against expropriation risk*	*Ethno-linguistic fragmen-tation*	*Log GDP per capita in 1995*	*Log GDP per capita in 1995*	*Ethno-linguistic fragmen-tation*	*Log GDP per capita in 1995*	*Ethno-linguistic fragmen-tation*	*Log GDP per capita in 1995*
Estimation method	*OLS*	*OLS*	*OLS*	*OLS*	*IV*	*OLS*	*IV*	*OLS*	*IV*
Intercept	8.929 (0.622)	4.825 (0.560)	0.341 (0.103)	6.282 (0.629)	4.237 (3.115)	0.234 (0.158)	5.495 (0.400)	0.239 (0.150)	5.494 (0.374)
Africa dummy	−0.874 (0.547)	0.750 (0.493)	0.518 (0.090)	−0.704 (0.233)	−1.597 (0.529)	0.521 (0.092)	−1.682 (0.425)	0.535 (0.079)	−1.682 (0.419)
Asia dummy	2.267 (0.684)	2.122 (0.616)	0.289 (0.113)	−0.616 (0.271)	−1.392 (0.941)	0.276 (0.126)	−1.135 (0.274)	0.297 (0.111)	−1.113 (0.269)
Distance to the equator	−0.124 (1.718)	−0.804 (1.547)	−0.945 (0.285)	0.190 (0.659)	1.824 (1.541)	−0.911 (0.286)	1.800 (0.827)	−0.905 (0.270)	1.829 (0.776)
Ethnolinguistic fragmentation				−0.518 (0.344)	1.943 (1.579)		1.844 (0.916)		1.906 (0.886)
Stock of TOEFL competence				−0.048 (0.061)	0.103 (0.328)				
Protection against expropriation risk				0.430 (0.060)	0.394 (0.141)	0.012 (0.026)	0.358 (0.057)	0.007 (0.024)	0.351 (0.055)
Proportion of European settlers in 1900	−0.000 (0.014)	0.042 (0.013)	0.005 (0.002)			0.005 (0.002)		0.005 (0.002)	
Constraint on the executive in 1900	0.522 (0.248)	0.247 (0.223)	−0.065 (0.041)			−0.036 (0.019)		−0.032 (0.017)	

(Continued)

Table 11.3 (Continued)

	5	6	7	8	9	10	11	12	13
Dependent variable	*Log stock of TOEFL competence*	*Protection against expropriation risk*	*Ethno-linguistic fragmen-tation*	*Log GDP per capita in 1995*	*Log GDP per capita in 1995*	*Ethno-linguistic fragmen-tation*	*Log GDP per capita in 1995*	*Ethno-linguistic fragmen-tation*	*Log GDP per capita in 1995*
Estimation method	*OLS*	*OLS*	*OLS*	*OLS*	*IV*	*OLS*	*IV*	*OLS*	*IV*
Democracy score in 1900	−0.355 (0.196)	−0.084 (0.177)	0.027 (0.032)						
Test of exogeneity of protection against expropriation risk: *p*-value					0.903				
Test of exogeneity of stock of TOEFL competence: *p*-value					0.756				
Test of exogeneity of ethnolinguistic fragmentation: *p*-value					0.088		0.008		0.005
R^2	0.451	0.437	0.581	0.729		0.576		0.596	
N	54	54	54	54	54	54	54	58	58

the continent dummies, the stock of TOEFL competence is not a statistically significant determinant of GDP per capita. Third, 'institutions' as measured by the protection against expropriation risk is a highly significant determinant of GDP per capita even once ethnolinguistic fragmentation and the stock of TOEFL competence are allowed to be endogenous. Fourth, the tests of the null hypotheses of the exogeneity of the three potentially endogenous RHS variables suggest rejection only for ethnolinguistic fragmentation, as shown by the p-value of 0.088 in the penultimate row of Column 9. In other words, it would appear reasonable, on statistical grounds, to assume that ethnolinguistic diversity is endogenous while protection against expropriation risk and TOEFL competence are exogenous (see Endnote 10).

This last result is extremely important and suggests that the existing literature may have been unduly hasty in ignoring the potential endogeneity of ethnolinguitic fragmentation while focusing all of its energies on endogenizing a measure of institutions. The upshot is that ethnolinguistic fragmentation (with the associated linguistic dimensions) has probably been blamed for feeble economic performance, whereas no such correlation may in fact exist, and the true causes for slow growth lie elsewhere.[13,14]

Given the lack of statistical significance of the stock of TOEFL knowledge in the structural equation, we drop it from the structural equations that follow. Moreover, given that the exogeneity of institutions as measured by the protection against expropriation risk is not rejected once ethnolinguistic fragmentation is allowed to be endogenous, we will henceforth assume that protection against expropriation risk is exogenous. Finally, given that ethnolinguistic fragmentation is the only variable for which exogeneity in the structural equation is rejected, we continue to allow it to be endogenous in the specifications that follow.

These assumptions lead to the first-stage reduced form for ethnolinguistic fragmentation presented in Column 10 of Table 11.3, and in which protection against expropriation risk is included given that, on the basis of the exogeneity tests discussed above, it will be assumed to be exogenous. Experimentation with the AJR instrument set yielded a specification of the structural equation from which the proportion of European settlers in 1900 and constraints on the executive in 1900, being the instruments, are excluded; they significantly affect ethnolinguistic fragmentation in 1960. Using this first-stage reduced form, where ethnolinguistic fragmentation is shown to be influenced by these two instruments, the resulting structural equation reported in Column 11 of Table 11.3 shows that ethnolinguistic fragmentation has a positive and statistically significant effect on the log of per-capita GDP in 1995, as does protection against expropriation risk.[15]

Back to the AJR Sample of Countries

One concern that could be raised with our results, which overturn the conventional wisdom with respect to the impact on growth of ethnolinguistic fragmentation, is that they are based on a slightly smaller sample than those of AJR. This is because we lose four observations (with respect to the standard AJR baseline IV results) because of missing data points in the stock of TOEFL competence variable. Given that we have now, on the basis of the econometric evidence, left out the stock of TOEFL competence from our empirical specification, these data can be included in further investigation. In the interests of brevity, only a subset of the corresponding results of this analysis is presented below.

Column 12 of Table 11.3 presents a first-stage reduced form for ethnolinguistic fragmentation in which only the statistically significant AJR instruments are retained ('proportion of European settlers' and 'constraints on the executive'). Both are (marginally) significant determinants of ethnolinguistic fragmentation in 1960. Column 13 presents the corresponding structural equation, in which ethnolinguistic fragmentation is assumed to be endogenous and protection against expropriation risk is assumed to be exogenous. As with the results presented earlier, we obtain a positive and statistically significant effect of protection against expropriation risk on log GDP per capita, as well as a positive and statistically significant effect of ethnolinguistic fragmentation. In quantitative terms (and using the metric explained earlier), a one standard deviation change in protection against expropriation risk (1.491, which is marginally greater than in the earlier 54 observation-strong dataset) leads to a 52% increase in GDP per capita. In contrast, a one standard deviation change in ethnolinguistic fragmentation (0.312) leads to a 59% increase in GDP per capita. These figures are obtained by multiplying the standard deviation by the estimated coefficient given in Column 13 of Table 11.3. For example, we see that 1.491 x 0.351 = 0.52. The quantitative impact of ethnolinguistic fragmentation on GDP per capita is, therefore, roughly equivalent to that of economic institutions. Moreover, contrary to received wisdom, we have made the econometric case that they both affect income per capita in the *same* direction.

Alternative Measures of Ethnolinguistic Fragmentation: Time to Shift the Burden of Proof?

Although our results in terms of a positive effect on GDP per capita of ethnolinguistic fragmentation once the latter is allowed to be endogenous are statistically robust and stem from an agnostic initial position concerning exogeneity, a question remains concerning the validity of the variable in and of itself. This is because the ethnolinguistic variable used in most of the empirical growth literature was constructed by Soviet geographers in the late 1950s and reflects a number of questionable assumptions. Interested readers are referred, for example, to Fearon (2003) for details.

Our purpose here is certainly not to descend into the arena in which alternative measures of ethnolinguistic fragmentation compete, yet it would appear worthwhile to ascertain whether our main result – that of ethnolinguistic fragmentation, once it is appropriately endogenized, has a positive impact on log GDP per capita – also holds when we use a different measure (and is not merely dependent upon using one or another definition of 'fragmentation' or 'multilingualism'). Given current research on the topic, and our preoccupation with linguistic as opposed to ethnic aspects of fragmentation, the most natural candidates are furnished by the 15 fragmentation measures recently proposed by Desmet *et al.* (2009, henceforth DOW), and which are constructed on the basis of linguistic genealogical trees, at varying degrees of linguistic aggregation.

Several aspects of these results are worth discussing. First, with the exception of the lowest level of linguistic aggregation (termed 'ELF1' by DOW), the exogeneity of linguistic fragmentation is always rejected. Second, with the exception of ELF 3 to ELF 6, the AJR instruments always provide a modicum of identification (meaning that they generate plausibly exogenous variation in these linguistic fragmentation variables, just as they did for the standard measure of ethnolinguistic fragmentation). Third, subject to these first two caveats, and thus for ELF 10 and above, the DOW fragmentation variables are associated with a positive and statistically significant impact on log GDP per capita. Given that the higher level of aggregation of the ELF variables used by DOW are those that are more highly correlated with the standard measure (though the correlation is far from being equal to 1), this should not come as a surprise.

The upshot is that for ELF 10 and above (meaning for six different measures of linguistic fragmentation), the results are broadly in line with those found using the standard measure of ethnolinguistic fragmentation. At the very least, and in terms of the issue of whether this variable is exogenously determined with respect to per capita income, our results suggest that it is perhaps time to shift the burden of proof: instead of automatically accepting the notion that linguistic diversity (which is reflected in measures of fragmentation) has a detrimental impact on economic performance, and expecting supporters of diversity to prove this notion wrong, there are solid grounds for considering linguistic diversity as *a priori* conducive to economic development – leaving it to advocates of monolingualism to provide proof positive that uniformity is better.

Concluding Remarks

Two main lessons can be derived from the econometric evidence presented in this chapter. First, widespread competence in a dominant language such as English is in no manner associated with a higher level of economic development, when the latter is measured by its most common incarnation of GDP per capita. When English language skills are no longer viewed as an exogenous variable emerging *ex nihilo,* but as a social feature that can co-vary with other variables, including income itself, we find that it is no longer associated with economic outcomes. When English language skills are handled in conjunction with ethnolinguistic fragmentation, however, it can, on statistical grounds, be treated as exogenous but ceases to have any notable effect on income. In short, English is not 'special' in terms of economic development or growth.

Second, we have turned to ethnolinguistic 'fragmentation', a label quite commonly used in the literature with a hint of a negative connotation, as it has often been blamed for poor economic performance. 'Fragmentation' is typically treated as exogenous. However, if we treat 'fragmentation' as an endogenous variable, and handle the issue with the same methods as we have done for English language skills, we find that ethnolinguistic diversity is associated not with lower, but with *higher* levels of per-capita income. This result challenges received wisdom in a fundamental way. Thus, the term 'fragmentation' might be replaced, to all intents and purposes, by the more positive-sounding '(societal) multilingualism'.

What is the alternative to the use of an international *lingua franca,* whether it be English or another? Typically, the alternatives are local languages, with lower numbers of L1 speakers worldwide. Despite the fact that a significantly smaller range of written materials (including for instructional purposes at all levels) are available in such languages, our fresh empirical evidence, based on an instrumental variables approach, indicates that ethnic and linguistic 'fragmentation', which surely must be the reflection of the widespread use of local languages, actually increases income per capita in a sample of ex-colonies that have been the object of considerable scrutiny in the empirical growth literature over the past decade.

If the lack of such instructional materials were remedied through adequate investment, broadening the range of domains (in the Fishman–Ferguson sense) in which local languages offer the same scope as dominant languages for access to knowledge, it is possible that the positive effect of linguistic fragmentation on income per capita could be boosted even further. The likelihood of this scenario is borne out by findings by Dutcher (1997) and Heugh (2006), suggesting that in developing countries, the use of local languages as a medium of instruction lowers drop-out and repetition rates, thereby leading to a higher aggregate stock of human capital; and human capital remains, in the long term, one of the keys of economic development. Though our empirical findings do not allow us to precisely identify the causal channels through which linguistic fragmentation increases income per capita, they are suggestive of the fact that language's impact on the development process has been, perhaps, seriously misinterpreted for many years.

Notes

(1) A number of contributions in applied linguistics provide detailed observations of communicational practices in economic contexts, and boldly interpret these practices as conducive to favourable economic outcomes, without, however, spelling out what these outcomes might be and why a causal relationship should emerge, and, of course, without offering any measurement of its magnitude. It is safer, in our view, to begin by ascertaining the existence of such a link, before venturing fine-grained interpretations of how it might unfold. For this reason, we shall leave aside the literature in critical sociolinguistics (e.g. Heller, 2007), and interactionist perspectives on language at work (e.g. Lüdi & Theme, 2002), including 'ethnomethodologically-inspired conversation analysis' (Mondada, 2007). A commentary on applied linguistic approaches to the study of multilingual practices in economic activity can be found in Grin *et al.* (2010), Chapter 2.

(2) The diversity index proposed by Greenberg in 1956, often called the 'A-index' in the literature, is equal to one minus what economists call the Herfindahl index. The various groups ($j = 1,\ldots,n$) in a set are each assigned a share x of the set, where the sum of these shares is equal to one, and $A = 1 - \sum_{j=1}^{n} (x_j)^2$. Lian and Oneal (1997) use a more complex index of diversity defined as: $\left(\sum_{j=1}^{n} \rho_j^2 - \rho_k^2\right) \times \left(\sum_{j=1}^{n} \rho_j^2\right)^{-2}$, where ρ_j is the percentage of the jth group and ρ_k is the percentage of the largest ethnic, linguistic or religious group in the country.

(3) For a pithy analysis of the economic implications of linguistic difference between holders of capital and suppliers of labour, see Lang (1986).

(4) So as to be in conformity with the year of our dependent variable (log GDP per capita in 1995), we use the measures of TOEFL test scores and examinees provided by the first edition of the *TOEFL Test and Score Manual Supplement* (1994-1995).

(5) Another way of understanding this is that a valid instrumental variable yields what is akin to a randomized control trial in which the level of the language variable will be randomly assigned to different countries. As such, any correlation between that portion of the language variable that is exogenously determined and our measure of economic development will be interpretable as a causal effect of English language competency on economic development.

(6) A similar argument is put forward in Mufwene (2001), where he contrasts 'settlement colonies' with 'exploitation colonies' (quoted in Ostler, 2010: 32).

(7) This why it is important that AJR use settler mortality at the time of colonization, and not an estimate of the mortality of the indigenous population. The latter

would, of course, be related to the resistance to various pathogens of the local population, and could be reasonably assumed to be a proxy for current resistance to various infectious diseases.

(8) This is the standard measure of ethnolinguistic fragmentation introduced in the literature by Mauro (1995) and subsequently popularized by such authors as Easterly and Levine (1997). We return to the measurement of ethnolinguistic fragmentation further on in the empirical analysis.

(9) When the ratio of the coefficient estimation divided by corresponding standard error is equal to or greater than 2, the coefficient can be regarded as statistically significant at the 5% level.

(10) It is nevertheless useful to recall them: First, we predict TOEFL competence using the first-stage reduced form presented in Column 1 of Table 11.2. Second, using the coefficients thus estimated and the value of the exogenous variables in Column 1, we can compute a predicted value of TOEFL competence for each country. If our instrumental variables are indeed valid, this predicted value of TOEFL competence will not be correlated with unobservables which affect GDP per capita. Third, instead of using the raw TOEFL values, we replace them by their respective predicted values as independent variables in the estimation of log GDP per capita (Column 3 of Table 11.2). The estimated coefficient associated with the estimated value of TOEFL competence will thereby reflect its causal impact on GDP per capita and will not reflect the causal relationship flowing in the other direction (from GDP per capita to TOEFL competence).

(11) Moreover, the p-value associated with the test of the null hypothesis of the exogeneity of the TOEFL competence variable is extremely small. In statistics, the p-value of a test corresponds to the probability that one will incorrectly reject the 'null hypothesis', which in this case is that TOEFL competence is exogenous. The smaller the p-value, therefore, the 'stronger' the rejection of the null hypothesis. In plainer terms, this means that it is so unlikely that TOEFL competence is unrelated to variables that also affect GDP per capita that we must treat it as endogenous, thereby justifying the IV approach.

(12) The idea underpinning this test is as follows: the residuals from the equation in Note 2 are treated as an additional independent variable in an estimation of GDP per capita. If the estimated coefficient associated with this term is statistically significant (as shown by the very small p-value), we conclude that our English language variable cannot be treated as exogenous.

(13) For a critique of the treatment of ethnicity in the mainstream development literature, see Arcand *et al.* (2000a, 2000b); these papers show that rather than fragmentation, it is polarization that hampers growth. This dovetails with recent results by Alesina and Zhuravskaya (2011), highlighting the negative impact of intergroup segregation on the quality of government.

(14) Note that, for comparison purposes, Column 8 of Table 11.3 presents the same equation estimated by OLS, and in which the three key variables are *not* allowed to be jointly endogenous. In contrast to the results reported in Column 9, we obtain the 'standard' result of a negative impact of ethnolinguistic fragmentation on GDP per capita.

(15) This result is in some sense the perfect 'pendant' to the standard AJR result, in which protection against expropriation risk is endogenous and has a positive and statistically significant impact on GDP per capita, whereas ethnolinguistic fragmentation has a negative and statistically significant effect. Recall that our specification

is to be preferred on statistical grounds in that, when both right-hand-side variables were allowed to be endogenous, the null hypothesis of exogeneity was rejected for ethnolinguistic fragmentation but was not for protection against expropriation risk.

References

Abou, S. and Haddad, K. (eds) (1997) *La diversité linguistique et culturelle et les enjeux du développement* (coll. L'Actualité scientifique). Montréal: AUPELF-UREF and Beirut, Université Saint-Joseph.

Acemoglu, D., Johnson, S. and Robinson, J. (2001) The colonial origins of comparative development: An empirical investigation. *American Economic Review* 91 (5), 1369-1401.

Akerlof, G. and Kranton, R. (2000) Economics and identity. *Quarterly Journal of Economics* CVX (3), 715-753.

Alesina, A. and LaFerrara, E. (2005) Ethnic diversity and economic performance. *Journal of Economic Literature* 43 (3), 762-800.

Alesina, A. and LaFerrara E. (2011) Segregation and the quality of government in a cross section of countries. *American Economic Review* 101, 1872-1911.

Arcand, J-L. (1996) Development economics and language: The earnest search for a mirage? *International Journal of the Sociology of Language* 121, 119-157.

Arcand, J-L., Guillaumont, P. and Guillaumont-Jeanneney, S. (2000a) How to make a tragedy: On the alleged effect of ethnicity on growth. *Journal of International Development* 12, 925-938.

Arcand, J-L., Guillaumont, P. and Guillaumont-Jeanneney, S. (2000b) Ethnicity, communication and growth. *WPS* 2000-20. Oxford: University of Oxford.

Barro, R. and McCleary, R. (2003) *Religion and Economic Growth*. NBER Working Paper No. 9682. Cambridge, MA: National Bureau of Economic Research.

Chaudenson, R. and de Robillard, D. (1990) *Langues, économie et développement*. Aix-Marseilles: Institut d'études créoles et francophones, Université de Provence.

Desmet, K., Ortuño-Ortín, I. and S. Weber (2009) Linguistic diversity and redistribution. *Journal of the European Economic Association* 7, 1291-1318.

Dutcher, N. (1997) *The Use of First and Second Languages in Education: A Review of International Experience*. Pacific Islands Discussion Paper Series 1. Washington, DC: The World Bank.

Easterly, W. and Levine, R. (1997) Africa's growth tragedy: Policies and ethnic divisions. *Quarterly Journal of Economics* 112, 1203-1250.

Fearon, J. (2003) Ethnic and cultural diversity by country. *Journal of Economic Growth* 8 (2), 195-222.

Grin, F. (ed.) (1996) Economic approaches to language and language planning. Theme issue of the *International Journal of the Sociology of Language* 121.

Grin, F. (2003) Economics and language planning. *Current Issues in Language Planning* 4 (1), 1-66.

Grin, F. (2010) Economics. In J. Fishman and O. García (eds) *Handbook of Language and Ethnic Identity* (pp. 70-88). Oxford: Oxford University Press.

Grin, F., Sfreddo C. and Vaillancourt, V. (2010) *The Economics of the Multilingual Workplace*. New York: Routledge.

Heller, M. (ed.) (2007) *Bilingualism: A Social Approach*. Basingstoke: Palgrave Macmillan.

Heugh, K. (2006) Cost implications of the provision of mother tongue and strong bilingual models of education in Africa. In H. Alidou and A. Boly (eds) *Optimizing Learning and Education in Africa- the Language Factor. A Stock-taking Research on Mother Tongue and Bilingual Education in Sub-Saharan Africa* (pp. 138-156). Paris: Association for the Development of Education in Africa.

Ku, H. and Zussman, A. (2010) Lingua franca: The role of English in international trade. *Journal of Economic Behavior and Organization* 75, 250-260.

Lamberton, D. (ed.) (2002) *The Economics of Language*. Cheltenham: Edward Elgar.

Lang, K. (1986) A language theory of discrimination. *Quarterly Journal of Economics* 101, 363-382.

Lian, B. and Oneal, J.R. (1997) Cultural diversity and economic development: A cross-national study of 98 countries, 1960-1985. *Economic Development and Cultural Change* 46 (1), 61-77.

Lüdi, G. and Theme, A. (2002) *Die Bedeutung einer lingua franca für Europa*. Baslerschriften zur europäischen Integration 60. Basel: Europainstitut der Universität Basel.

Mauro, P. (1995) Corruption and growth. *Quarterly Journal of Economics* CX (3), 681-712.

Mondada, L. (2007) Bilingualism and the analysis of talk at work: Code-switching as a resource for the organisation of action and interaction. In M. Heller (ed.) *Bilingualism: A Social Approach* (pp. 297-318). Basingstoke: Palgrave Macmillan.

Mufwene, S. (2001) *The Ecology of Language Evolution*. Cambridge: Cambridge University Press.

Nettle, D. (2000) Linguistic fragmentation and the wealth of nations: The Fishman-Pool hypothesis re-examined. *Economic Development and Cultural Change* 48, 335-348.

Noguer, M. and Siscart, M. (2003) Language as a barrier to international trade? An empirical investigation. Unpublished mimeo.

Ostler, N. (2010) *The Last Lingua Franca. English until the Return of Babel*. London: Allen Lane.

Seargeant, P. and Erling, E. (2011) The discourse of 'English as a language for international development': Policy assumptions and practical challenges. In H. Coleman (ed.) *Dreams and Realities: Developing Countries and the English Language* (pp. 255-274). London: British Council.

Vaillancourt, F. (1985) *Économie et langue*. Québec: Conseil de la langue française.

Index